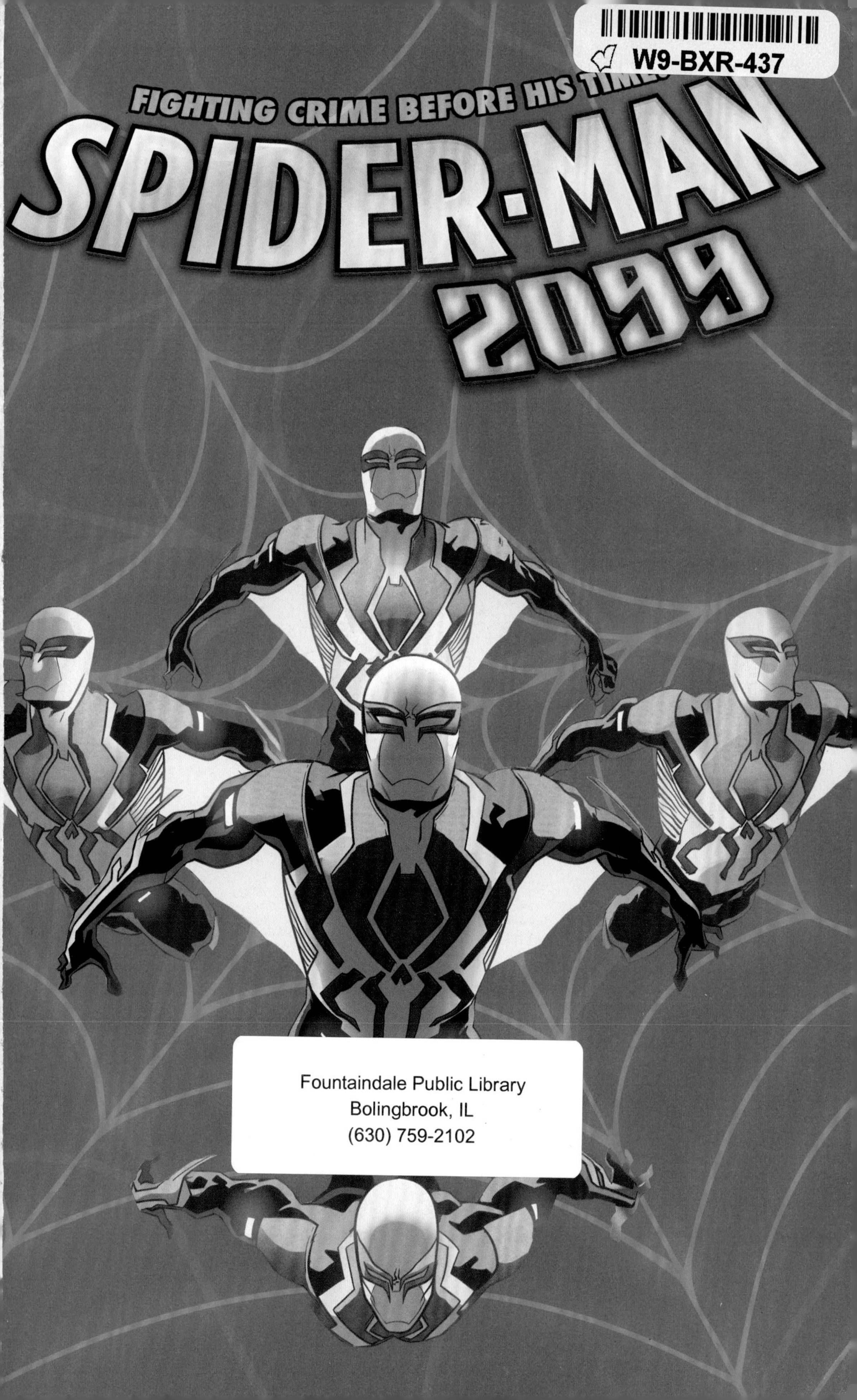
FIGHTING CRIME BEFORE HIS TIME
SPIDER-MAN
2099

FIGHTING CRIME BEFORE HIS TIME!

SPIDER-MAN 2099

CIVIL WAR II

PETER DAVID
writer

WILL SLINEY
artist

RACHELLE ROSENBERG
colorist

VC's CORY PETIT
letterer

FRANCESCO MATTINA
cover art

CHARLES BEACHAM
editor

MARK PANICCIA
senior editor

SPIDER-MAN created by **STAN LEE & STEVE DITKO**

---

collection editor **SARAH BRUNSTAD**
associate managing editor **KATERI WOODY**
editor, special projects **MARK D. BEAZLEY**
senior editor, special projects **JENNIFER GRÜNWALD**
vp production & special projects **JEFF YOUNGQUIST**
book design **ADAM DEL RE**

svp print, sales & marketing **DAVID GABRIEL**
editor in chief **AXEL ALONSO**
chief creative officer **JOE QUESADA**
publisher **DAN BUCKLEY**
executive producer **ALAN FINE**

SPIDER-MAN 2099 VOL. 5: CIVIL WAR II. Contains material originally published in magazine form as SPIDER-MAN 2099 #11-16. First printing 2016. ISBN# 978-1-302-90281-0. Published by MARVEL WORLDWIDE, INC., a subsidiary of MARVEL ENTERTAINMENT, LLC. OFFICE OF PUBLICATION: 135 West 50th Street, New York, NY 10020. Copyright © 2016 MARVEL No similarity between any of the names, characters, persons, and/or institutions in this magazine with those of any living or dead person or institution is intended, and any such similarity which may exist is purely coincidental. **Printed in Canada.** ALAN FINE, President, Marvel Entertainment; DAN BUCKLEY, President, TV, Publishing & Brand Management; JOE QUESADA, Chief Creative Officer; TOM BREVOORT, SVP of Publishing; DAVID BOGART, SVP of Business Affairs & Operations, Publishing & Partnership; C.B. CEBULSKI, VP of Brand Management & Development, Asia; DAVID GABRIEL, SVP of Sales & Marketing, Publishing; JEFF YOUNGQUIST, VP of Production & Special Projects; DAN CARR, Executive Director of Publishing Technology; ALEX MORALES, Director of Publishing Operations; SUSAN CRESPI, Production Manager; STAN LEE, Chairman Emeritus. For information regarding advertising in Marvel Comics or on Marvel.com, please contact Vit DeBellis, Integrated Sales Manager, at vdebellis@marvel.com. For Marvel subscription inquiries, please call 888-511-5480. **Manufactured between 11/25/2016 and 1/2/2017 by SOLISCO PRINTERS, SCOTT, QC, CANADA.**

10 9 8 7 6 5 4 3 2 1

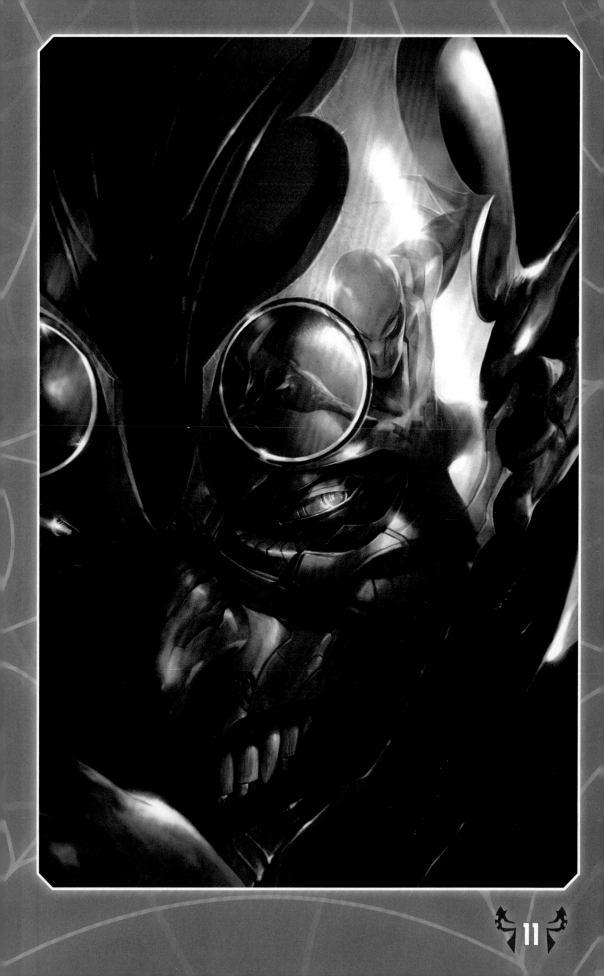

MIGUEL O'HARA WAS A YOUNG GENETICS GENIUS EMPLOYED AT THE MEGACORPORATION ALCHEMAX IN THE FUTURE CITY OF NUEVA YORK! ONE OF HIS EXPERIMENTS–TO REPLICATE THE POWERS OF THE PRESENT-DAY SPIDER-MAN–WAS TURNED AGAINST HIM AND REWROTE HIS DNA TO MAKE IT 50 PERCENT SPIDER! AFTER LEARNING HOW TO USE HIS AMAZING NEW ABILITIES, MIGUEL BECAME...

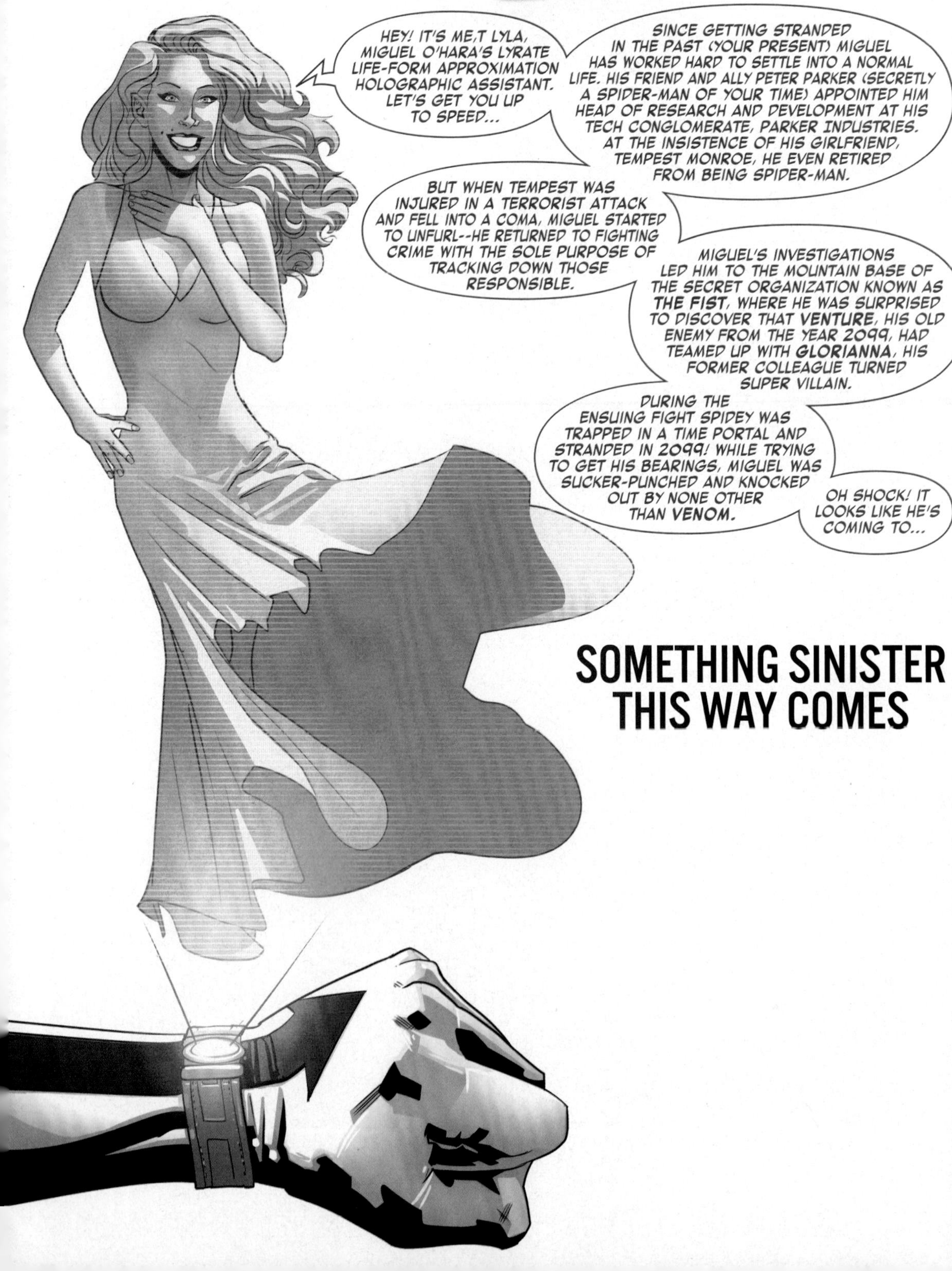
HEY! IT'S ME,T LYLA, MIGUEL O'HARA'S LYRATE LIFE-FORM APPROXIMATION HOLOGRAPHIC ASSISTANT. LET'S GET YOU UP TO SPEED...
SINCE GETTING STRANDED IN THE PAST (YOUR PRESENT) MIGUEL HAS WORKED HARD TO SETTLE INTO A NORMAL LIFE. HIS FRIEND AND ALLY PETER PARKER (SECRETLY A SPIDER-MAN OF YOUR TIME) APPOINTED HIM HEAD OF RESEARCH AND DEVELOPMENT AT HIS TECH CONGLOMERATE, PARKER INDUSTRIES. AT THE INSISTENCE OF HIS GIRLFRIEND, TEMPEST MONROE, HE EVEN RETIRED FROM BEING SPIDER-MAN.
BUT WHEN TEMPEST WAS INJURED IN A TERRORIST ATTACK AND FELL INTO A COMA, MIGUEL STARTED TO UNFURL--HE RETURNED TO FIGHTING CRIME WITH THE SOLE PURPOSE OF TRACKING DOWN THOSE RESPONSIBLE.
MIGUEL'S INVESTIGATIONS LED HIM TO THE MOUNTAIN BASE OF THE SECRET ORGANIZATION KNOWN AS **THE FIST**, WHERE HE WAS SURPRISED TO DISCOVER THAT **VENTURE**, HIS OLD ENEMY FROM THE YEAR 2099, HAD TEAMED UP WITH **GLORIANNA**, HIS FORMER COLLEAGUE TURNED SUPER VILLAIN.
DURING THE ENSUING FIGHT SPIDEY WAS TRAPPED IN A TIME PORTAL AND STRANDED IN 2099! WHILE TRYING TO GET HIS BEARINGS, MIGUEL WAS SUCKER-PUNCHED AND KNOCKED OUT BY NONE OTHER THAN **VENOM**.
OH SHOCK! IT LOOKS LIKE HE'S COMING TO...

SOMETHING SINISTER THIS WAY COMES

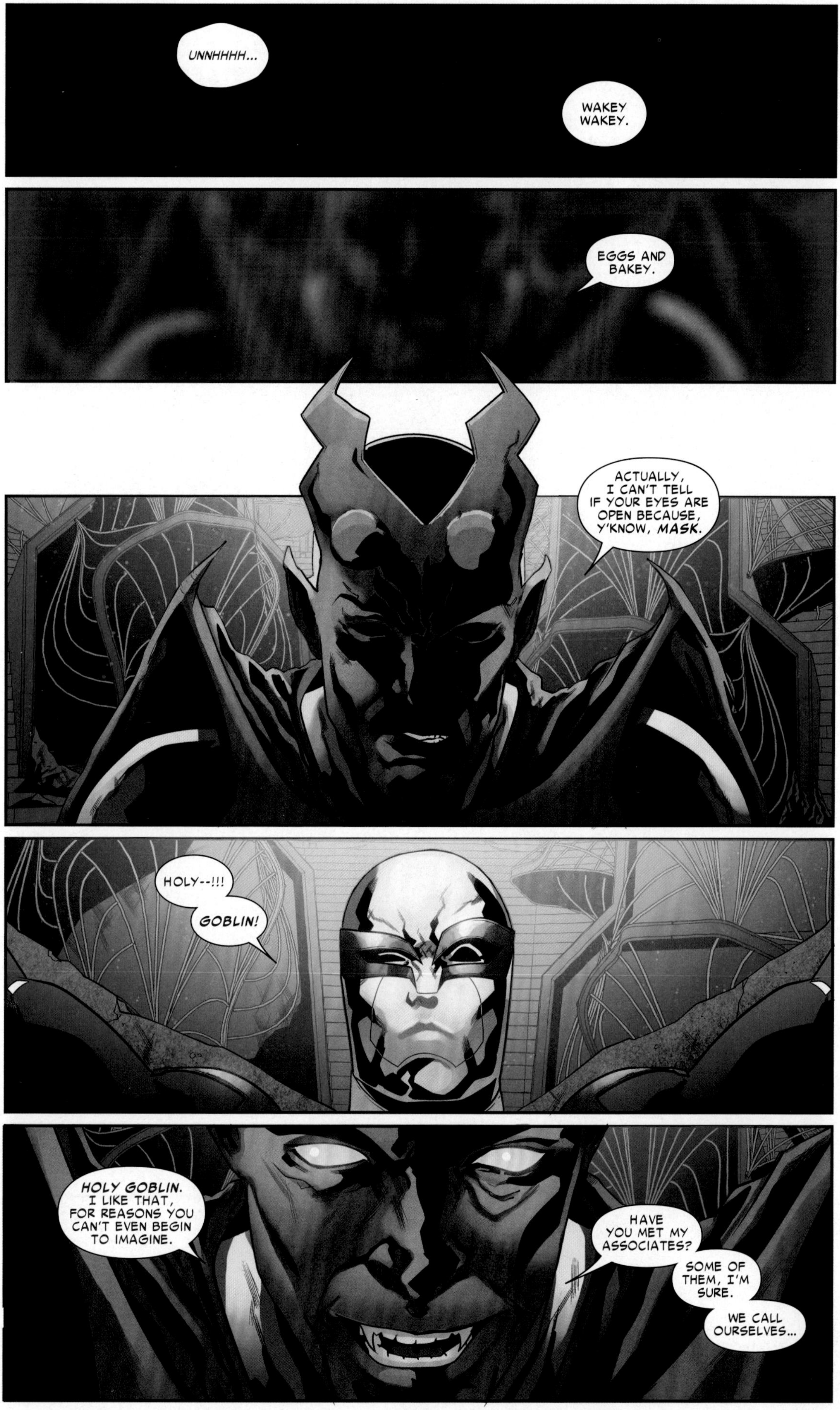
UNNHHHH...
WAKEY WAKEY.
EGGS AND BAKEY.
ACTUALLY, I CAN'T TELL IF YOUR EYES ARE OPEN BECAUSE, Y'KNOW, MASK.
HOLY--!!!
GOBLIN!
HOLY GOBLIN. I LIKE THAT, FOR REASONS YOU CAN'T EVEN BEGIN TO IMAGINE.
HAVE YOU MET MY ASSOCIATES?
SOME OF THEM, I'M SURE.
WE CALL OURSELVES...

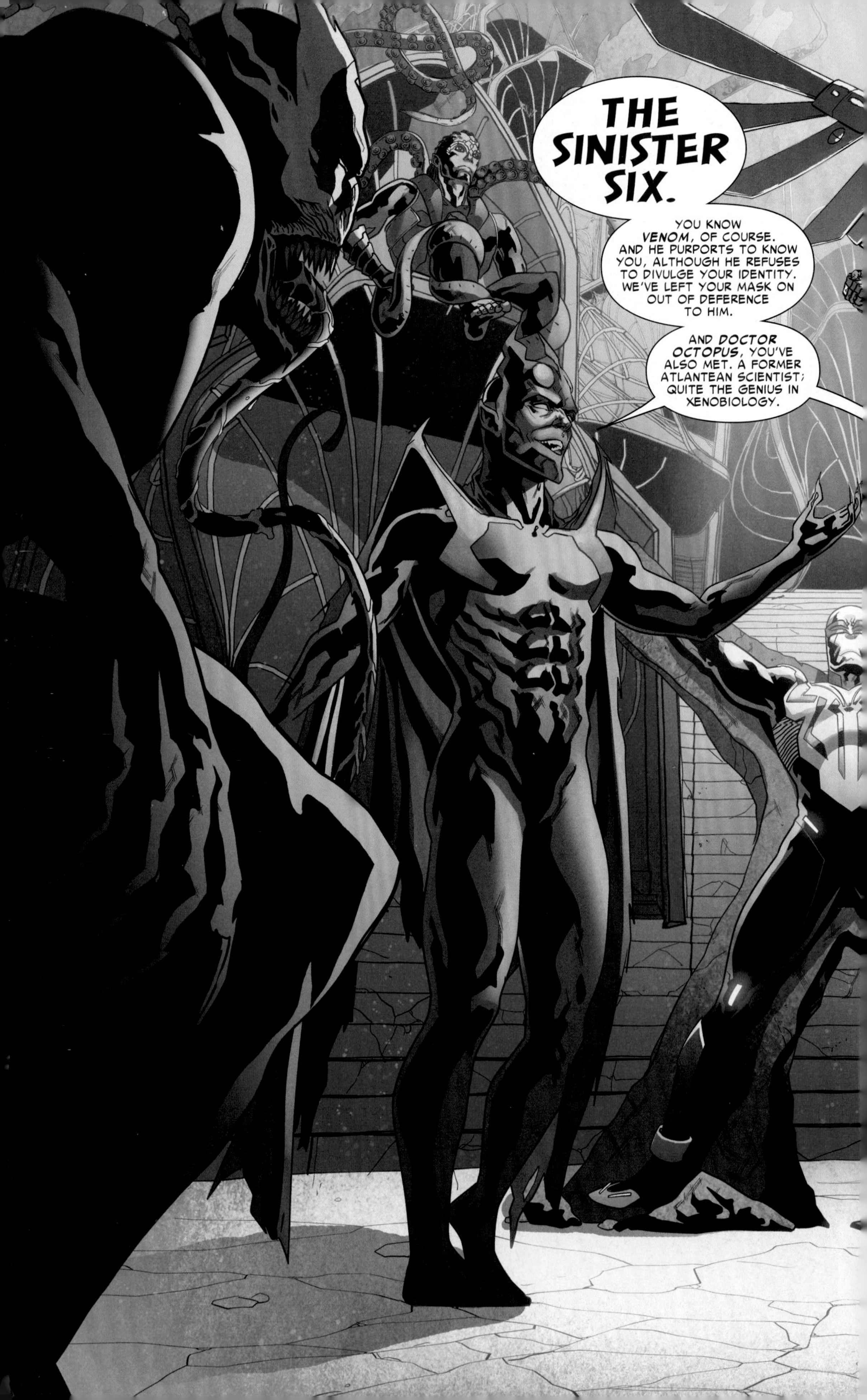
THE SINISTER SIX.
YOU KNOW VENOM, OF COURSE. AND HE PURPORTS TO KNOW YOU, ALTHOUGH HE REFUSES TO DIVULGE YOUR IDENTITY. WE'VE LEFT YOUR MASK ON OUT OF DEFERENCE TO HIM.
AND DOCTOR OCTOPUS, YOU'VE ALSO MET. A FORMER ATLANTEAN SCIENTIST; QUITE THE GENIUS IN XENOBIOLOGY.

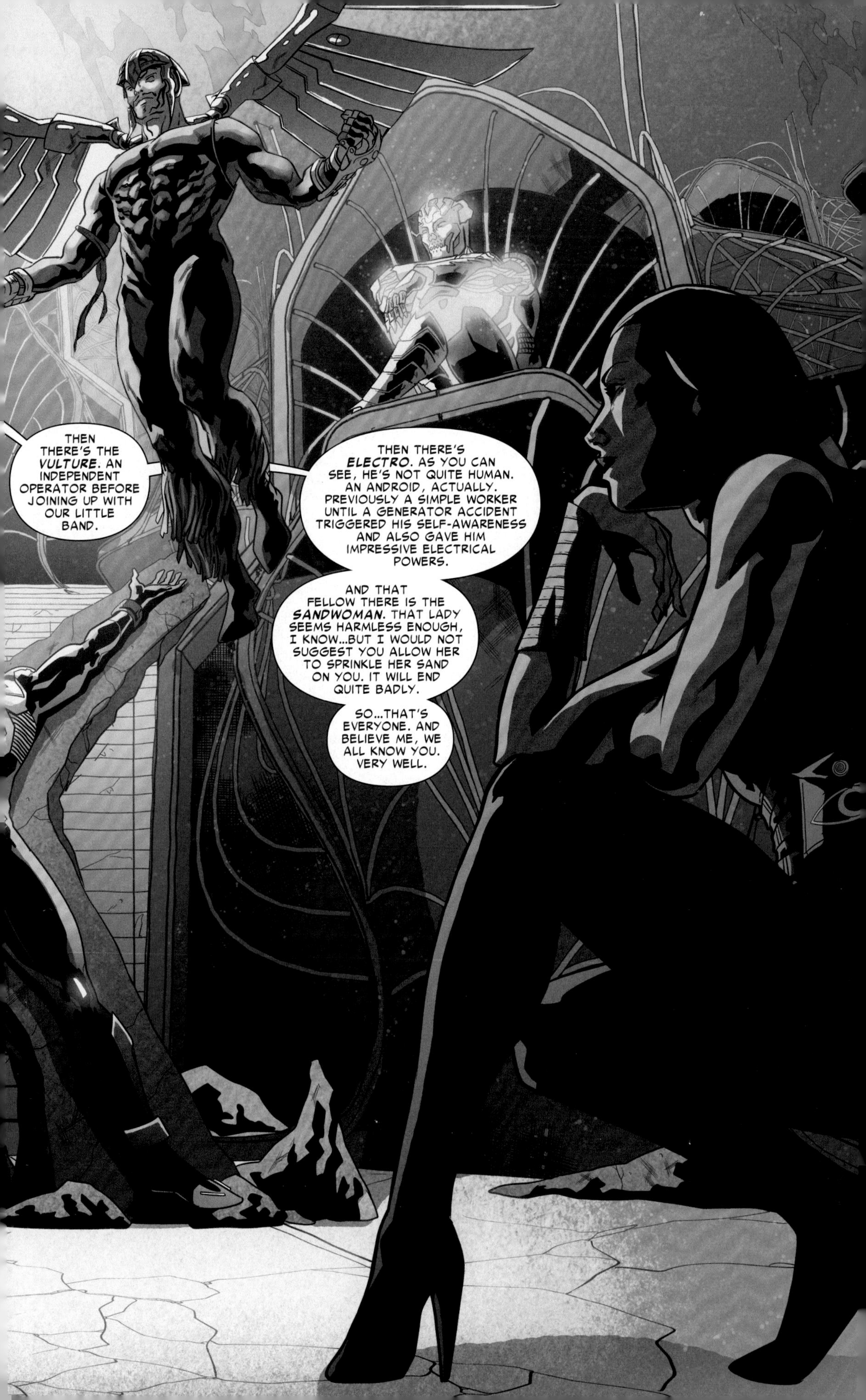
THEN THERE'S THE ***VULTURE***. AN INDEPENDENT OPERATOR BEFORE JOINING UP WITH OUR LITTLE BAND.
THEN THERE'S ***ELECTRO***. AS YOU CAN SEE, HE'S NOT QUITE HUMAN. AN ANDROID, ACTUALLY. PREVIOUSLY A SIMPLE WORKER UNTIL A GENERATOR ACCIDENT TRIGGERED HIS SELF-AWARENESS AND ALSO GAVE HIM IMPRESSIVE ELECTRICAL POWERS.
AND THAT FELLOW THERE IS THE ***SANDWOMAN***. THAT LADY SEEMS HARMLESS ENOUGH, I KNOW...BUT I WOULD NOT SUGGEST YOU ALLOW HER TO SPRINKLE HER SAND ON YOU. IT WILL END QUITE BADLY.
SO...THAT'S EVERYONE. AND BELIEVE ME, WE ALL KNOW YOU. VERY WELL.

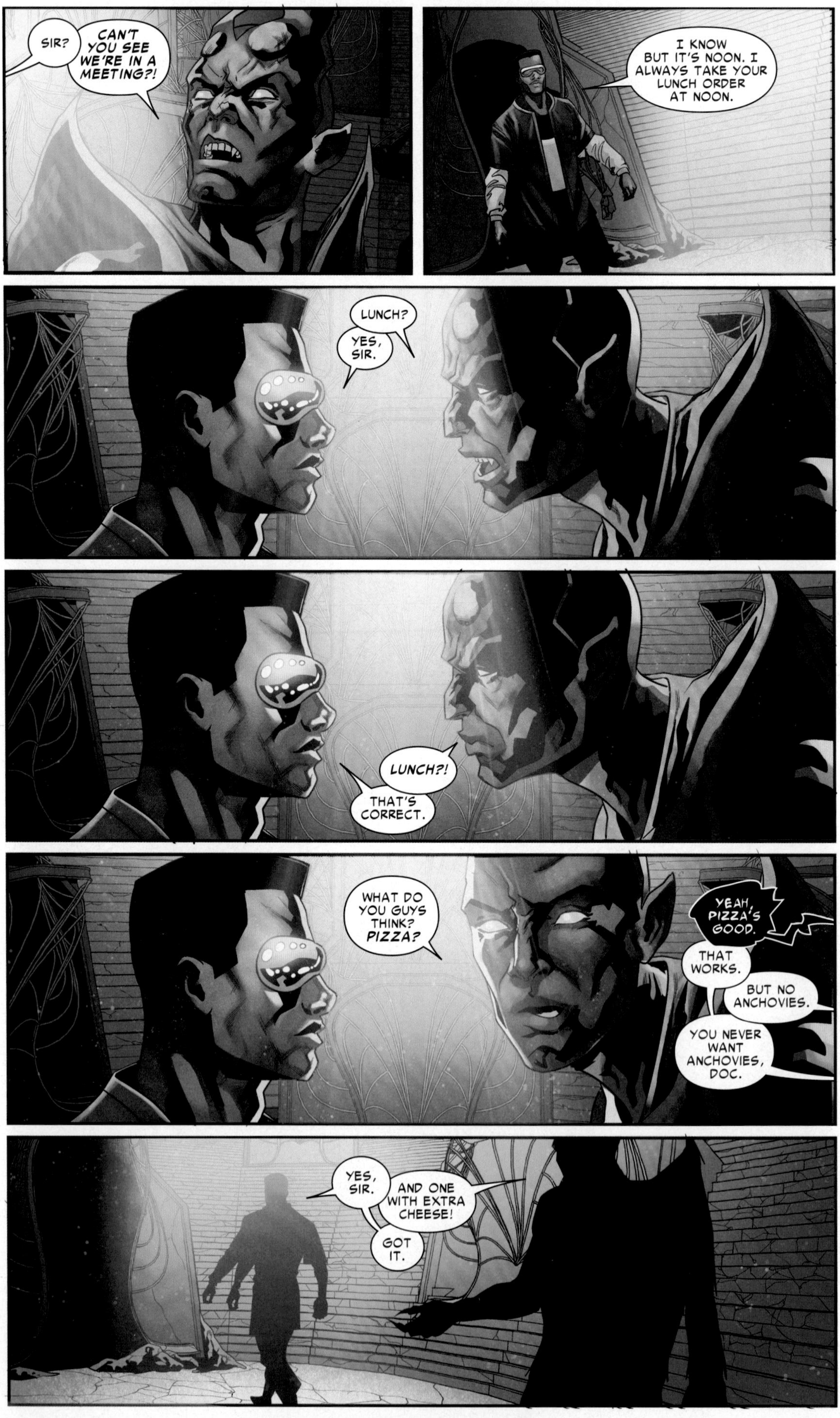
SIR?
CAN'T YOU SEE WE'RE IN A MEETING?!
I KNOW BUT IT'S NOON. I ALWAYS TAKE YOUR LUNCH ORDER AT NOON.
LUNCH?
YES, SIR.
LUNCH?!
THAT'S CORRECT.
WHAT DO YOU GUYS THINK? PIZZA?
YEAH, PIZZA'S GOOD.
THAT WORKS.
BUT NO ANCHOVIES.
YOU NEVER WANT ANCHOVIES, DOC.
YES, SIR.
AND ONE WITH EXTRA CHEESE!
GOT IT.

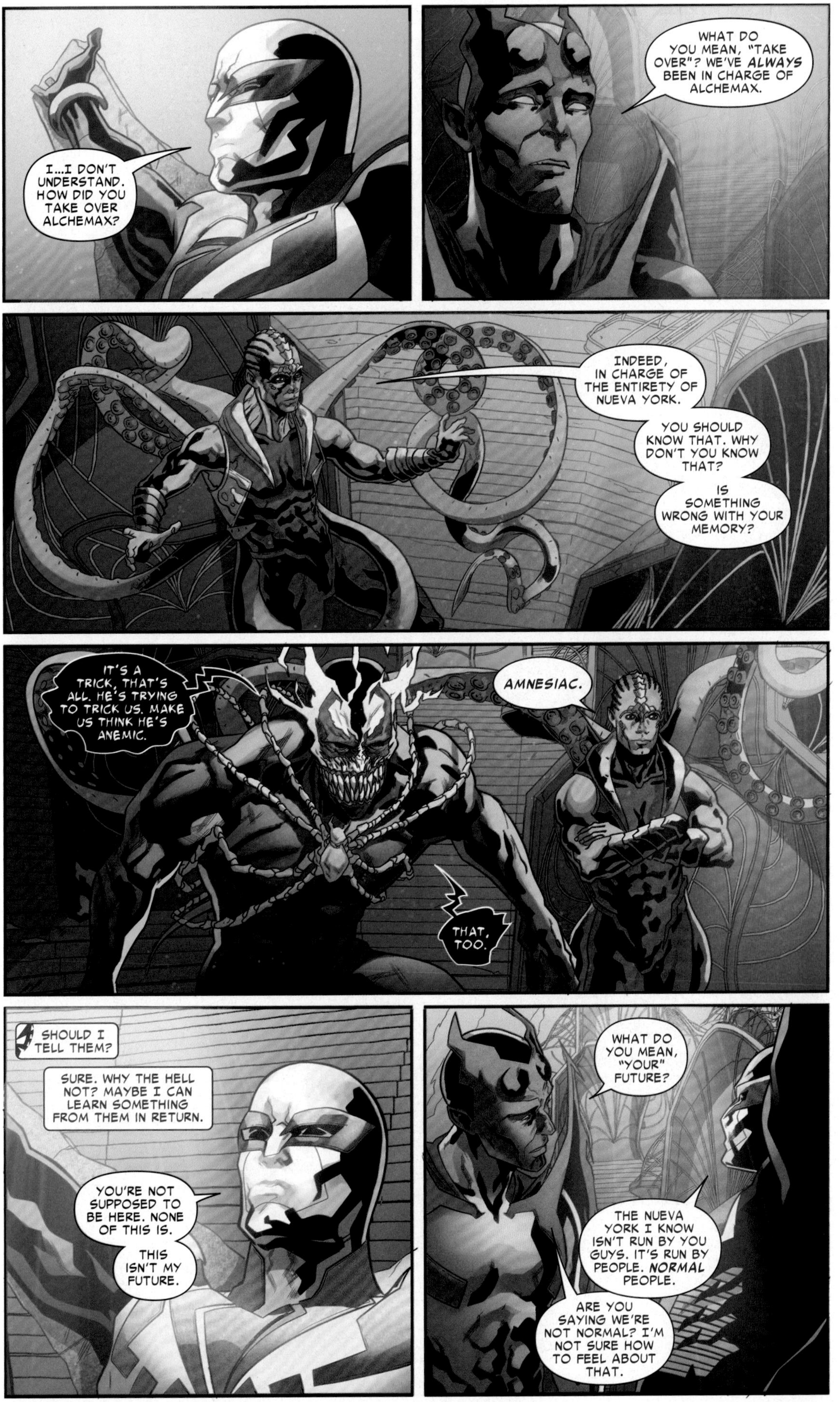
I...I DON'T UNDERSTAND. HOW DID YOU TAKE OVER ALCHEMAX?
WHAT DO YOU MEAN, "TAKE OVER"? WE'VE ALWAYS BEEN IN CHARGE OF ALCHEMAX.
INDEED, IN CHARGE OF THE ENTIRETY OF NUEVA YORK.
YOU SHOULD KNOW THAT. WHY DON'T YOU KNOW THAT?
IS SOMETHING WRONG WITH YOUR MEMORY?
IT'S A TRICK, THAT'S ALL. HE'S TRYING TO TRICK US. MAKE US THINK HE'S ANEMIC.
AMNESIAC.
THAT, TOO.
SHOULD I TELL THEM?
SURE. WHY THE HELL NOT? MAYBE I CAN LEARN SOMETHING FROM THEM IN RETURN.
YOU'RE NOT SUPPOSED TO BE HERE. NONE OF THIS IS.
THIS ISN'T MY FUTURE.
WHAT DO YOU MEAN, "YOUR" FUTURE?
THE NUEVA YORK I KNOW ISN'T RUN BY YOU GUYS. IT'S RUN BY PEOPLE. NORMAL PEOPLE.
ARE YOU SAYING WE'RE NOT NORMAL? I'M NOT SURE HOW TO FEEL ABOUT THAT.

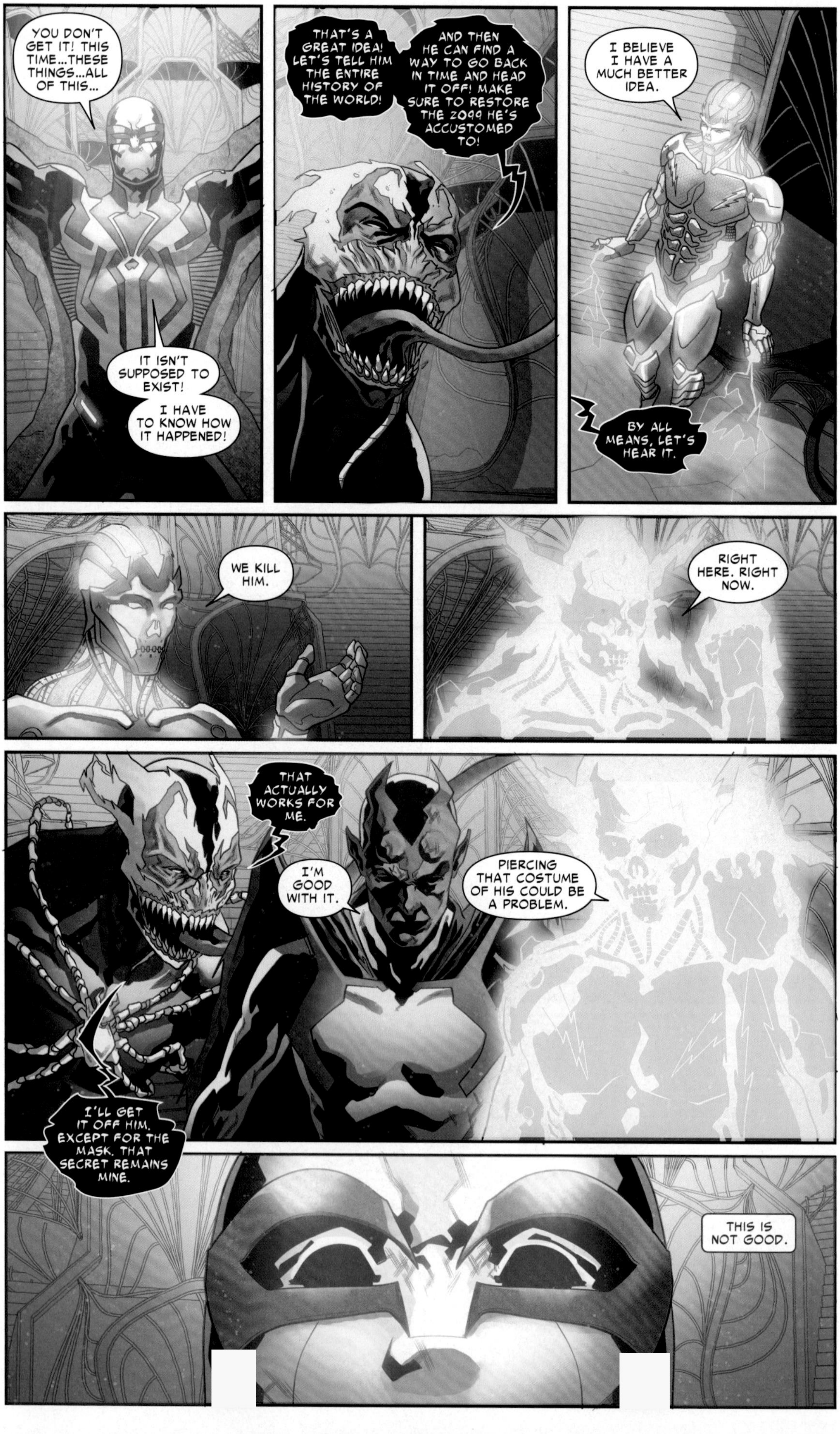
YOU DON'T GET IT! THIS TIME...THESE THINGS...ALL OF THIS...
IT ISN'T SUPPOSED TO EXIST!
I HAVE TO KNOW HOW IT HAPPENED!
THAT'S A GREAT IDEA! LET'S TELL HIM THE ENTIRE HISTORY OF THE WORLD!
AND THEN HE CAN FIND A WAY TO GO BACK IN TIME AND HEAD IT OFF! MAKE SURE TO RESTORE THE 2099 HE'S ACCUSTOMED TO!
I BELIEVE I HAVE A MUCH BETTER IDEA.
BY ALL MEANS, LET'S HEAR IT.
WE KILL HIM.
RIGHT HERE. RIGHT NOW.
THAT ACTUALLY WORKS FOR ME.
I'M GOOD WITH IT.
PIERCING THAT COSTUME OF HIS COULD BE A PROBLEM.
I'LL GET IT OFF HIM. EXCEPT FOR THE MASK. THAT SECRET REMAINS MINE.
THIS IS NOT GOOD.

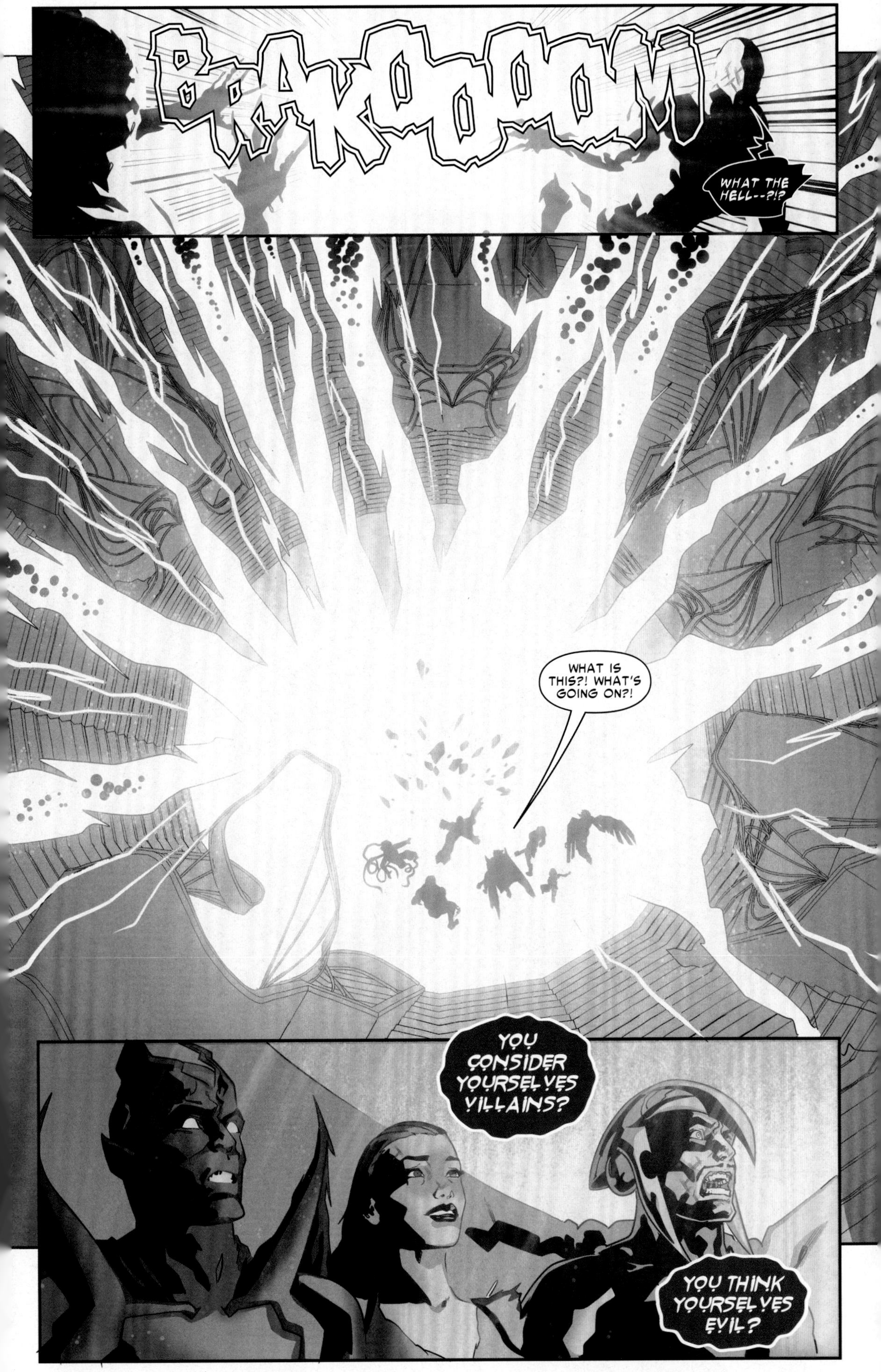
BRAKOOOOM
WHAT THE HELL--?!?
WHAT IS THIS?! WHAT'S GOING ON?!
YOU CONSIDER YOURSELVES VILLAINS?
YOU THINK YOURSELVES EVIL?

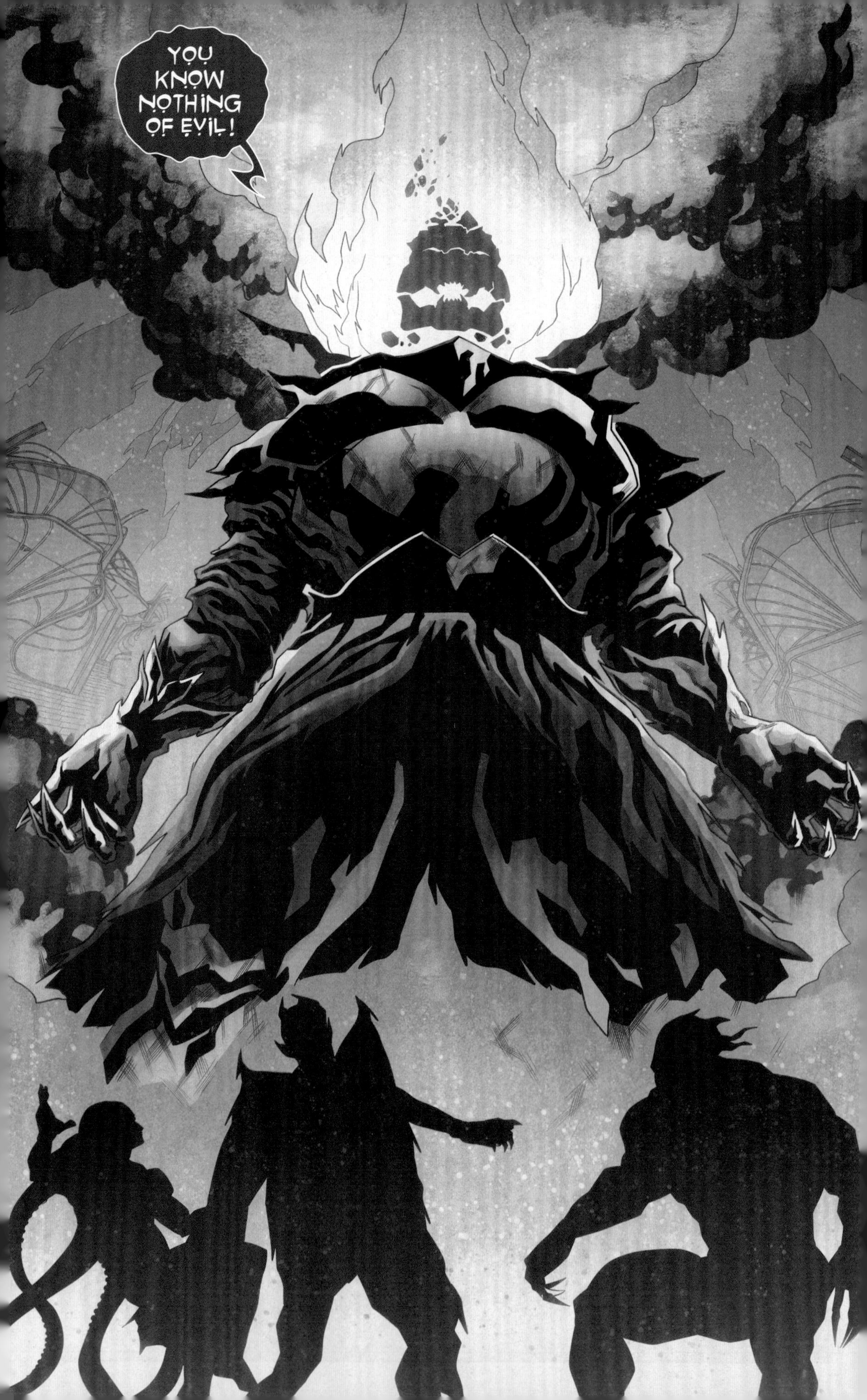
YOU KNOW NOTHING OF EVIL!

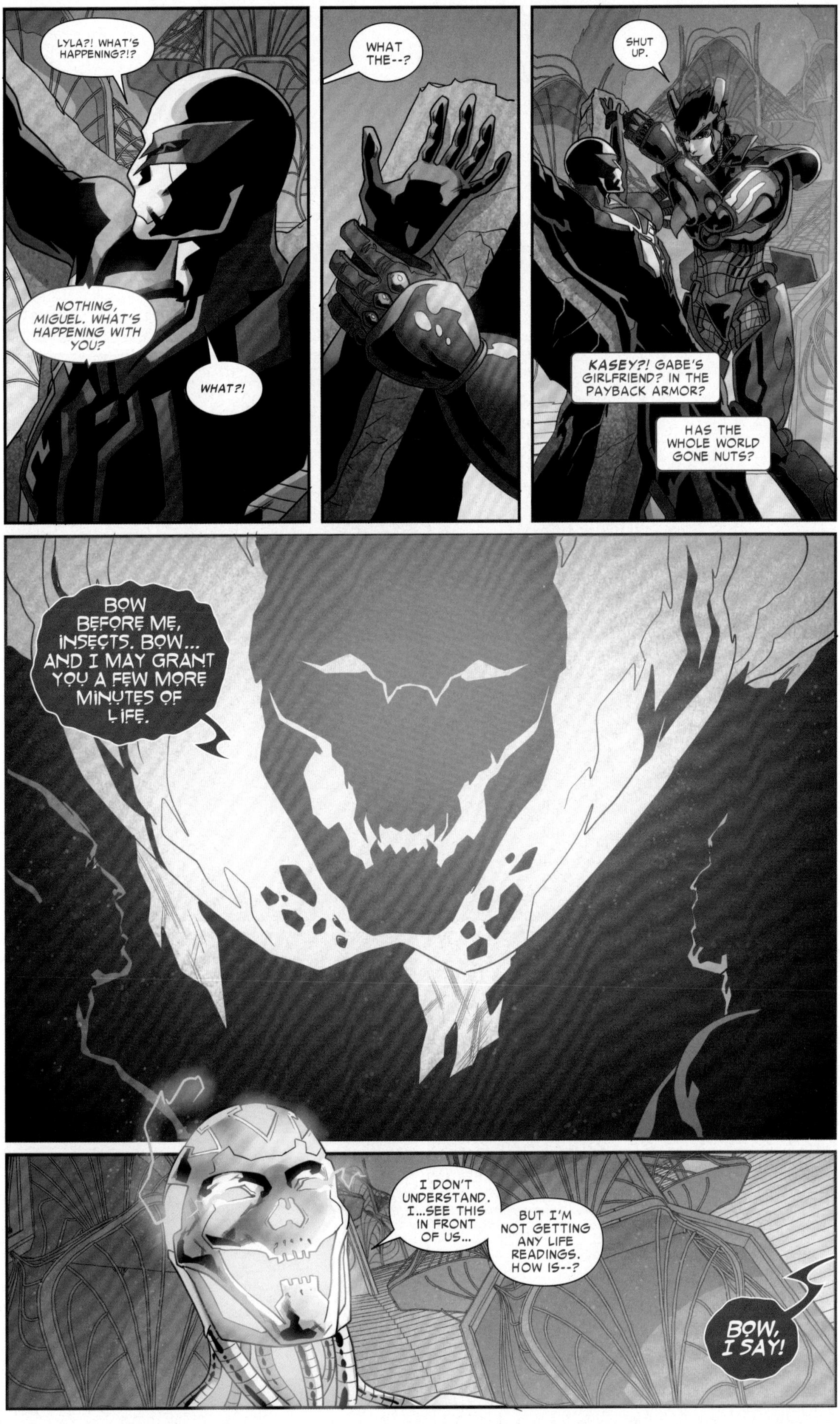
LYLA?! WHAT'S HAPPENING?!?
NOTHING, MIGUEL. WHAT'S HAPPENING WITH YOU?
WHAT?!
WHAT THE--?
SHUT UP.
KASEY?! GABE'S GIRLFRIEND? IN THE PAYBACK ARMOR?
HAS THE WHOLE WORLD GONE NUTS?
BOW BEFORE ME, INSECTS. BOW... AND I MAY GRANT YOU A FEW MORE MINUTES OF LIFE.
I DON'T UNDERSTAND. I...SEE THIS IN FRONT OF US...
BUT I'M NOT GETTING ANY LIFE READINGS. HOW IS--?
BOW, I SAY!

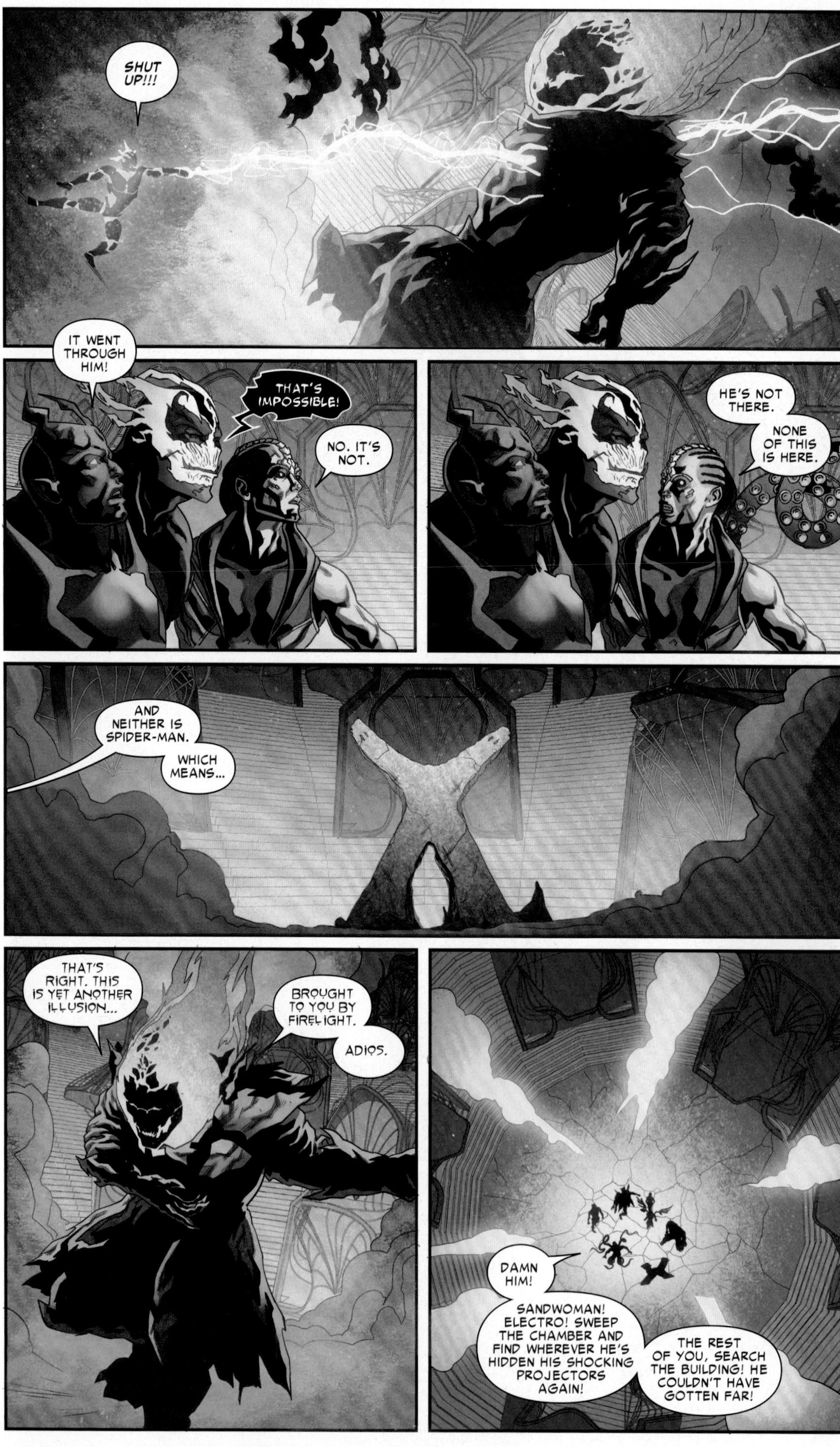
SHUT UP!!!
IT WENT THROUGH HIM!
THAT'S IMPOSSIBLE!
NO. IT'S NOT.
HE'S NOT THERE.
NONE OF THIS IS HERE.
AND NEITHER IS SPIDER-MAN.
WHICH MEANS...
THAT'S RIGHT. THIS IS YET ANOTHER ILLUSION...
BROUGHT TO YOU BY FIRELIGHT.
ADIOS.
DAMN HIM!
SANDWOMAN! ELECTRO! SWEEP THE CHAMBER AND FIND WHEREVER HE'S HIDDEN HIS SHOCKING PROJECTORS AGAIN!
THE REST OF YOU, SEARCH THE BUILDING! HE COULDN'T HAVE GOTTEN FAR!

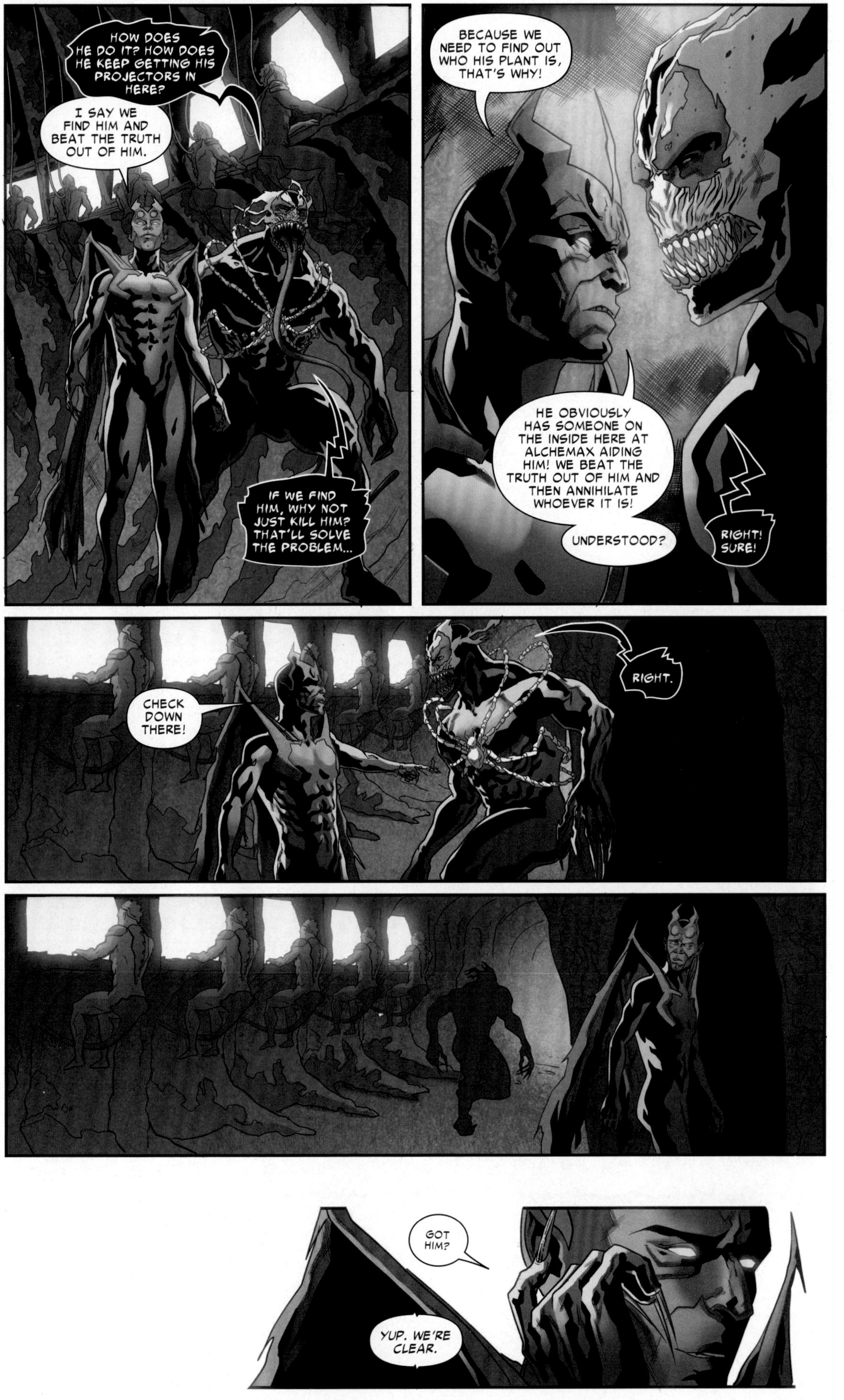
HOW DOES HE DO IT? HOW DOES HE KEEP GETTING HIS PROJECTORS IN HERE?
I SAY WE FIND HIM AND BEAT THE TRUTH OUT OF HIM.
IF WE FIND HIM, WHY NOT JUST KILL HIM? THAT'LL SOLVE THE PROBLEM...
BECAUSE WE NEED TO FIND OUT WHO HIS PLANT IS, THAT'S WHY!
HE OBVIOUSLY HAS SOMEONE ON THE INSIDE HERE AT ALCHEMAX AIDING HIM! WE BEAT THE TRUTH OUT OF HIM AND THEN ANNIHILATE WHOEVER IT IS!
UNDERSTOOD?
RIGHT! SURE!
CHECK DOWN THERE!
RIGHT.
GOT HIM?
YUP. WE'RE CLEAR.

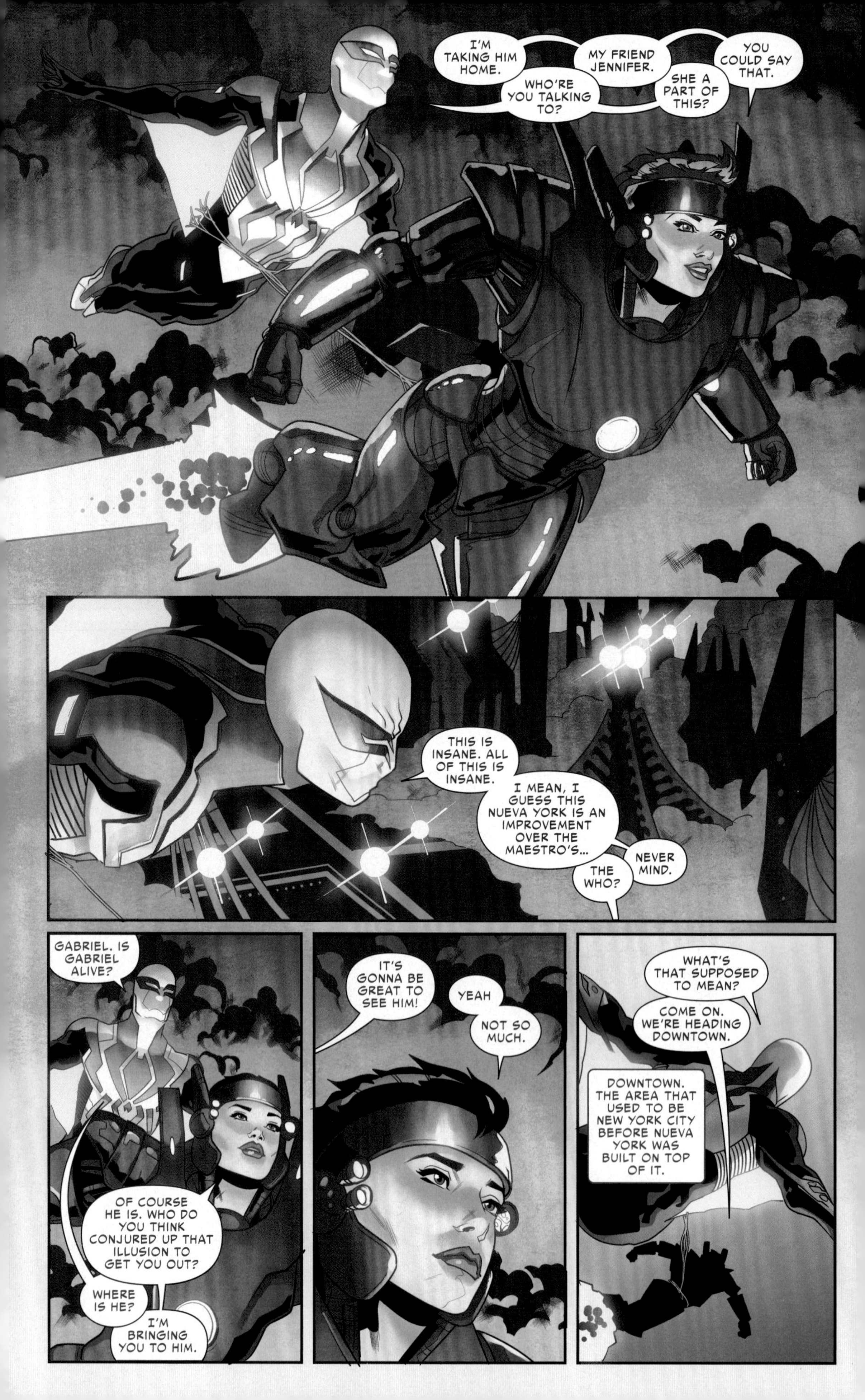
I'M TAKING HIM HOME.
WHO'RE YOU TALKING TO?
MY FRIEND JENNIFER.
SHE A PART OF THIS?
YOU COULD SAY THAT.
THIS IS INSANE. ALL OF THIS IS INSANE.
I MEAN, I GUESS THIS NUEVA YORK IS AN IMPROVEMENT OVER THE MAESTRO'S...
THE WHO?
NEVER MIND.
GABRIEL. IS GABRIEL ALIVE?
OF COURSE HE IS. WHO DO YOU THINK CONJURED UP THAT ILLUSION TO GET YOU OUT?
WHERE IS HE?
I'M BRINGING YOU TO HIM.
IT'S GONNA BE GREAT TO SEE HIM!
YEAH
NOT SO MUCH.
WHAT'S THAT SUPPOSED TO MEAN?
COME ON. WE'RE HEADING DOWNTOWN.
DOWNTOWN. THE AREA THAT USED TO BE NEW YORK CITY BEFORE NUEVA YORK WAS BUILT ON TOP OF IT.

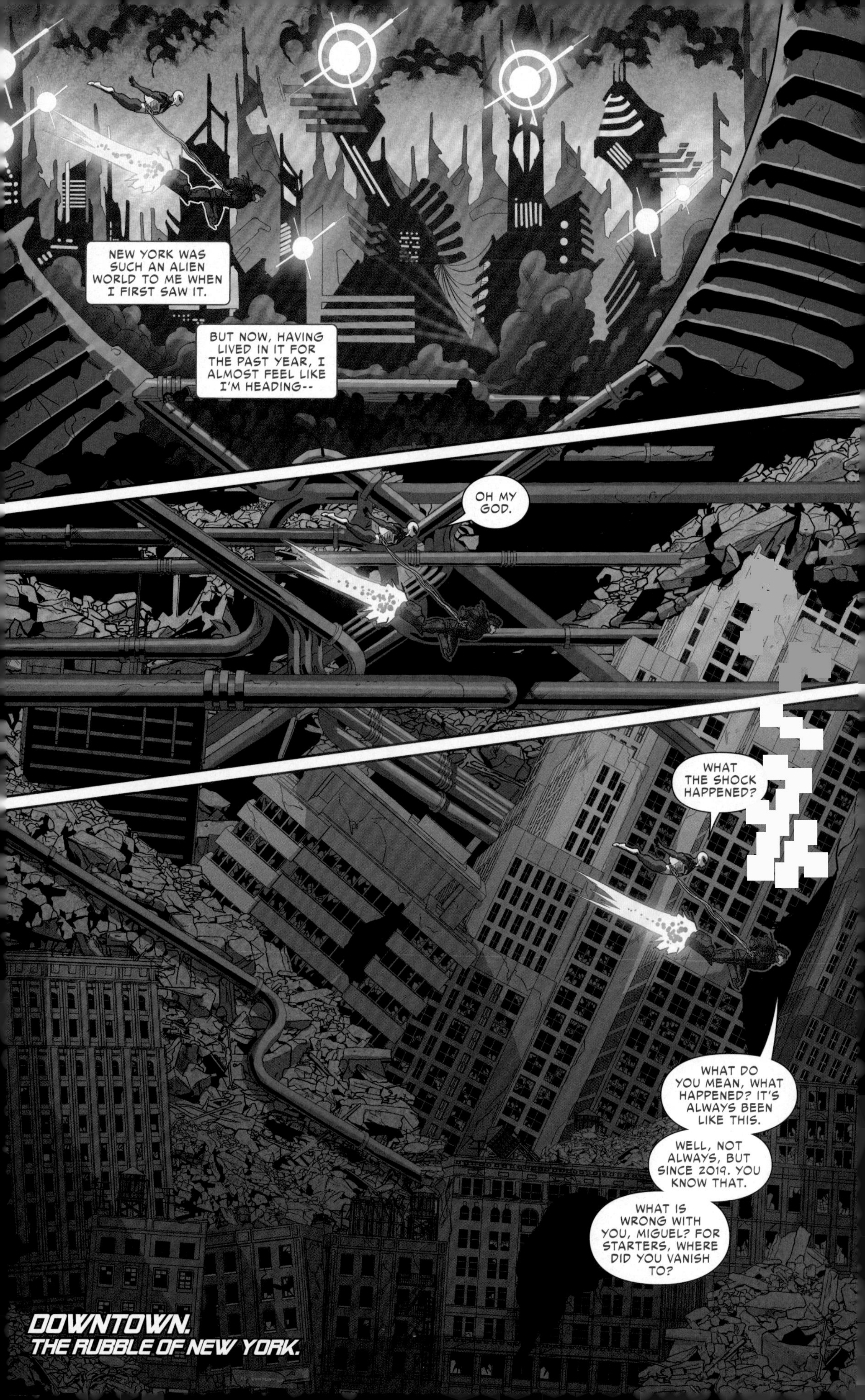
NEW YORK WAS SUCH AN ALIEN WORLD TO ME WHEN I FIRST SAW IT.
BUT NOW, HAVING LIVED IN IT FOR THE PAST YEAR, I ALMOST FEEL LIKE I'M HEADING--
OH MY GOD.
WHAT THE SHOCK HAPPENED?
DOWNTOWN. THE RUBBLE OF NEW YORK.
WHAT DO YOU MEAN, WHAT HAPPENED? IT'S ALWAYS BEEN LIKE THIS.
WELL, NOT ALWAYS, BUT SINCE 2019. YOU KNOW THAT.
WHAT IS WRONG WITH YOU, MIGUEL? FOR STARTERS, WHERE DID YOU VANISH TO?

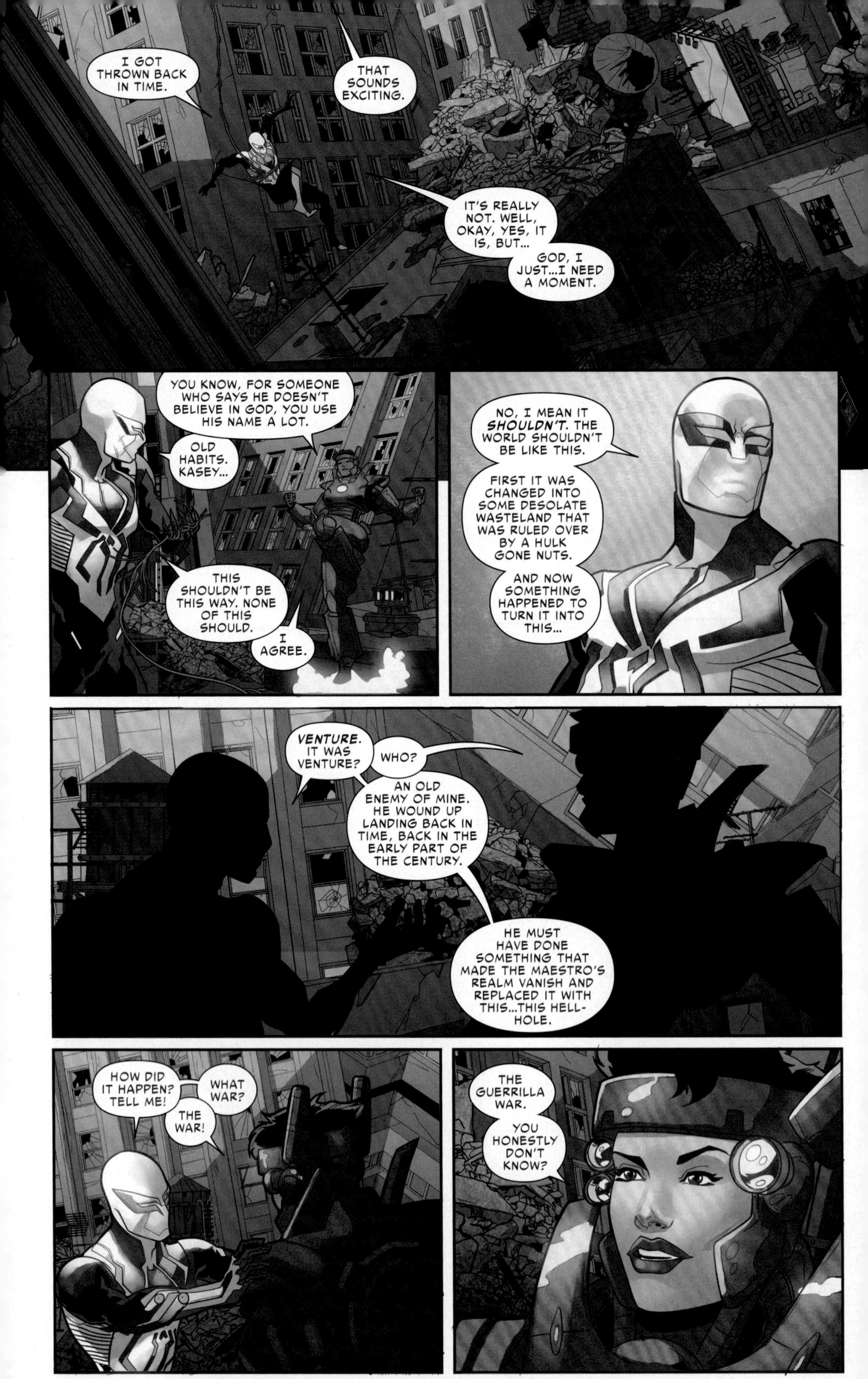

I GOT THROWN BACK IN TIME.
THAT SOUNDS EXCITING.
IT'S REALLY NOT. WELL, OKAY, YES, IT IS, BUT...
GOD, I JUST...I NEED A MOMENT.
YOU KNOW, FOR SOMEONE WHO SAYS HE DOESN'T BELIEVE IN GOD, YOU USE HIS NAME A LOT.
OLD HABITS. KASEY...
THIS SHOULDN'T BE THIS WAY. NONE OF THIS SHOULD.
I AGREE.
NO, I MEAN IT *SHOULDN'T*. THE WORLD SHOULDN'T BE LIKE THIS.
FIRST IT WAS CHANGED INTO SOME DESOLATE WASTELAND THAT WAS RULED OVER BY A HULK GONE NUTS.
AND NOW SOMETHING HAPPENED TO TURN IT INTO THIS...
VENTURE. IT WAS VENTURE?
WHO?
AN OLD ENEMY OF MINE. HE WOUND UP LANDING BACK IN TIME, BACK IN THE EARLY PART OF THE CENTURY.
HE MUST HAVE DONE SOMETHING THAT MADE THE MAESTRO'S REALM VANISH AND REPLACED IT WITH THIS...THIS HELL-HOLE.
HOW DID IT HAPPEN? TELL ME!
WHAT WAR?
THE WAR!
THE GUERRILLA WAR.
YOU HONESTLY DON'T KNOW?

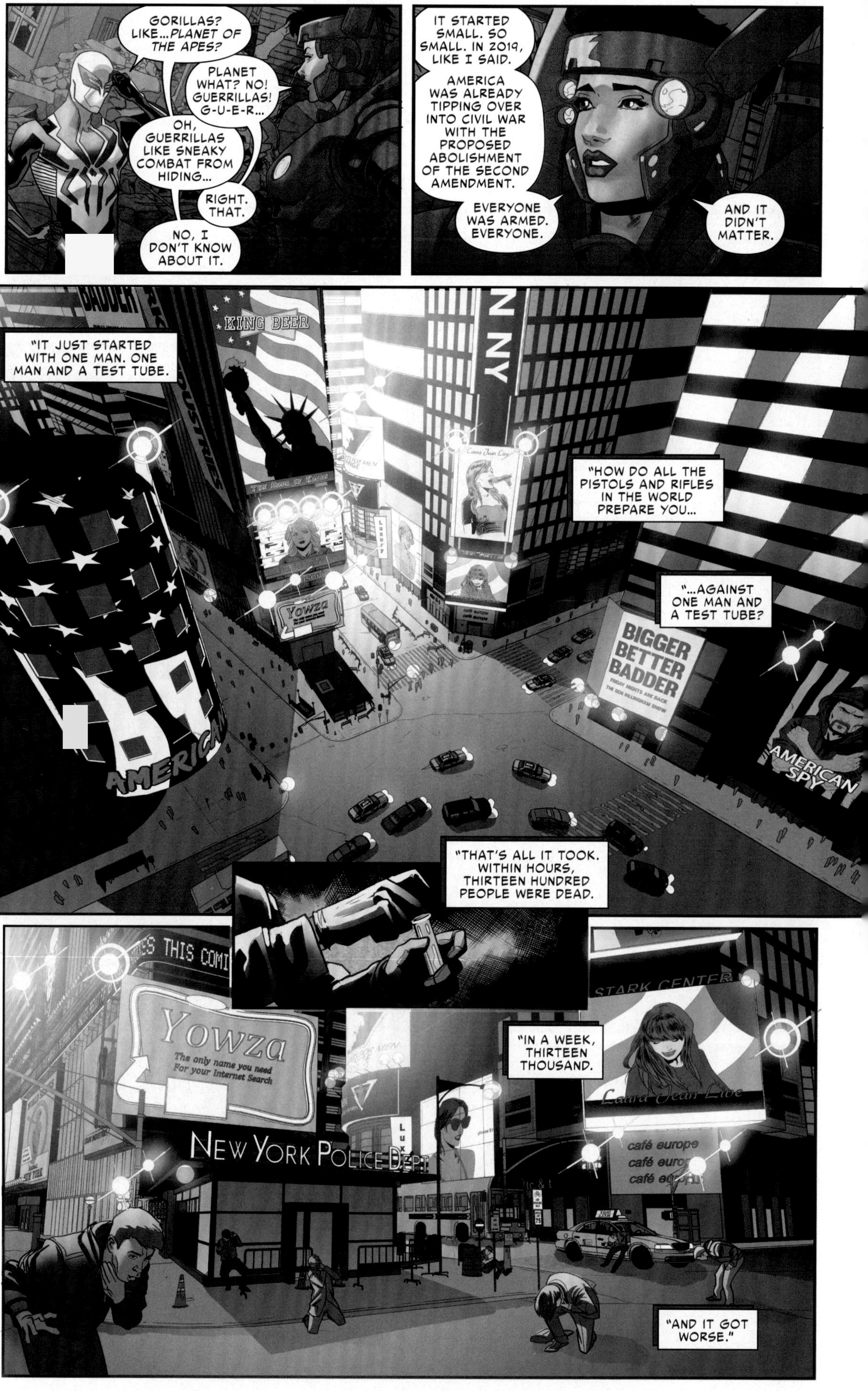
GORILLAS? LIKE...PLANET OF THE APES?
PLANET WHAT? NO! GUERRILLAS! G-U-E-R...
OH, GUERRILLAS LIKE SNEAKY COMBAT FROM HIDING...
RIGHT. THAT.
NO, I DON'T KNOW ABOUT IT.
IT STARTED SMALL. SO SMALL. IN 2019, LIKE I SAID.
AMERICA WAS ALREADY TIPPING OVER INTO CIVIL WAR WITH THE PROPOSED ABOLISHMENT OF THE SECOND AMENDMENT.
EVERYONE WAS ARMED. EVERYONE.
AND IT DIDN'T MATTER.
"IT JUST STARTED WITH ONE MAN. ONE MAN AND A TEST TUBE.
KING BEER
"HOW DO ALL THE PISTOLS AND RIFLES IN THE WORLD PREPARE YOU...
"...AGAINST ONE MAN AND A TEST TUBE?
Yowza
BIGGER BETTER BADDER
AMERICAN SPY
AMERICAN
"THAT'S ALL IT TOOK. WITHIN HOURS, THIRTEEN HUNDRED PEOPLE WERE DEAD.
Yowza
The only name you need For your Internet Search
NEW YORK POLICE DEPT
STARK CENTER
Laura Jean Live
café europe
"IN A WEEK, THIRTEEN THOUSAND.
"AND IT GOT WORSE."

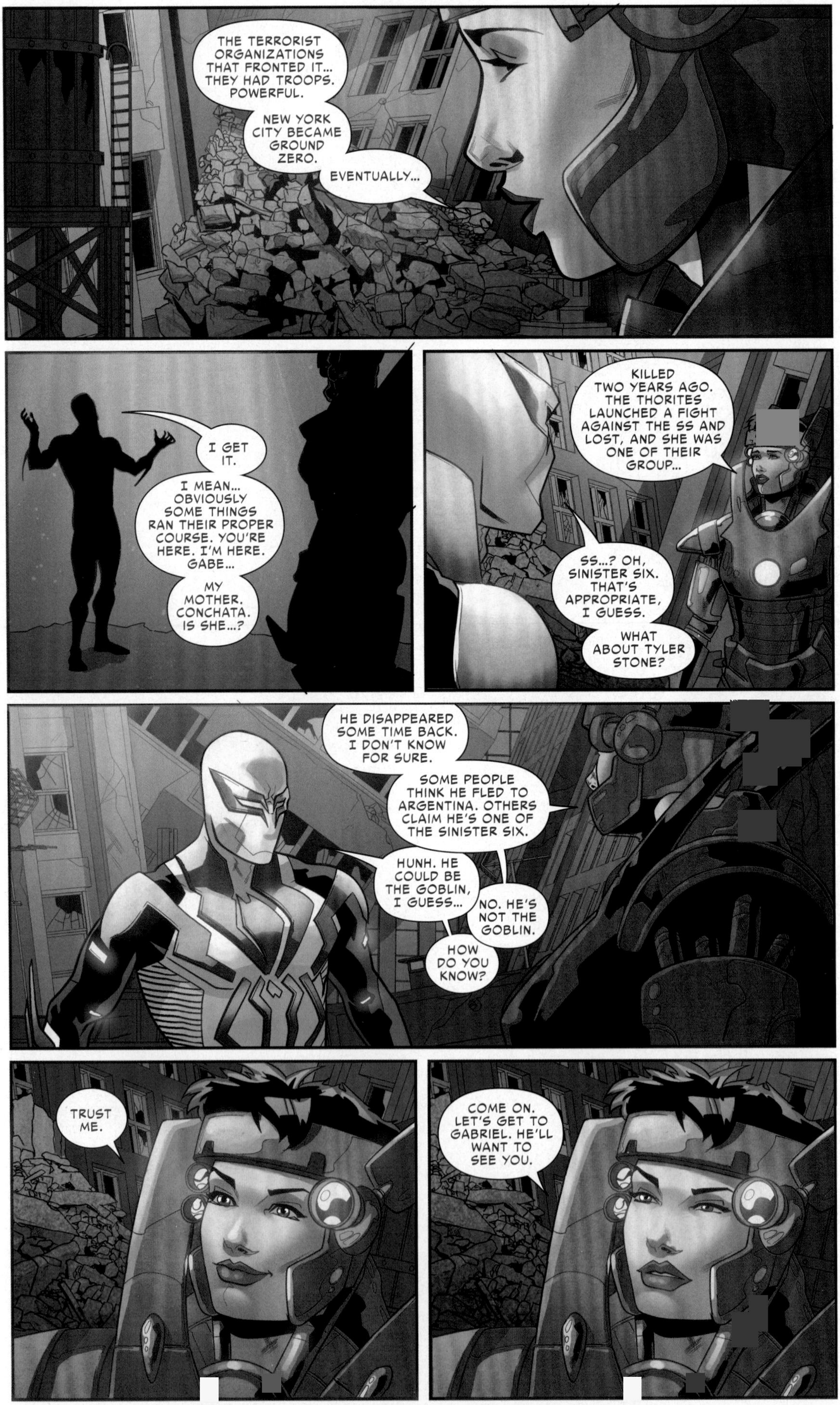
THE TERRORIST ORGANIZATIONS THAT FRONTED IT... THEY HAD TROOPS. POWERFUL.
NEW YORK CITY BECAME GROUND ZERO.
EVENTUALLY...
I GET IT.
I MEAN... OBVIOUSLY SOME THINGS RAN THEIR PROPER COURSE. YOU'RE HERE. I'M HERE. GABE...
MY MOTHER. CONCHATA. IS SHE...?
KILLED TWO YEARS AGO. THE THORITES LAUNCHED A FIGHT AGAINST THE SS AND LOST, AND SHE WAS ONE OF THEIR GROUP...
SS...? OH, SINISTER SIX. THAT'S APPROPRIATE, I GUESS.
WHAT ABOUT TYLER STONE?
HE DISAPPEARED SOME TIME BACK. I DON'T KNOW FOR SURE.
SOME PEOPLE THINK HE FLED TO ARGENTINA. OTHERS CLAIM HE'S ONE OF THE SINISTER SIX.
HUNH. HE COULD BE THE GOBLIN, I GUESS...
NO. HE'S NOT THE GOBLIN.
HOW DO YOU KNOW?
TRUST ME.
COME ON. LET'S GET TO GABRIEL. HE'LL WANT TO SEE YOU.

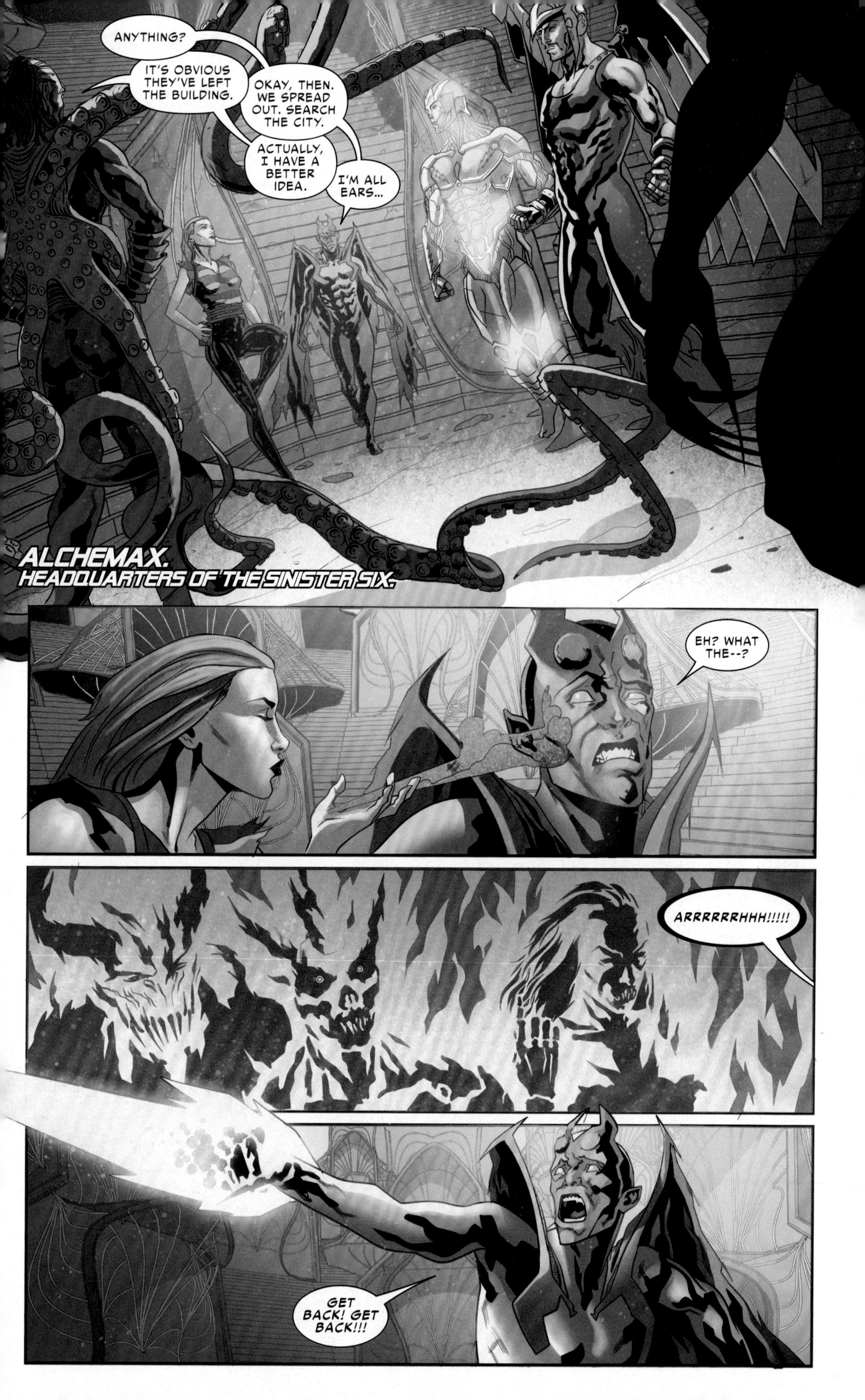
ANYTHING?
IT'S OBVIOUS THEY'VE LEFT THE BUILDING.
OKAY, THEN. WE SPREAD OUT. SEARCH THE CITY.
ACTUALLY, I HAVE A BETTER IDEA.
I'M ALL EARS...
ALCHEMAX.
HEADQUARTERS OF THE SINISTER SIX.
EH? WHAT THE--?
ARRRRRRHHH!!!!!
GET BACK! GET BACK!!!

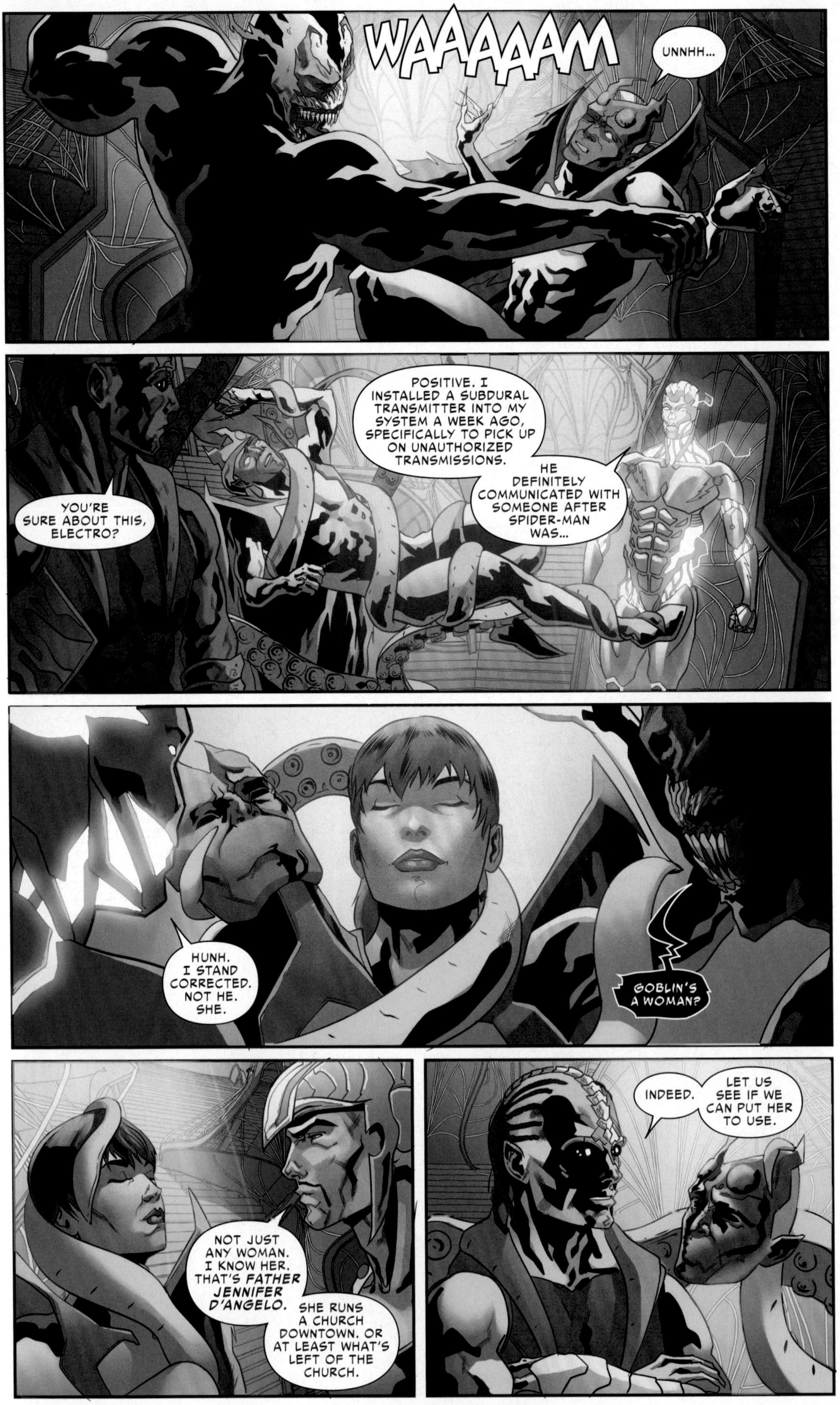
WAAAAAM
UNNHH...
YOU'RE SURE ABOUT THIS, ELECTRO?
POSITIVE. I INSTALLED A SUBDURAL TRANSMITTER INTO MY SYSTEM A WEEK AGO, SPECIFICALLY TO PICK UP ON UNAUTHORIZED TRANSMISSIONS.
HE DEFINITELY COMMUNICATED WITH SOMEONE AFTER SPIDER-MAN WAS...
HUNH. I STAND CORRECTED. NOT HE. SHE.
GOBLIN'S A WOMAN?
NOT JUST ANY WOMAN. I KNOW HER. THAT'S FATHER JENNIFER D'ANGELO.
SHE RUNS A CHURCH DOWNTOWN. OR AT LEAST WHAT'S LEFT OF THE CHURCH.
INDEED.
LET US SEE IF WE CAN PUT HER TO USE.

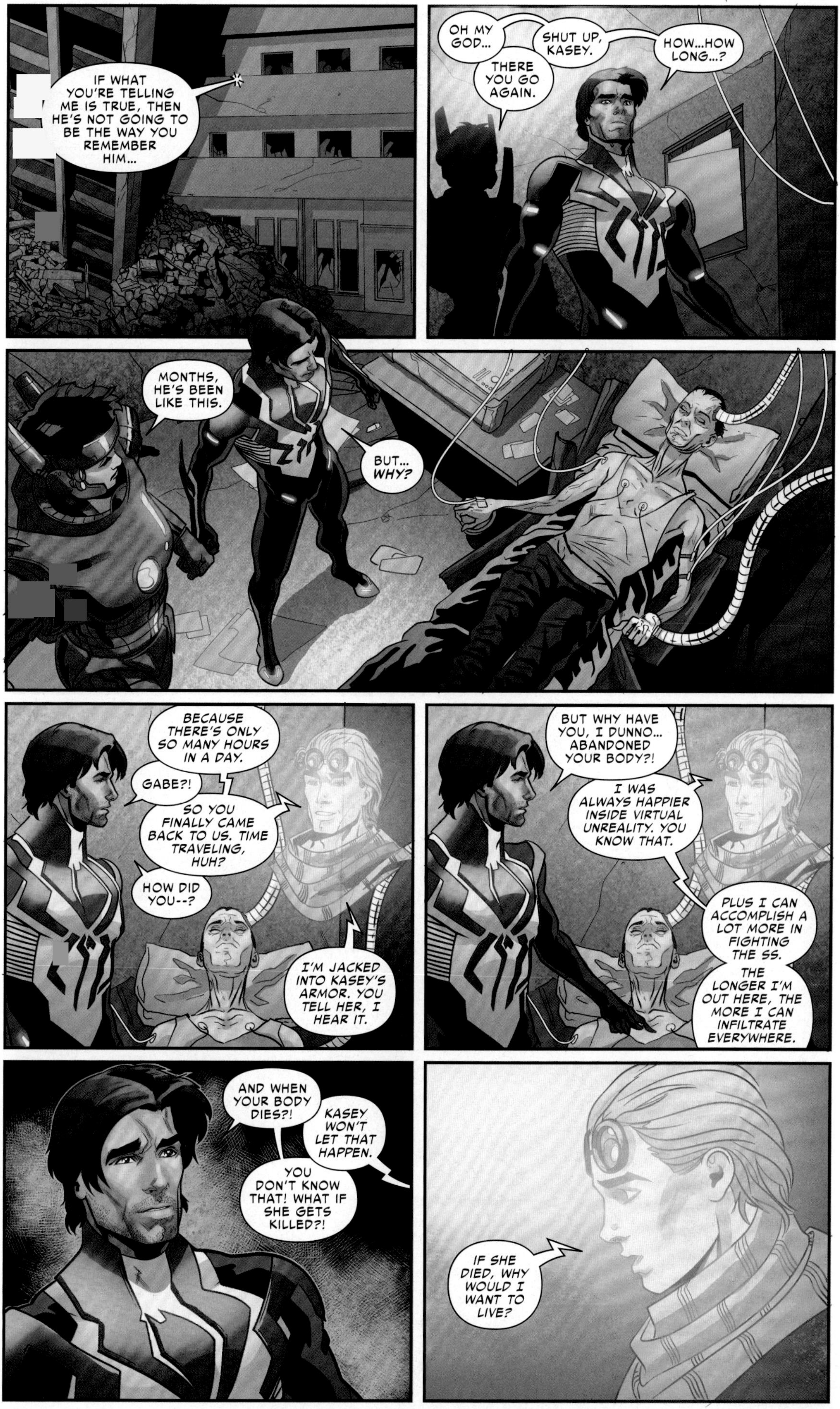
IF WHAT YOU'RE TELLING ME IS TRUE, THEN HE'S NOT GOING TO BE THE WAY YOU REMEMBER HIM...
OH MY GOD...
SHUT UP, KASEY.
THERE YOU GO AGAIN.
HOW...HOW LONG...?
MONTHS, HE'S BEEN LIKE THIS.
BUT... WHY?
BECAUSE THERE'S ONLY SO MANY HOURS IN A DAY.
GABE?!
SO YOU FINALLY CAME BACK TO US. TIME TRAVELING, HUH?
HOW DID YOU--?
I'M JACKED INTO KASEY'S ARMOR. YOU TELL HER, I HEAR IT.
BUT WHY HAVE YOU, I DUNNO... ABANDONED YOUR BODY?!
I WAS ALWAYS HAPPIER INSIDE VIRTUAL UNREALITY. YOU KNOW THAT.
PLUS I CAN ACCOMPLISH A LOT MORE IN FIGHTING THE SS.
THE LONGER I'M OUT HERE, THE MORE I CAN INFILTRATE EVERYWHERE.
AND WHEN YOUR BODY DIES?!
KASEY WON'T LET THAT HAPPEN.
YOU DON'T KNOW THAT! WHAT IF SHE GETS KILLED?!
IF SHE DIED, WHY WOULD I WANT TO LIVE?

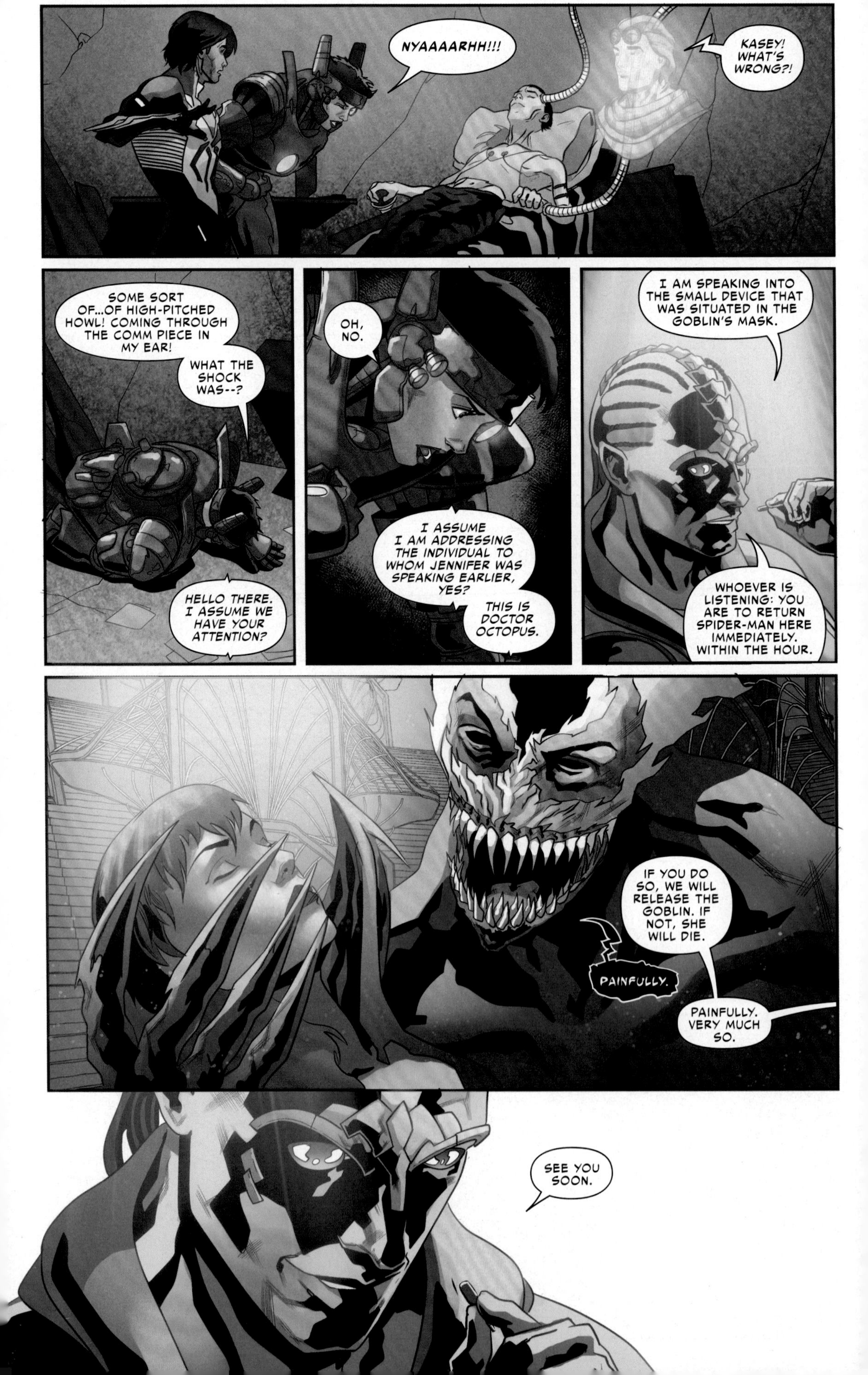
NYAAAARHH!!!
KASEY! WHAT'S WRONG?!
SOME SORT OF...OF HIGH-PITCHED HOWL! COMING THROUGH THE COMM PIECE IN MY EAR!
WHAT THE SHOCK WAS--?
HELLO THERE. I ASSUME WE HAVE YOUR ATTENTION?
OH, NO.
I ASSUME I AM ADDRESSING THE INDIVIDUAL TO WHOM JENNIFER WAS SPEAKING EARLIER, YES?
THIS IS DOCTOR OCTOPUS.
I AM SPEAKING INTO THE SMALL DEVICE THAT WAS SITUATED IN THE GOBLIN'S MASK.
WHOEVER IS LISTENING: YOU ARE TO RETURN SPIDER-MAN HERE IMMEDIATELY. WITHIN THE HOUR.
IF YOU DO SO, WE WILL RELEASE THE GOBLIN. IF NOT, SHE WILL DIE.
PAINFULLY.
PAINFULLY. VERY MUCH SO.
SEE YOU SOON.

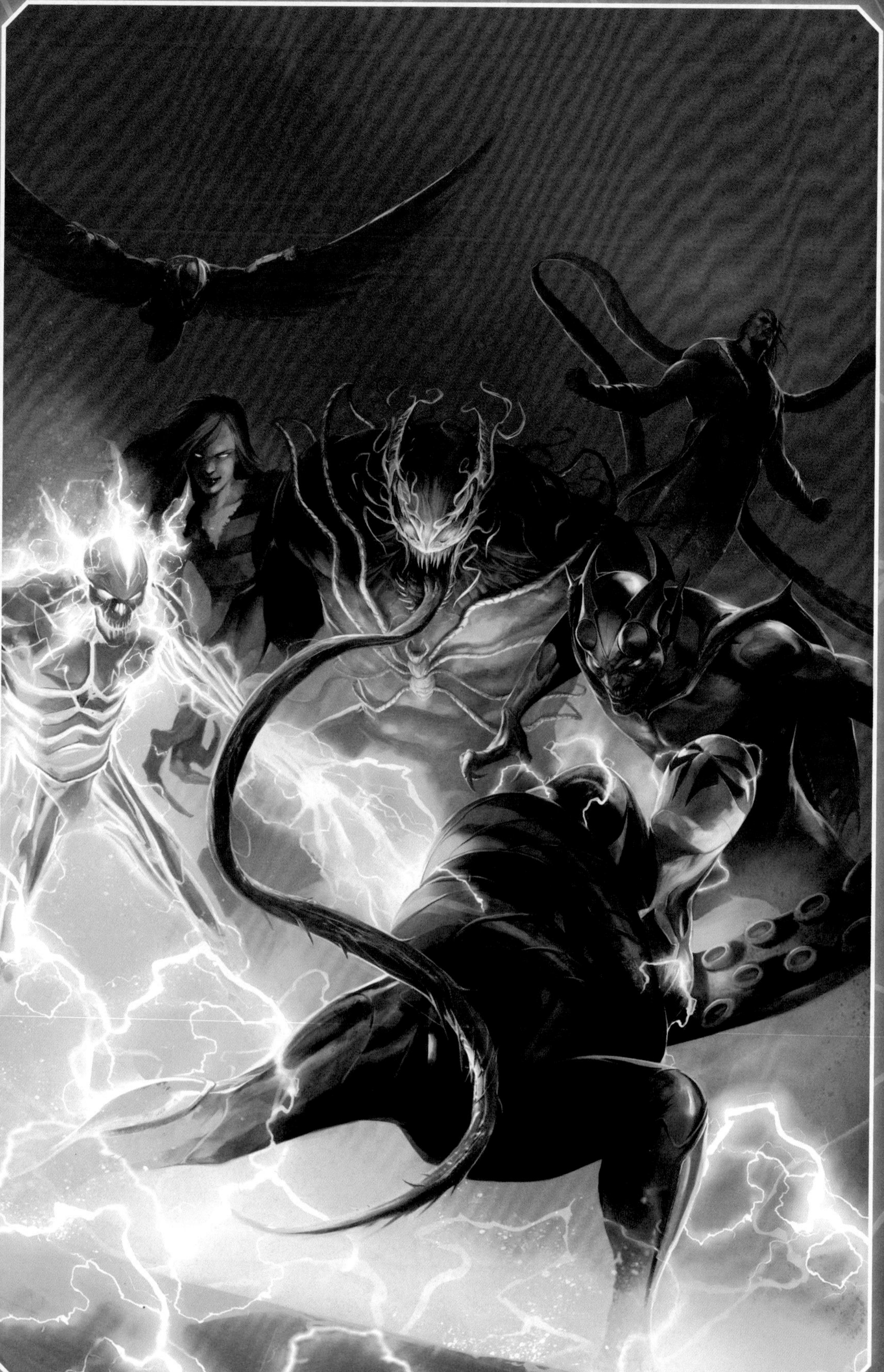

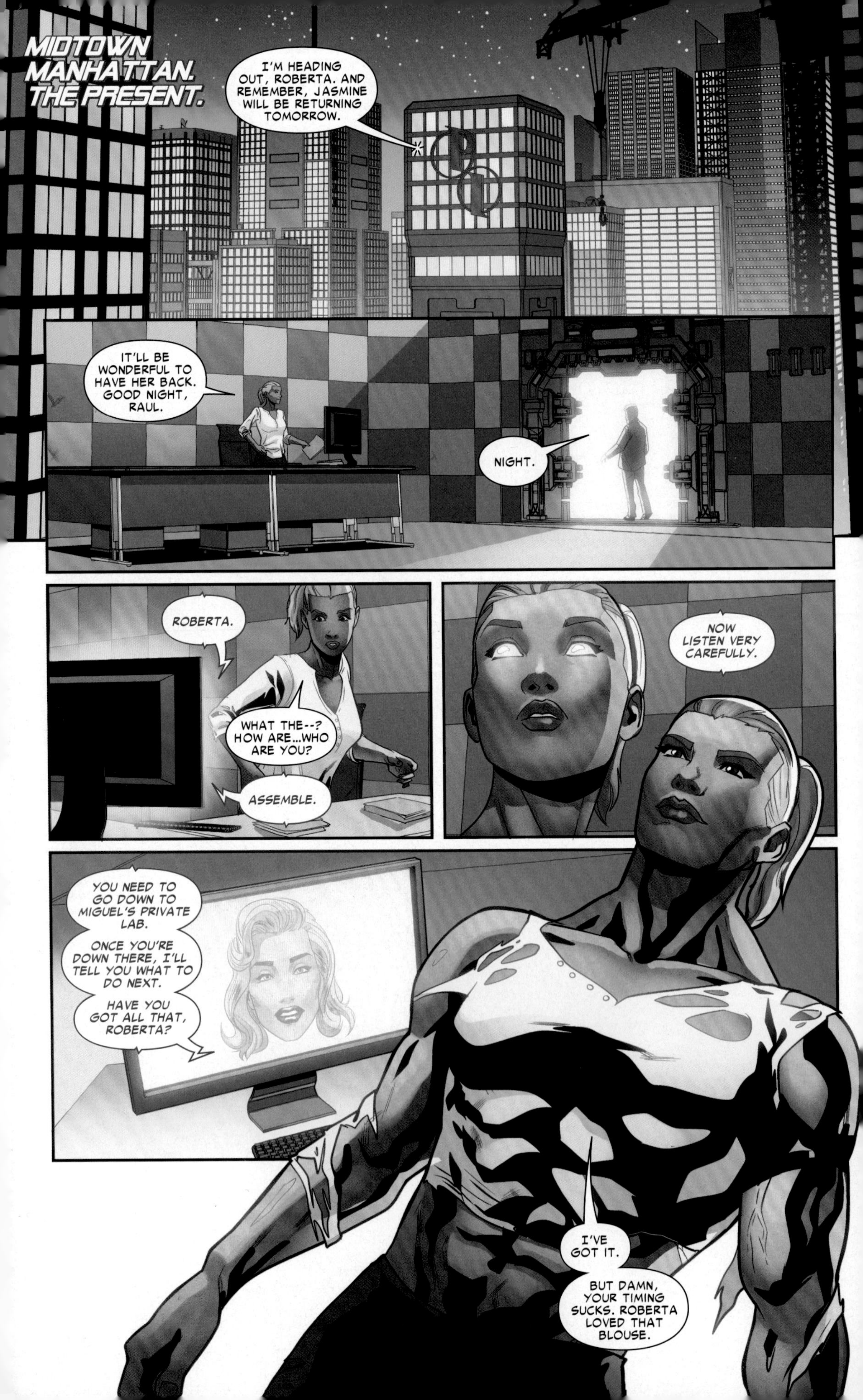
MIDTOWN MANHATTAN. THE PRESENT.
I'M HEADING OUT, ROBERTA. AND REMEMBER, JASMINE WILL BE RETURNING TOMORROW.
IT'LL BE WONDERFUL TO HAVE HER BACK. GOOD NIGHT, RAUL.
NIGHT.
ROBERTA.
WHAT THE--? HOW ARE...WHO ARE YOU?
ASSEMBLE.
NOW LISTEN VERY CAREFULLY.
YOU NEED TO GO DOWN TO MIGUEL'S PRIVATE LAB.
ONCE YOU'RE DOWN THERE, I'LL TELL YOU WHAT TO DO NEXT.
HAVE YOU GOT ALL THAT, ROBERTA?
I'VE GOT IT.
BUT DAMN, YOUR TIMING SUCKS. ROBERTA LOVED THAT BLOUSE.

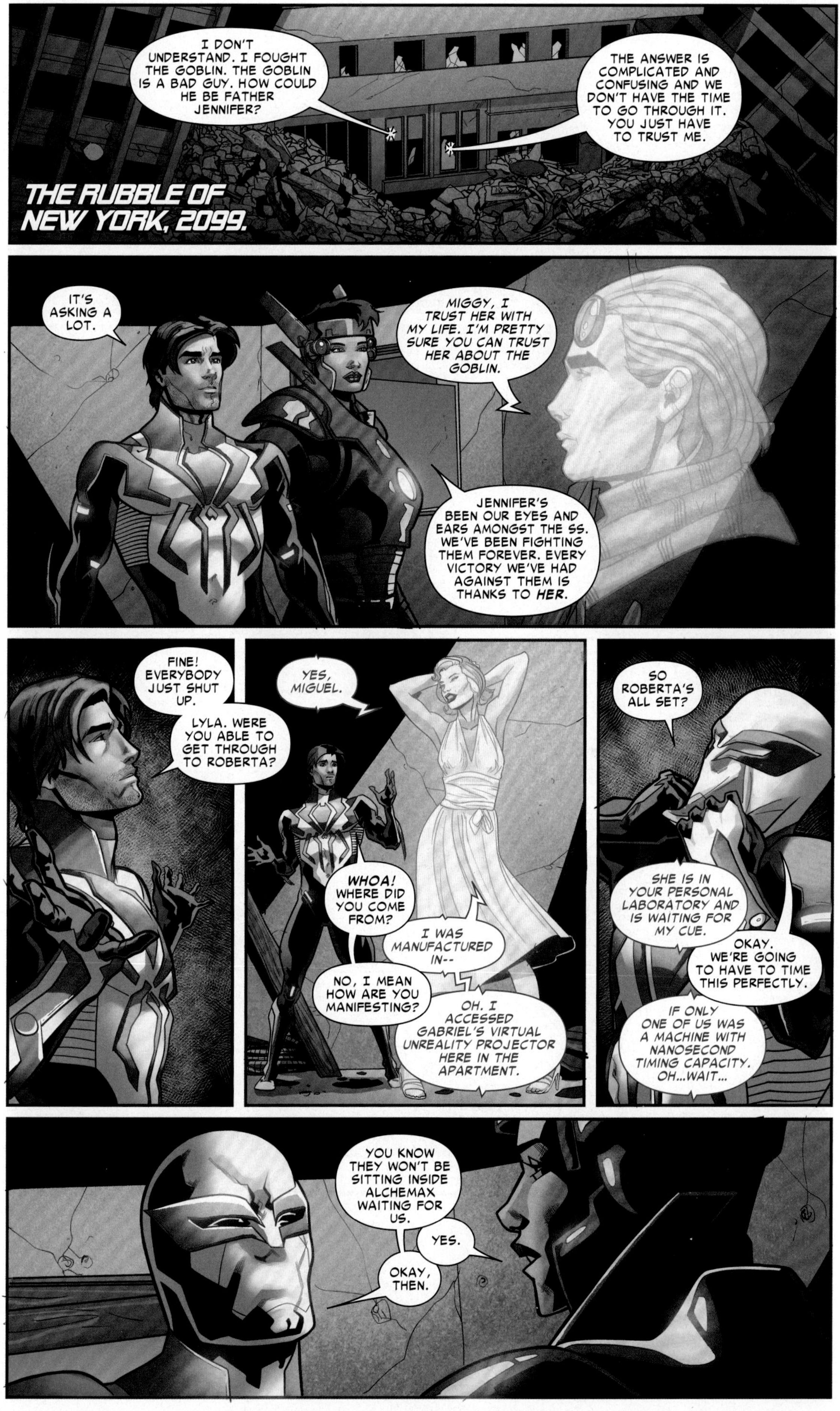
I DON'T UNDERSTAND. I FOUGHT THE GOBLIN. THE GOBLIN IS A BAD GUY. HOW COULD HE BE FATHER JENNIFER?
THE ANSWER IS COMPLICATED AND CONFUSING AND WE DON'T HAVE THE TIME TO GO THROUGH IT. YOU JUST HAVE TO TRUST ME.
THE RUBBLE OF NEW YORK, 2099.
IT'S ASKING A LOT.
MIGGY, I TRUST HER WITH MY LIFE. I'M PRETTY SURE YOU CAN TRUST HER ABOUT THE GOBLIN.
JENNIFER'S BEEN OUR EYES AND EARS AMONGST THE SS. WE'VE BEEN FIGHTING THEM FOREVER. EVERY VICTORY WE'VE HAD AGAINST THEM IS THANKS TO HER.
FINE! EVERYBODY JUST SHUT UP.
LYLA. WERE YOU ABLE TO GET THROUGH TO ROBERTA?
YES, MIGUEL.
WHOA! WHERE DID YOU COME FROM?
I WAS MANUFACTURED IN--
NO, I MEAN HOW ARE YOU MANIFESTING?
OH. I ACCESSED GABRIEL'S VIRTUAL UNREALITY PROJECTOR HERE IN THE APARTMENT.
SO ROBERTA'S ALL SET?
SHE IS IN YOUR PERSONAL LABORATORY AND IS WAITING FOR MY CUE.
OKAY. WE'RE GOING TO HAVE TO TIME THIS PERFECTLY.
IF ONLY ONE OF US WAS A MACHINE WITH NANOSECOND TIMING CAPACITY. OH...WAIT...
YOU KNOW THEY WON'T BE SITTING INSIDE ALCHEMAX WAITING FOR US.
YES.
OKAY, THEN.

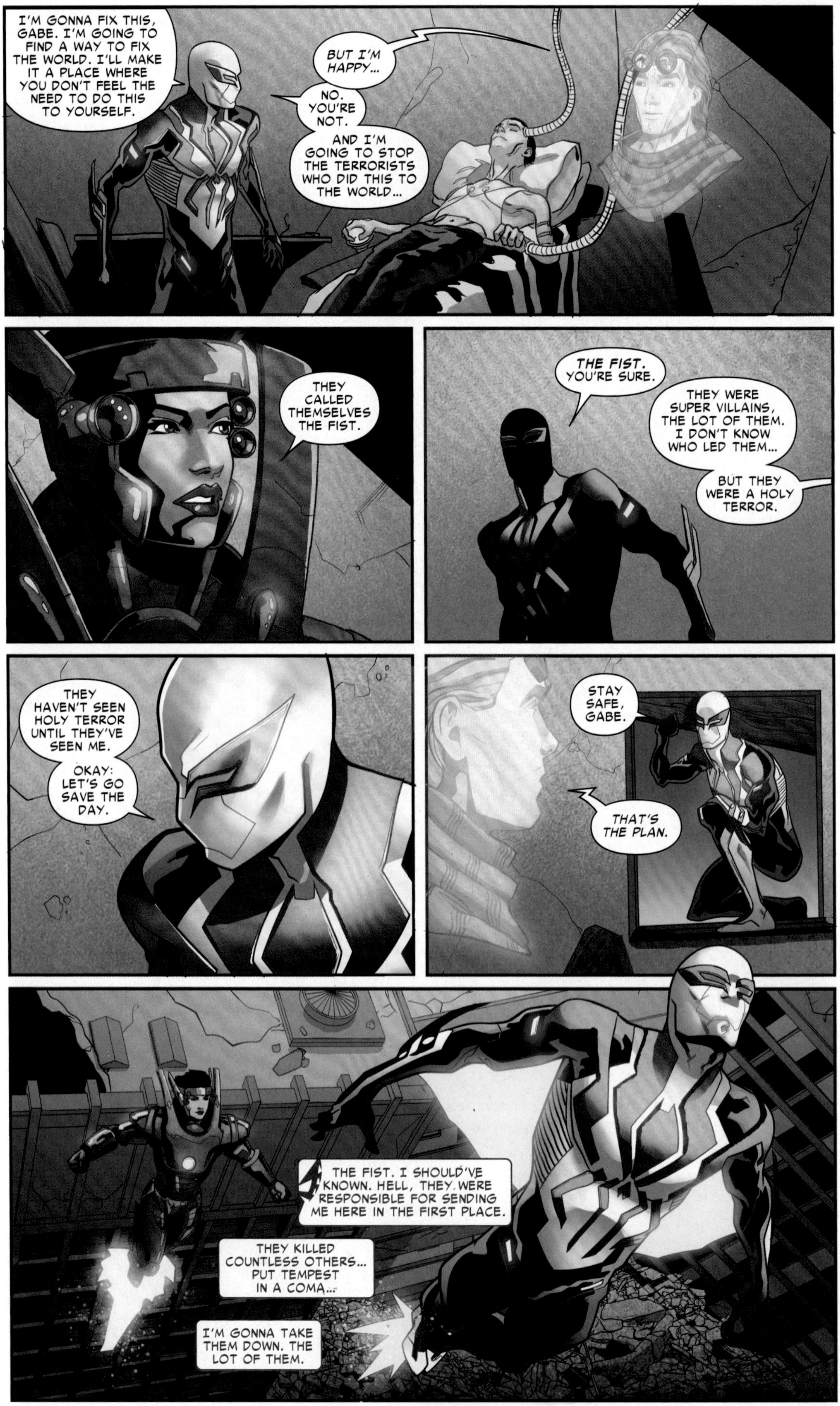
I'M GONNA FIX THIS, GABE. I'M GOING TO FIND A WAY TO FIX THE WORLD. I'LL MAKE IT A PLACE WHERE YOU DON'T FEEL THE NEED TO DO THIS TO YOURSELF.
BUT I'M HAPPY...
NO. YOU'RE NOT.
AND I'M GOING TO STOP THE TERRORISTS WHO DID THIS TO THE WORLD...
THEY CALLED THEMSELVES THE FIST.
THE FIST. YOU'RE SURE.
THEY WERE SUPER VILLAINS, THE LOT OF THEM. I DON'T KNOW WHO LED THEM...
BUT THEY WERE A HOLY TERROR.
THEY HAVEN'T SEEN HOLY TERROR UNTIL THEY'VE SEEN ME.
OKAY: LET'S GO SAVE THE DAY.
STAY SAFE, GABE.
THAT'S THE PLAN.
THE FIST. I SHOULD'VE KNOWN. HELL, THEY WERE RESPONSIBLE FOR SENDING ME HERE IN THE FIRST PLACE.
THEY KILLED COUNTLESS OTHERS... PUT TEMPEST IN A COMA...
I'M GONNA TAKE THEM DOWN. THE LOT OF THEM.

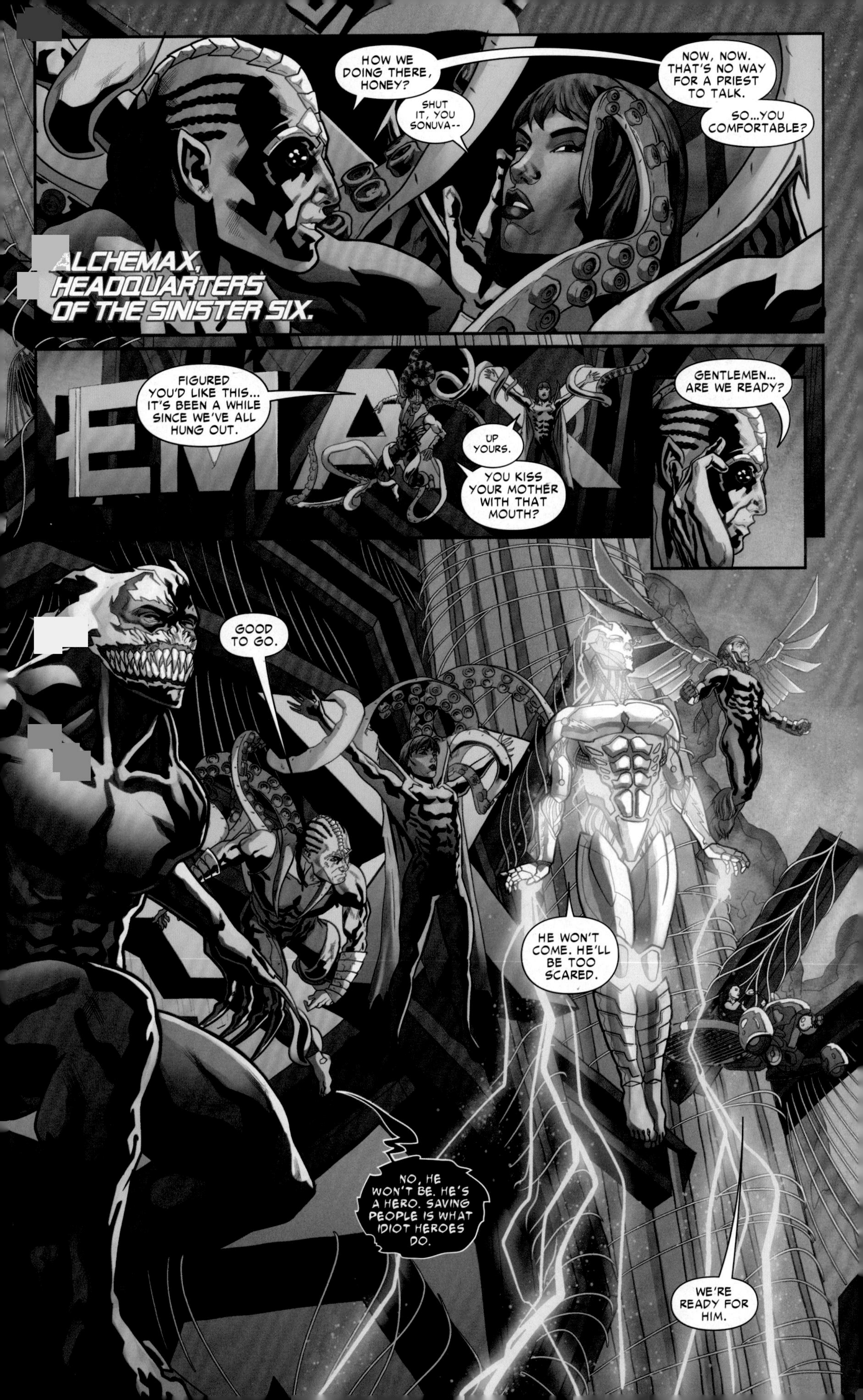
ALCHEMAX, HEADQUARTERS OF THE SINISTER SIX.
HOW WE DOING THERE, HONEY?
SHUT IT, YOU SONUVA--
NOW, NOW. THAT'S NO WAY FOR A PRIEST TO TALK.
SO...YOU COMFORTABLE?
FIGURED YOU'D LIKE THIS... IT'S BEEN A WHILE SINCE WE'VE ALL HUNG OUT.
UP YOURS.
YOU KISS YOUR MOTHER WITH THAT MOUTH?
GENTLEMEN... ARE WE READY?
GOOD TO GO.
HE WON'T COME. HE'LL BE TOO SCARED.
NO, HE WON'T BE. HE'S A HERO. SAVING PEOPLE IS WHAT IDIOT HEROES DO.
WE'RE READY FOR HIM.

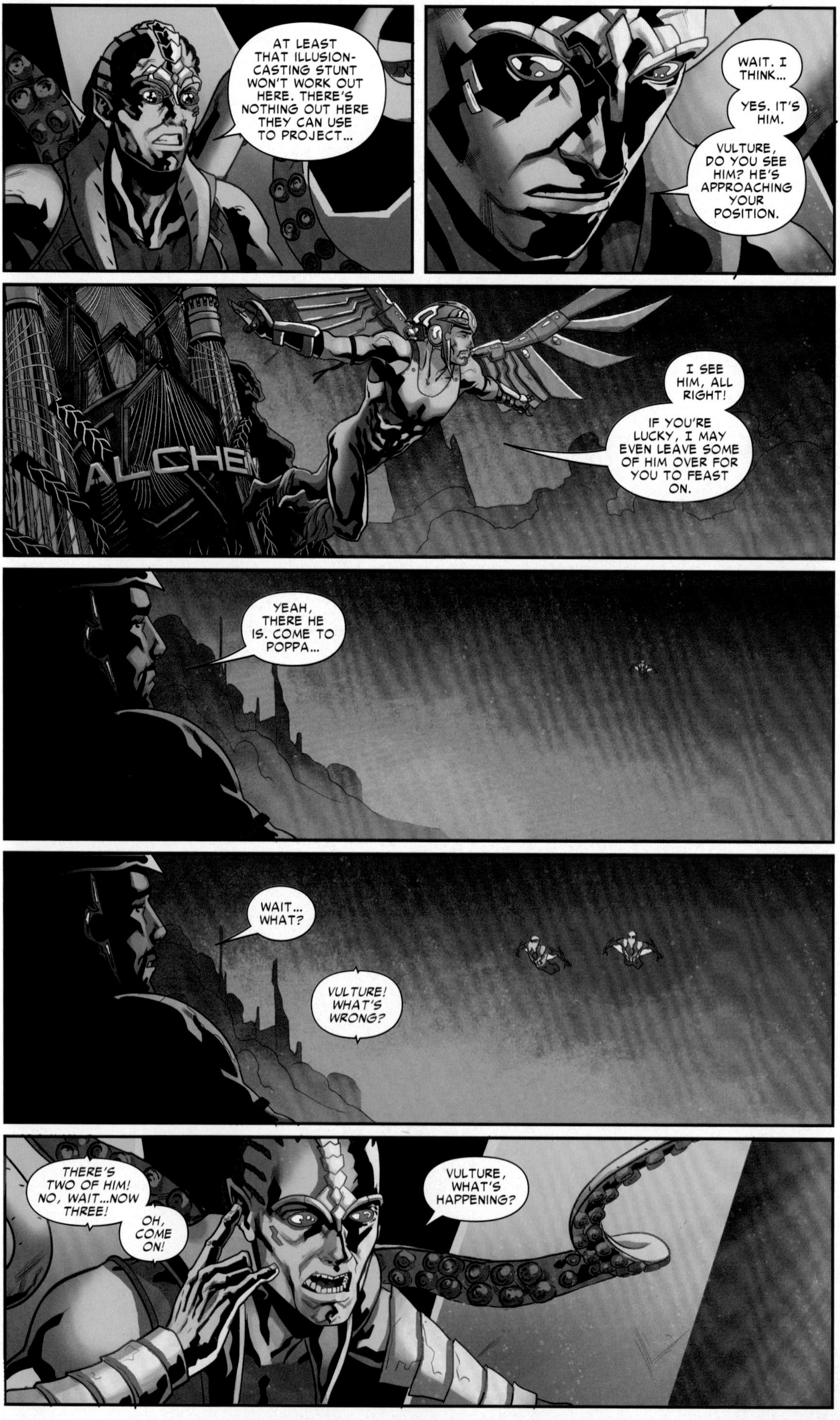
AT LEAST THAT ILLUSION-CASTING STUNT WON'T WORK OUT HERE. THERE'S NOTHING OUT HERE THEY CAN USE TO PROJECT...
WAIT. I THINK...
YES. IT'S HIM.
VULTURE, DO YOU SEE HIM? HE'S APPROACHING YOUR POSITION.
I SEE HIM, ALL RIGHT!
IF YOU'RE LUCKY, I MAY EVEN LEAVE SOME OF HIM OVER FOR YOU TO FEAST ON.
ALCHEM
YEAH, THERE HE IS. COME TO POPPA...
WAIT... WHAT?
VULTURE! WHAT'S WRONG?
THERE'S TWO OF HIM! NO, WAIT...NOW THREE!
OH, COME ON!
VULTURE, WHAT'S HAPPENING?

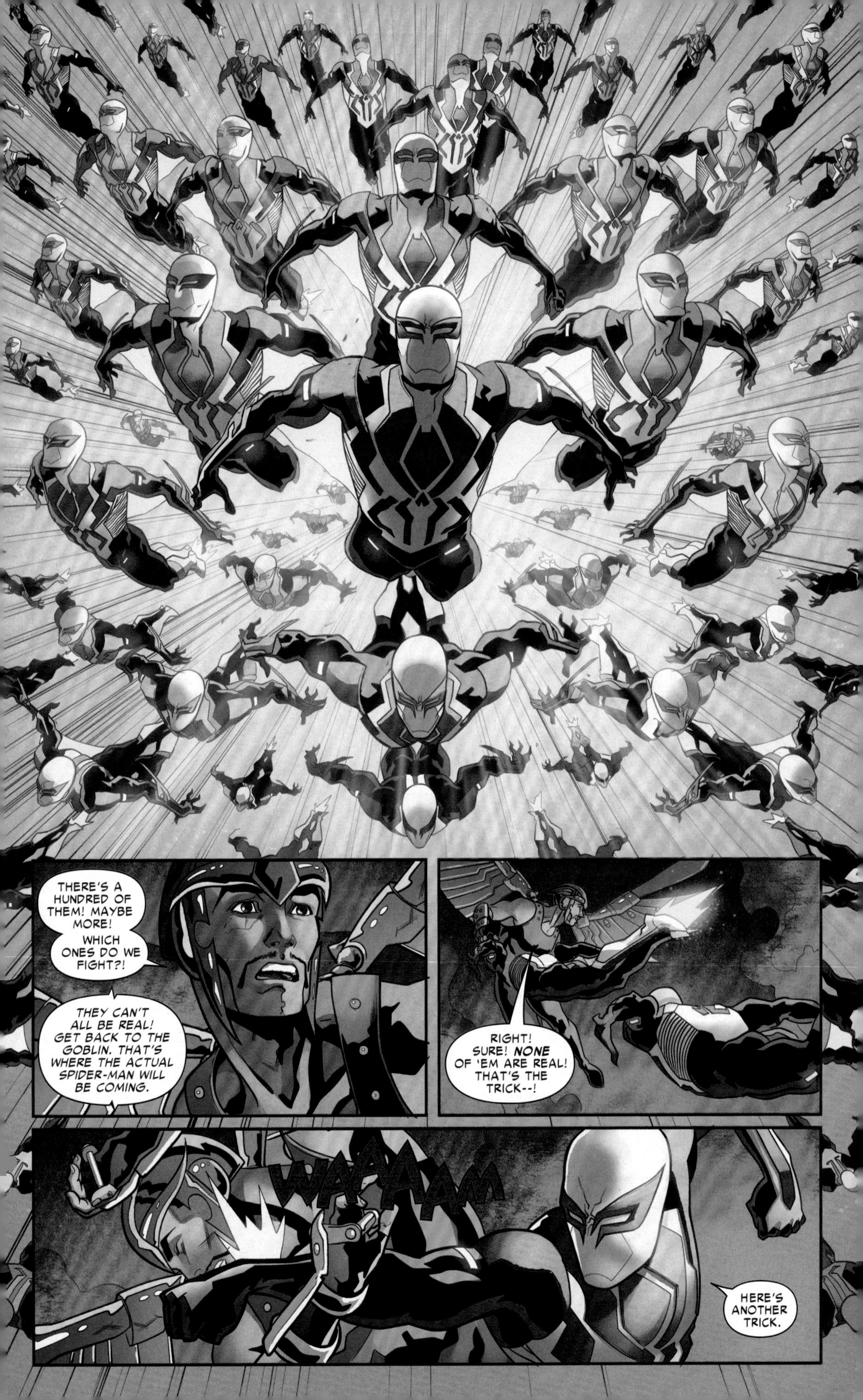
THERE'S A HUNDRED OF THEM! MAYBE MORE!
WHICH ONES DO WE FIGHT?!
THEY CAN'T ALL BE REAL! GET BACK TO THE GOBLIN. THAT'S WHERE THE ACTUAL SPIDER-MAN WILL BE COMING.
RIGHT! SURE! NONE OF 'EM ARE REAL! THAT'S THE TRICK--!
WHAAAAM
HERE'S ANOTHER TRICK.

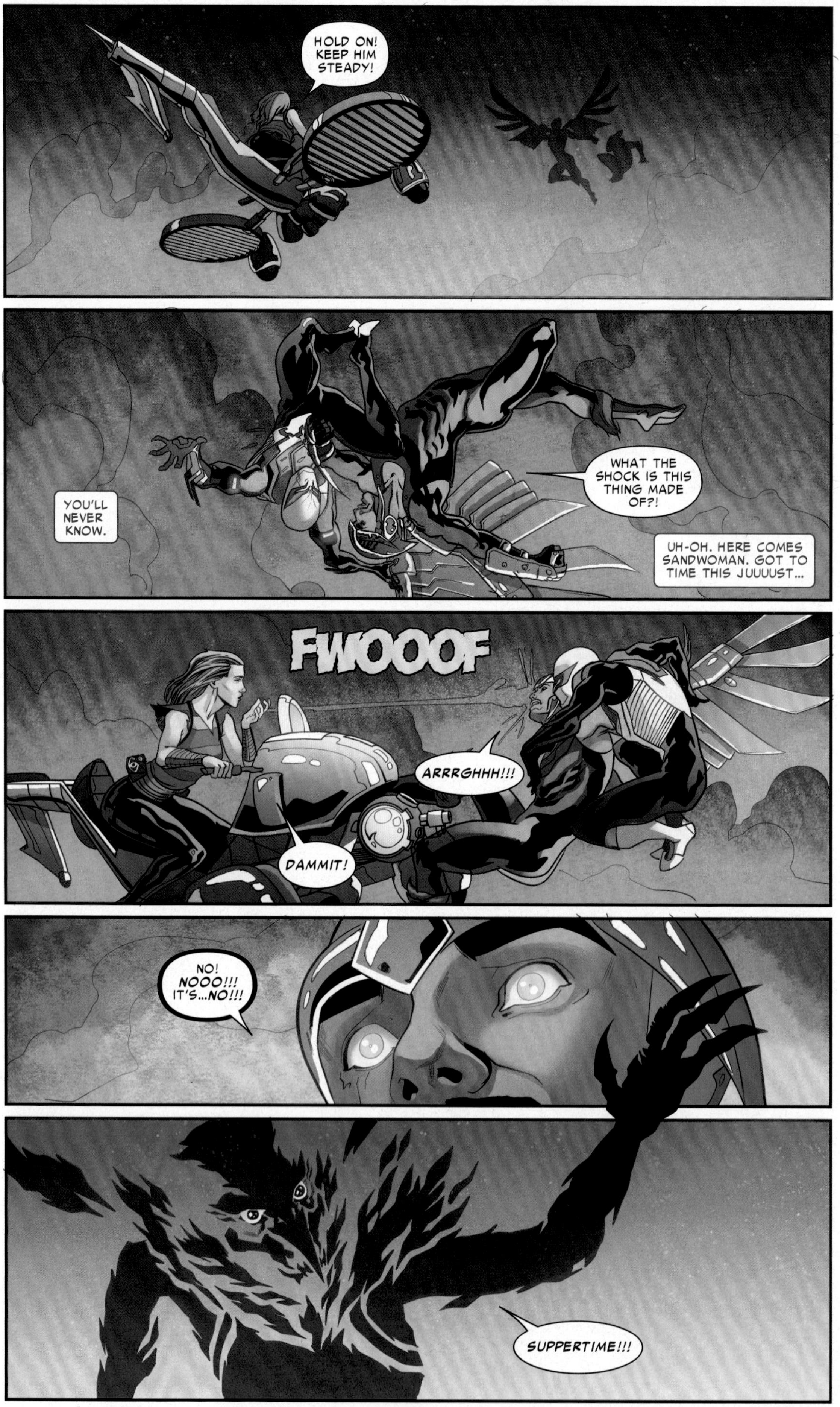
HOLD ON! KEEP HIM STEADY!
YOU'LL NEVER KNOW.
WHAT THE SHOCK IS THIS THING MADE OF?!
UH-OH. HERE COMES SANDWOMAN. GOT TO TIME THIS JUUUUST...
FWOOOF
ARRRGHHH!!!
DAMMIT!
NO! NOOO!!! IT'S...NO!!!
SUPPERTIME!!!

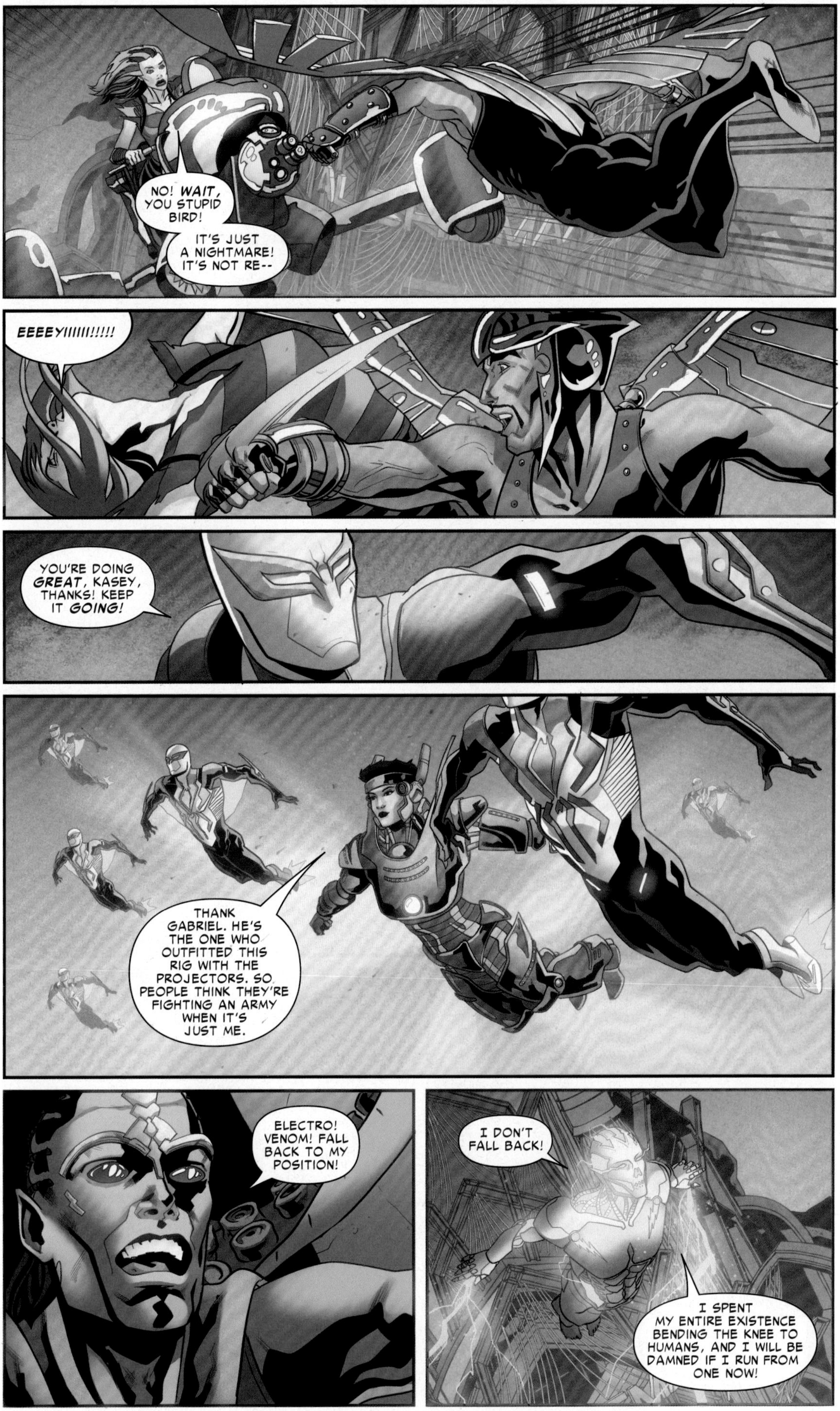
NO! WAIT, YOU STUPID BIRD!
IT'S JUST A NIGHTMARE! IT'S NOT RE--
EEEEYIIIIII!!!!!!
YOU'RE DOING GREAT, KASEY, THANKS! KEEP IT GOING!
THANK GABRIEL. HE'S THE ONE WHO OUTFITTED THIS RIG WITH THE PROJECTORS. SO PEOPLE THINK THEY'RE FIGHTING AN ARMY WHEN IT'S JUST ME.
ELECTRO! VENOM! FALL BACK TO MY POSITION!
I DON'T FALL BACK!
I SPENT MY ENTIRE EXISTENCE BENDING THE KNEE TO HUMANS, AND I WILL BE DAMNED IF I RUN FROM ONE NOW!

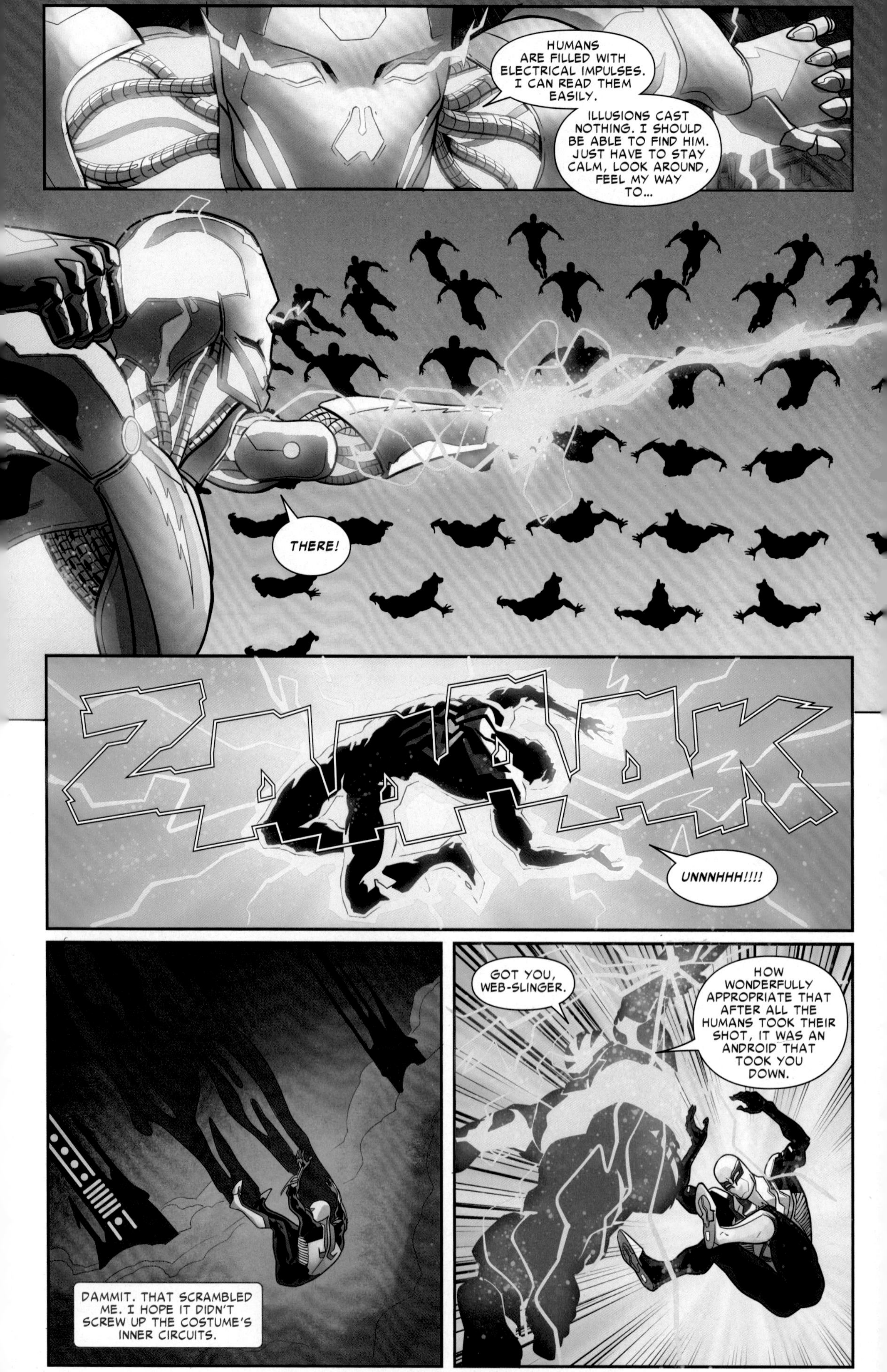
HUMANS ARE FILLED WITH ELECTRICAL IMPULSES. I CAN READ THEM EASILY.
ILLUSIONS CAST NOTHING. I SHOULD BE ABLE TO FIND HIM. JUST HAVE TO STAY CALM, LOOK AROUND, FEEL MY WAY TO...
THERE!
ZAAAK
UNNNHHH!!!!
DAMMIT. THAT SCRAMBLED ME. I HOPE IT DIDN'T SCREW UP THE COSTUME'S INNER CIRCUITS.
GOT YOU, WEB-SLINGER.
HOW WONDERFULLY APPROPRIATE THAT AFTER ALL THE HUMANS TOOK THEIR SHOT, IT WAS AN ANDROID THAT TOOK YOU DOWN.

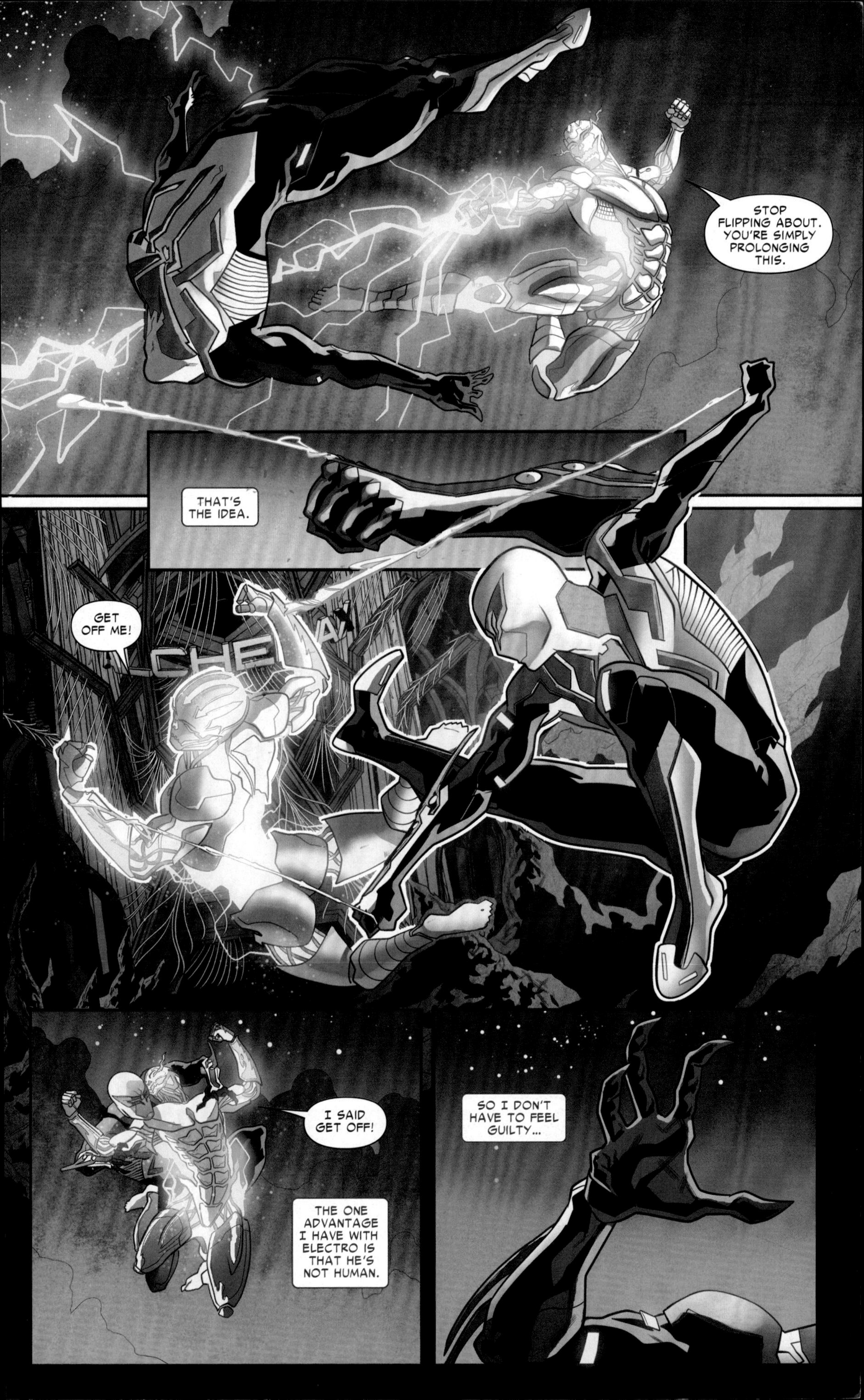
STOP FLIPPING ABOUT. YOU'RE SIMPLY PROLONGING THIS.
THAT'S THE IDEA.
GET OFF ME!
I SAID GET OFF!
THE ONE ADVANTAGE I HAVE WITH ELECTRO IS THAT HE'S NOT HUMAN.
SO I DON'T HAVE TO FEEL GUILTY...

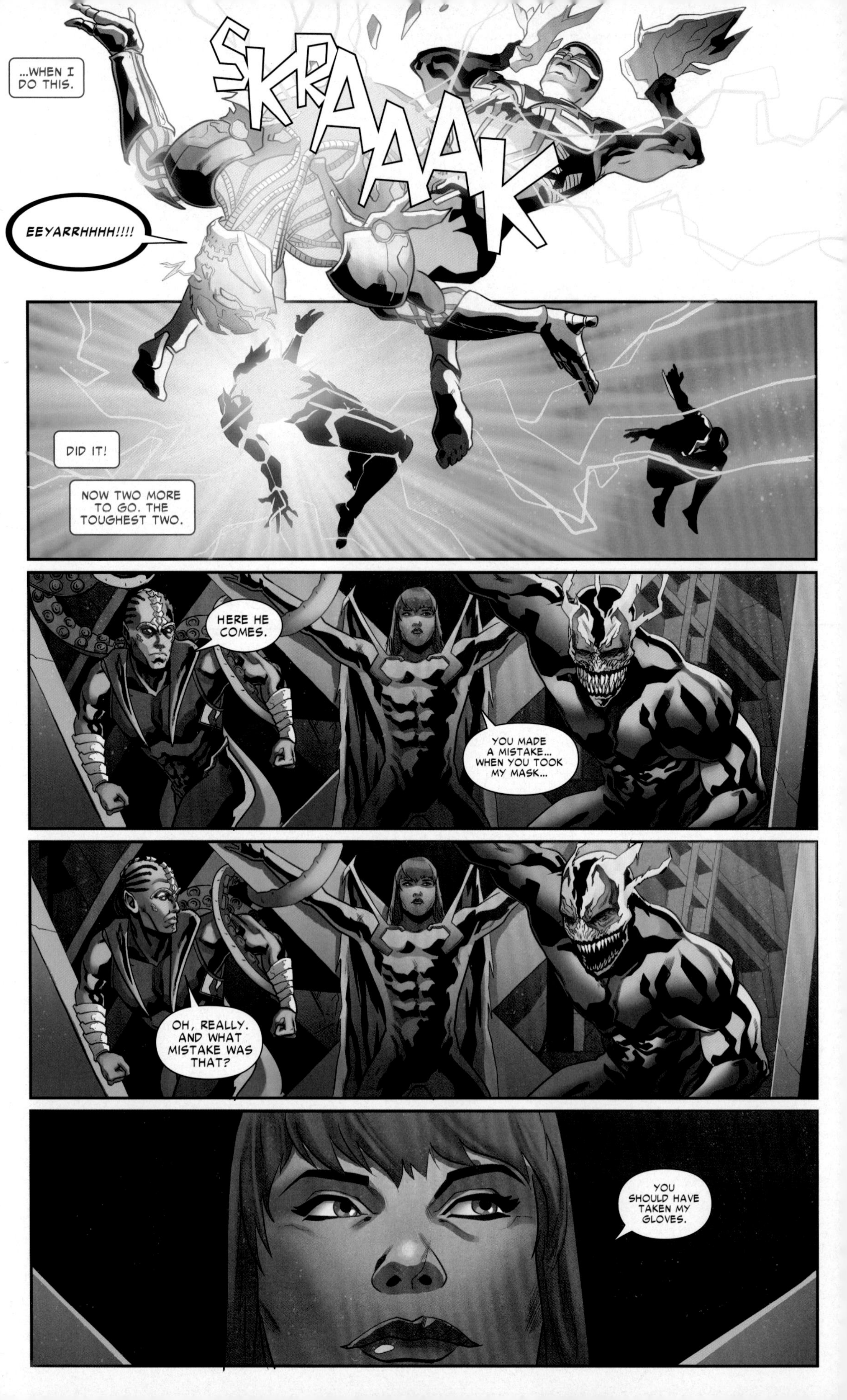
...WHEN I DO THIS.
SKRAAAK
EEYARRHHHH!!!!
DID IT!
NOW TWO MORE TO GO. THE TOUGHEST TWO.
HERE HE COMES.
YOU MADE A MISTAKE... WHEN YOU TOOK MY MASK...
OH, REALLY. AND WHAT MISTAKE WAS THAT?
YOU SHOULD HAVE TAKEN MY GLOVES.

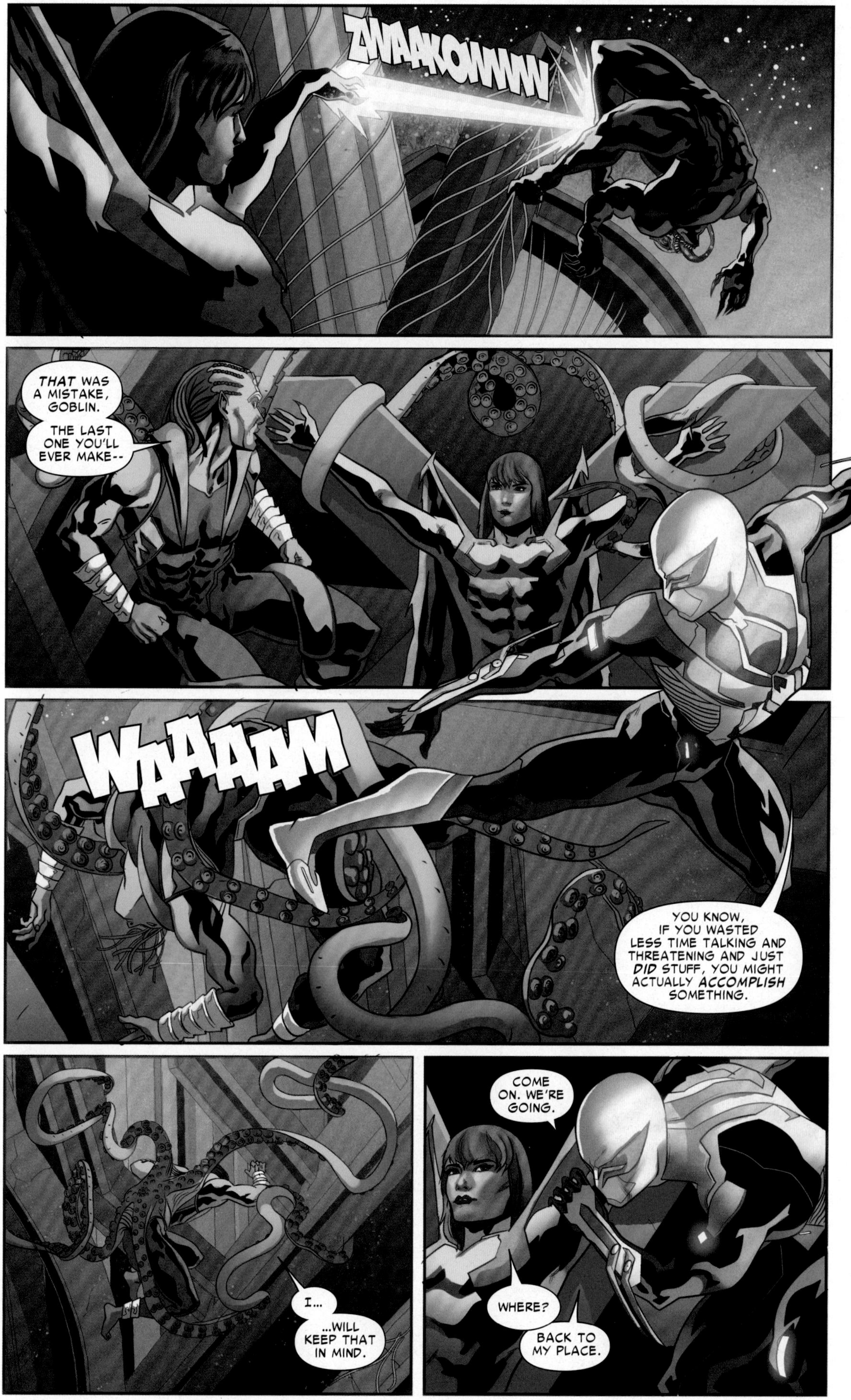
ZWAAKOWWW
THAT WAS A MISTAKE, GOBLIN.
THE LAST ONE YOU'LL EVER MAKE--
WAAAAM
YOU KNOW, IF YOU WASTED LESS TIME TALKING AND THREATENING AND JUST DID STUFF, YOU MIGHT ACTUALLY ACCOMPLISH SOMETHING.
I...
...WILL KEEP THAT IN MIND.
COME ON. WE'RE GOING.
WHERE?
BACK TO MY PLACE.

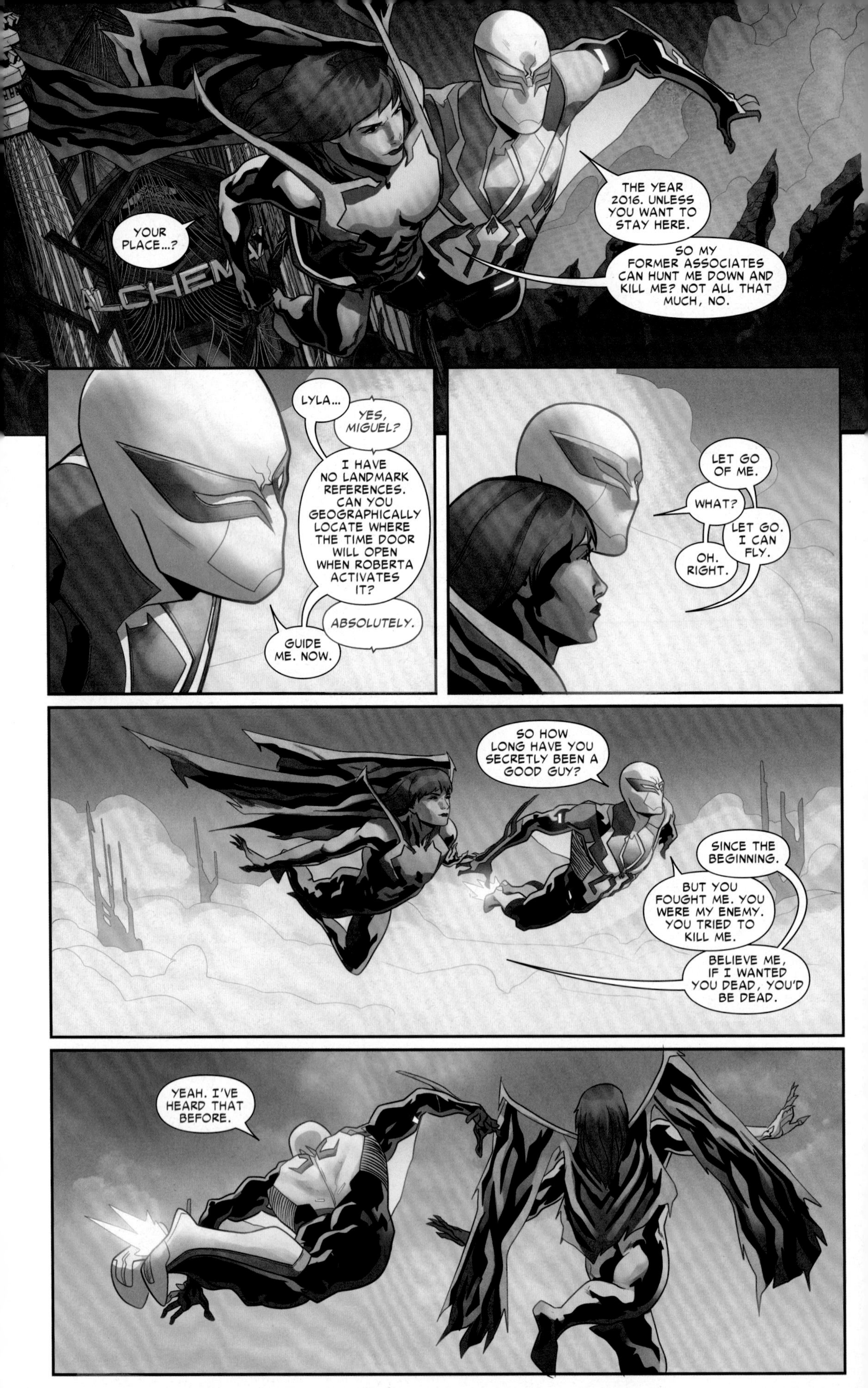
YOUR PLACE...?
THE YEAR 2016. UNLESS YOU WANT TO STAY HERE.
SO MY FORMER ASSOCIATES CAN HUNT ME DOWN AND KILL ME? NOT ALL THAT MUCH, NO.
ALCHEM
LYLA...
YES, MIGUEL?
I HAVE NO LANDMARK REFERENCES. CAN YOU GEOGRAPHICALLY LOCATE WHERE THE TIME DOOR WILL OPEN WHEN ROBERTA ACTIVATES IT?
ABSOLUTELY.
GUIDE ME. NOW.
LET GO OF ME.
WHAT?
LET GO. I CAN FLY.
OH. RIGHT.
SO HOW LONG HAVE YOU SECRETLY BEEN A GOOD GUY?
SINCE THE BEGINNING.
BUT YOU FOUGHT ME. YOU WERE MY ENEMY. YOU TRIED TO KILL ME.
BELIEVE ME, IF I WANTED YOU DEAD, YOU'D BE DEAD.
YEAH. I'VE HEARD THAT BEFORE.

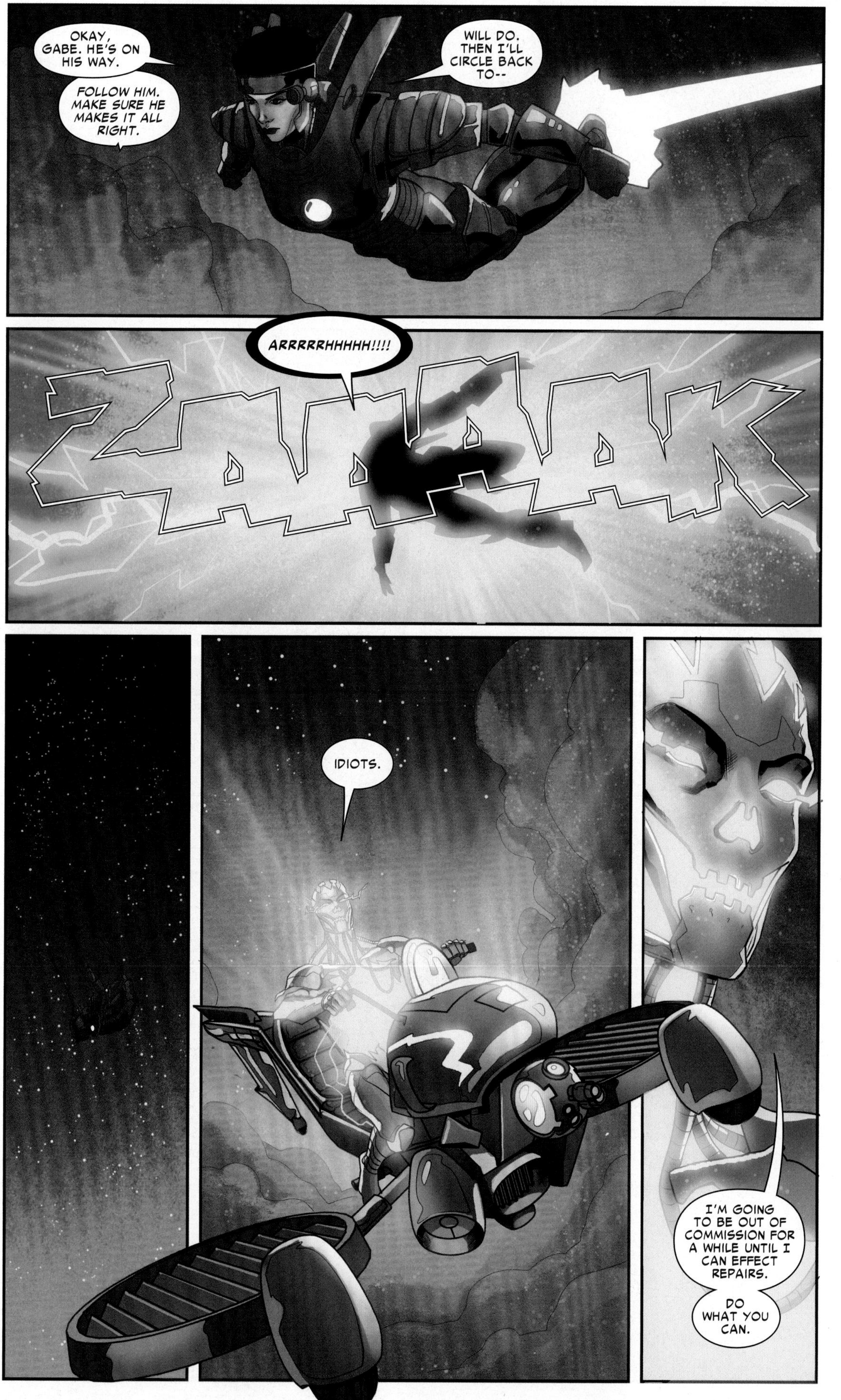
OKAY, GABE. HE'S ON HIS WAY.
FOLLOW HIM. MAKE SURE HE MAKES IT ALL RIGHT.
WILL DO. THEN I'LL CIRCLE BACK TO--
ARRRRRHHHHH!!!!
ZAAAAK
IDIOTS.
I'M GOING TO BE OUT OF COMMISSION FOR A WHILE UNTIL I CAN EFFECT REPAIRS.
DO WHAT YOU CAN.

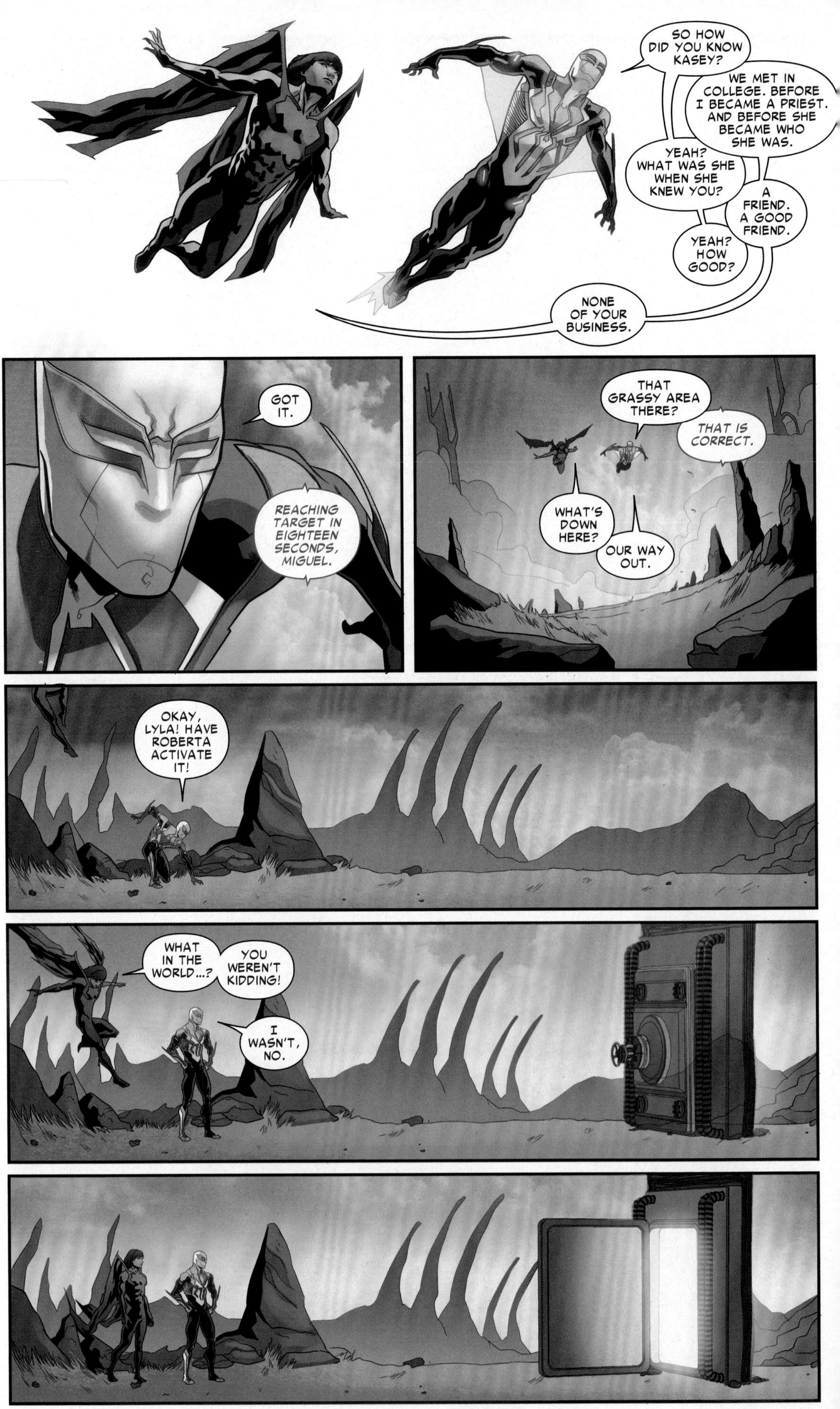

SO HOW DID YOU KNOW KASEY?
WE MET IN COLLEGE. BEFORE I BECAME A PRIEST. AND BEFORE SHE BECAME WHO SHE WAS.
YEAH? WHAT WAS SHE WHEN SHE KNEW YOU?
A FRIEND. A GOOD FRIEND.
YEAH? HOW GOOD?
NONE OF YOUR BUSINESS.
GOT IT.
REACHING TARGET IN EIGHTEEN SECONDS, MIGUEL.
THAT GRASSY AREA THERE?
THAT IS CORRECT.
WHAT'S DOWN HERE?
OUR WAY OUT.
OKAY, LYLA! HAVE ROBERTA ACTIVATE IT!
WHAT IN THE WORLD...?
YOU WEREN'T KIDDING!
I WASN'T, NO.

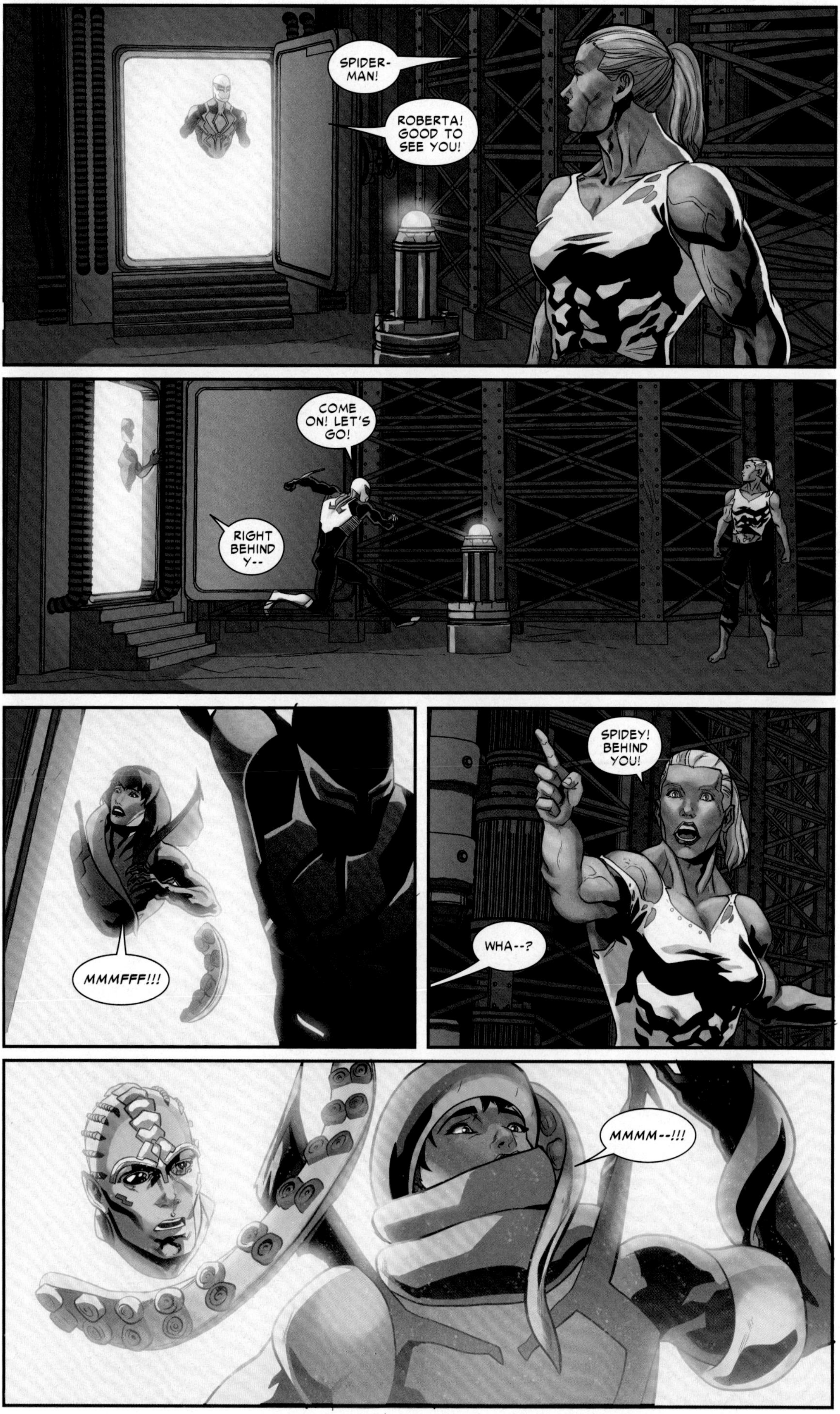
SPIDER-MAN!
ROBERTA! GOOD TO SEE YOU!
COME ON! LET'S GO!
RIGHT BEHIND Y--
MMMFFF!!!
SPIDEY! BEHIND YOU!
WHA--?
MMMM--!!!

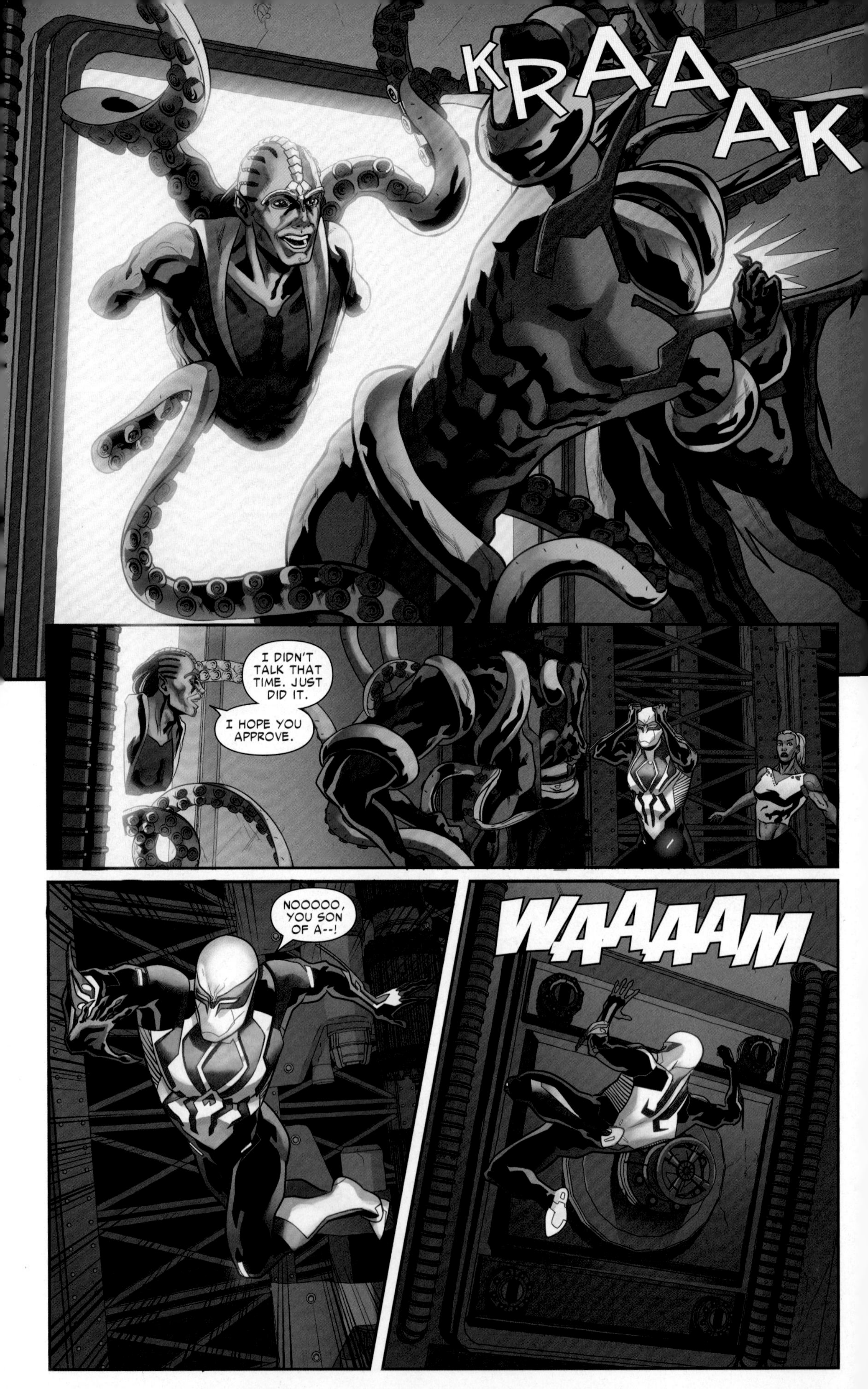
KRAAAK
I DIDN'T TALK THAT TIME. JUST DID IT.
I HOPE YOU APPROVE.
NOOOOO, YOU SON OF A--!
WAAAAM

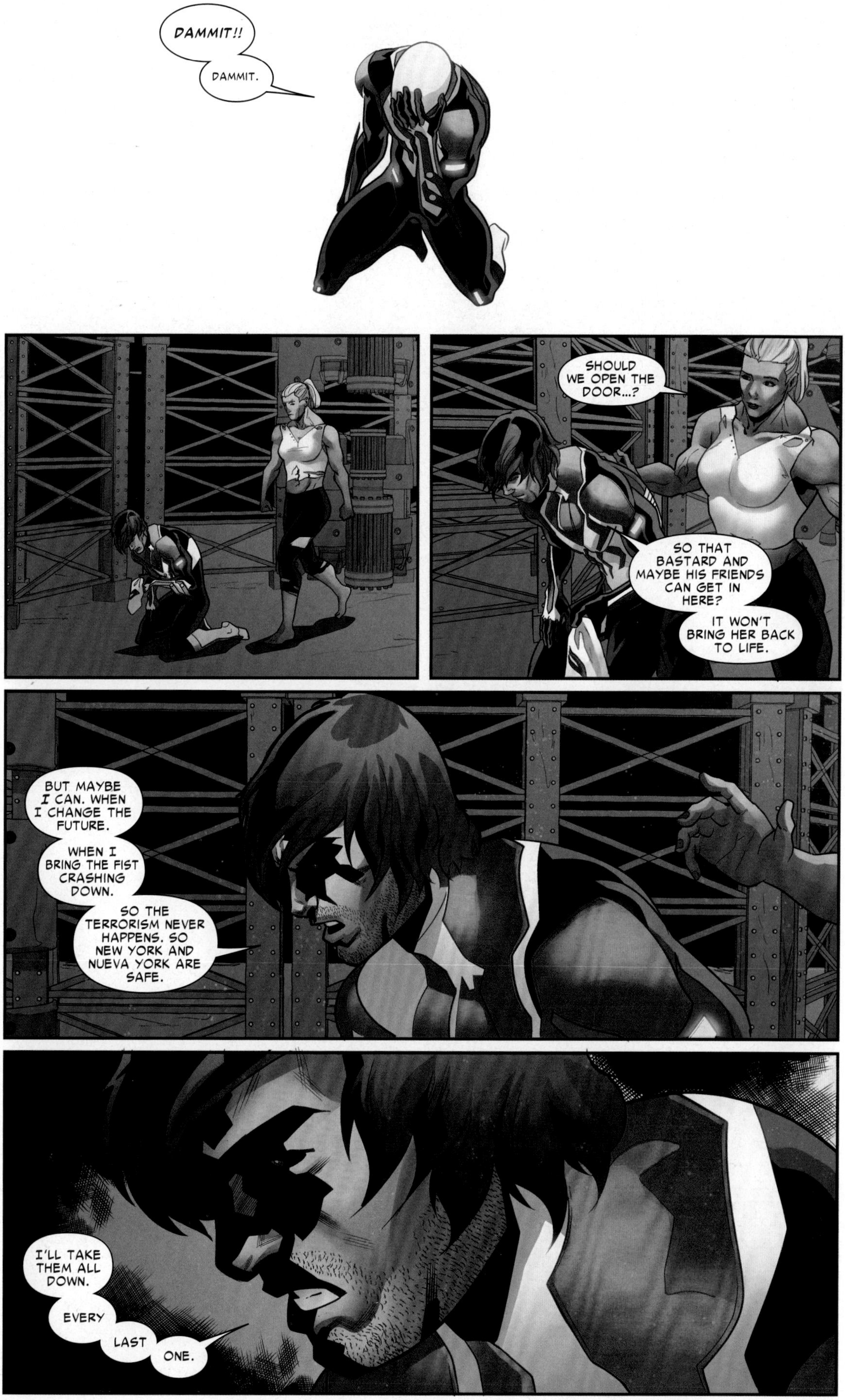
DAMMIT!!
DAMMIT.
SHOULD WE OPEN THE DOOR...?
SO THAT BASTARD AND MAYBE HIS FRIENDS CAN GET IN HERE?
IT WON'T BRING HER BACK TO LIFE.
BUT MAYBE I CAN. WHEN I CHANGE THE FUTURE.
WHEN I BRING THE FIST CRASHING DOWN.
SO THE TERRORISM NEVER HAPPENS. SO NEW YORK AND NUEVA YORK ARE SAFE.
I'LL TAKE THEM ALL DOWN.
EVERY
LAST
ONE.

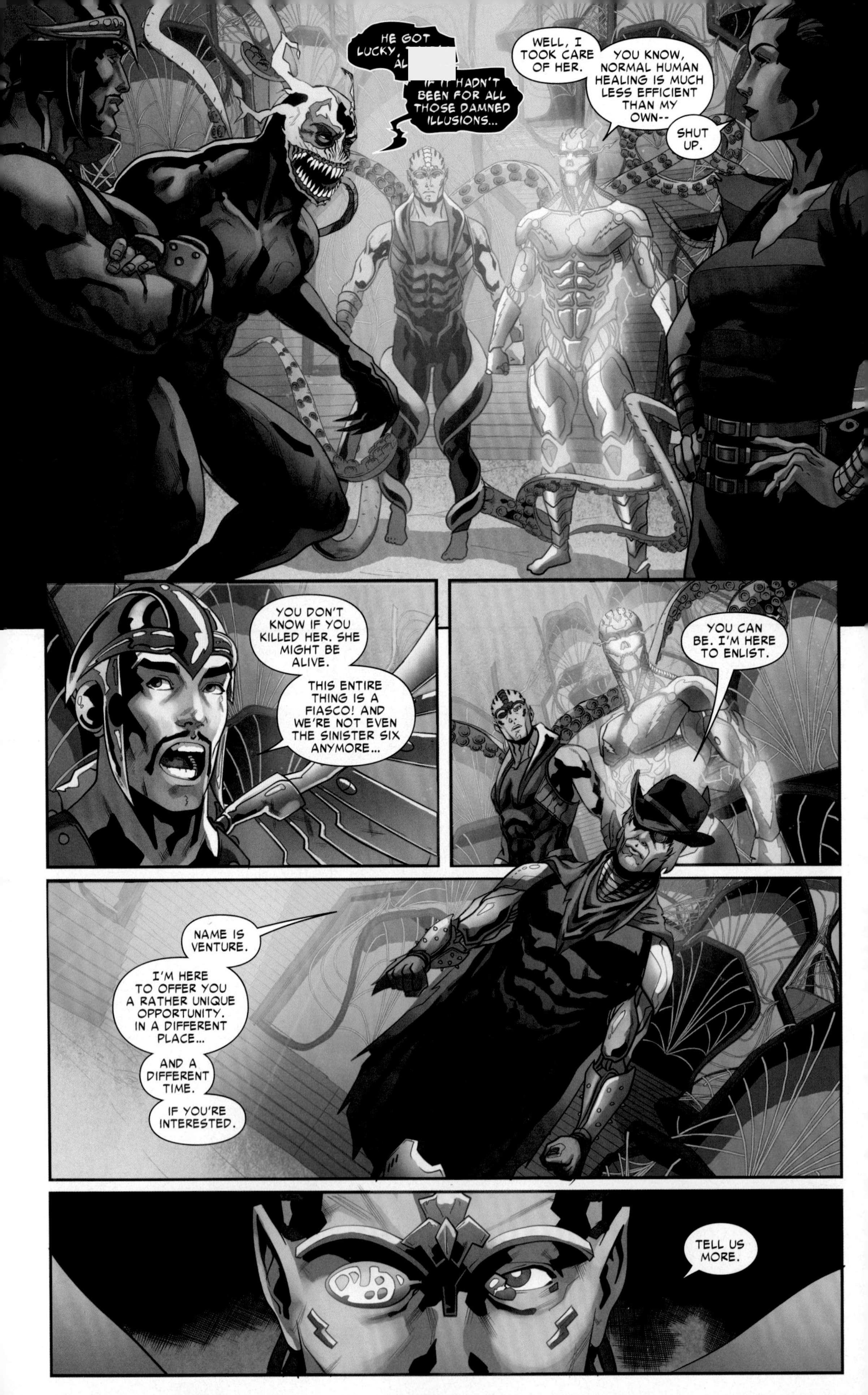

HE GOT LUCKY, [redacted] IF IT HADN'T BEEN FOR ALL THOSE DAMNED ILLUSIONS...
WELL, I TOOK CARE OF HER.
YOU KNOW, NORMAL HUMAN HEALING IS MUCH LESS EFFICIENT THAN MY OWN--
SHUT UP.
YOU DON'T KNOW IF YOU KILLED HER. SHE MIGHT BE ALIVE.
THIS ENTIRE THING IS A FIASCO! AND WE'RE NOT EVEN THE SINISTER SIX ANYMORE...
YOU CAN BE. I'M HERE TO ENLIST.
NAME IS VENTURE.
I'M HERE TO OFFER YOU A RATHER UNIQUE OPPORTUNITY. IN A DIFFERENT PLACE...
AND A DIFFERENT TIME.
IF YOU'RE INTERESTED.
TELL US MORE.

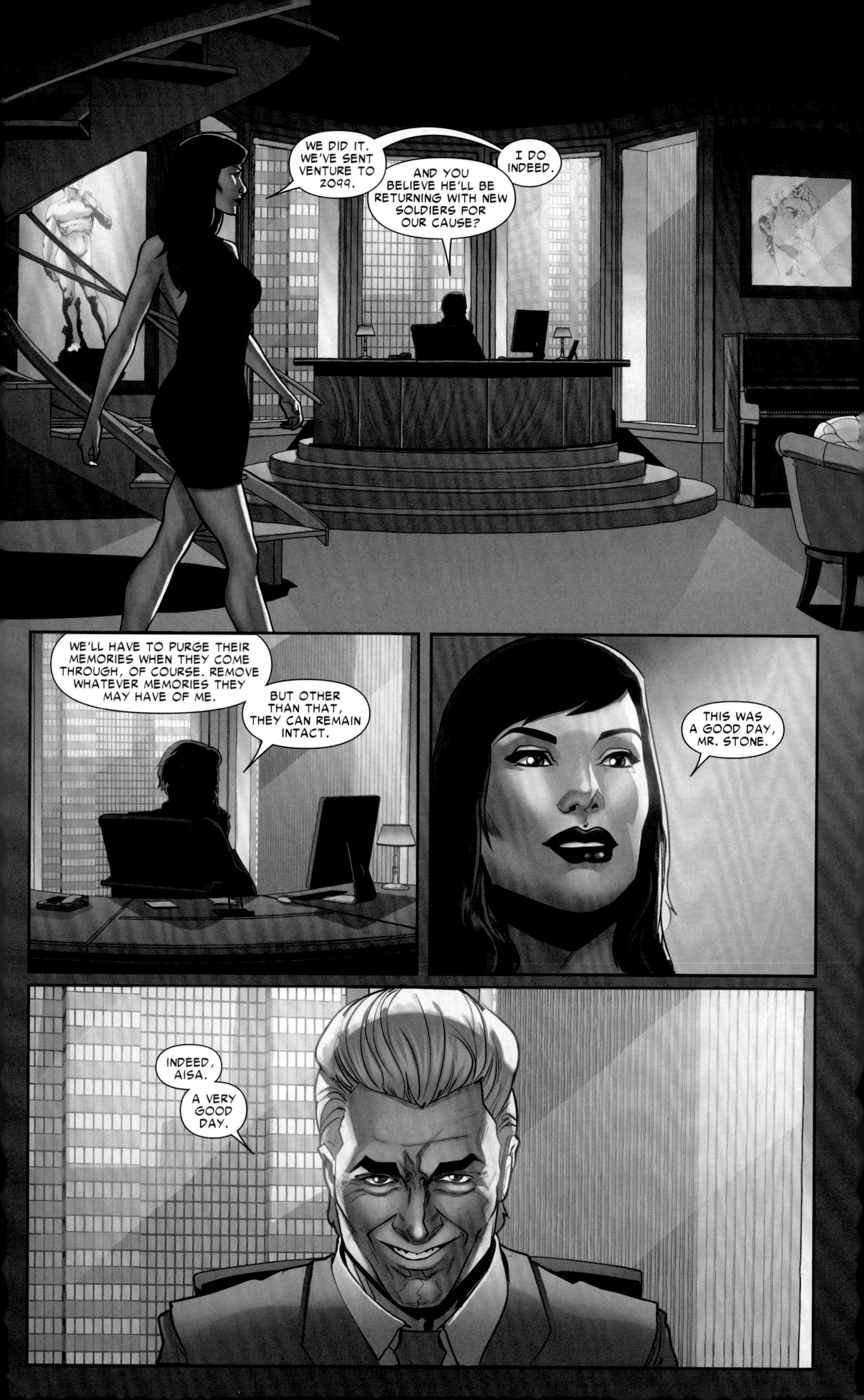
WE DID IT. WE'VE SENT VENTURE TO 2099.
AND YOU BELIEVE HE'LL BE RETURNING WITH NEW SOLDIERS FOR OUR CAUSE?
I DO INDEED.
WE'LL HAVE TO PURGE THEIR MEMORIES WHEN THEY COME THROUGH, OF COURSE. REMOVE WHATEVER MEMORIES THEY MAY HAVE OF ME.
BUT OTHER THAN THAT, THEY CAN REMAIN INTACT.
THIS WAS A GOOD DAY, MR. STONE.
INDEED, AISA.
A VERY GOOD DAY.

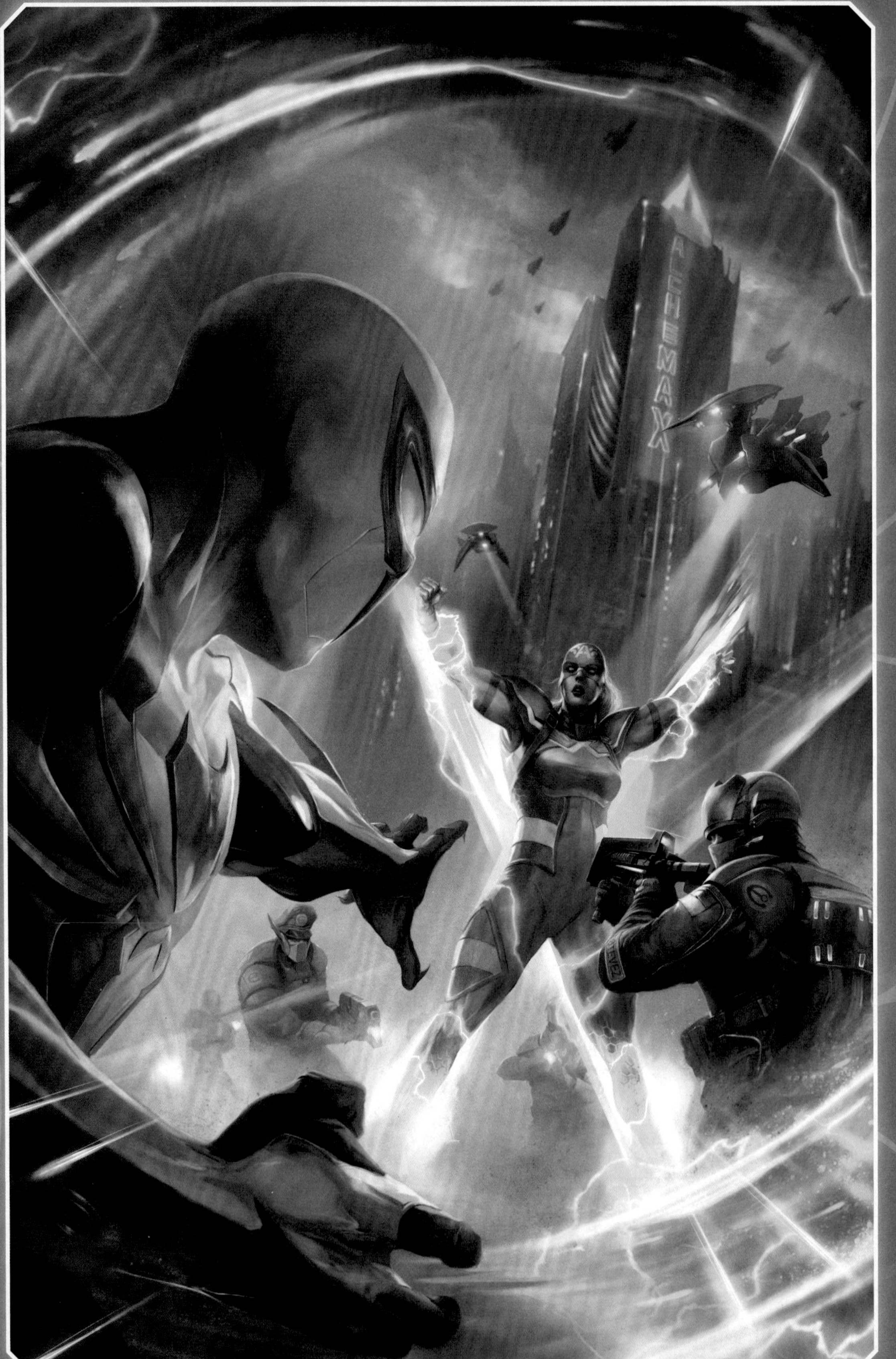
ALCHEMAX

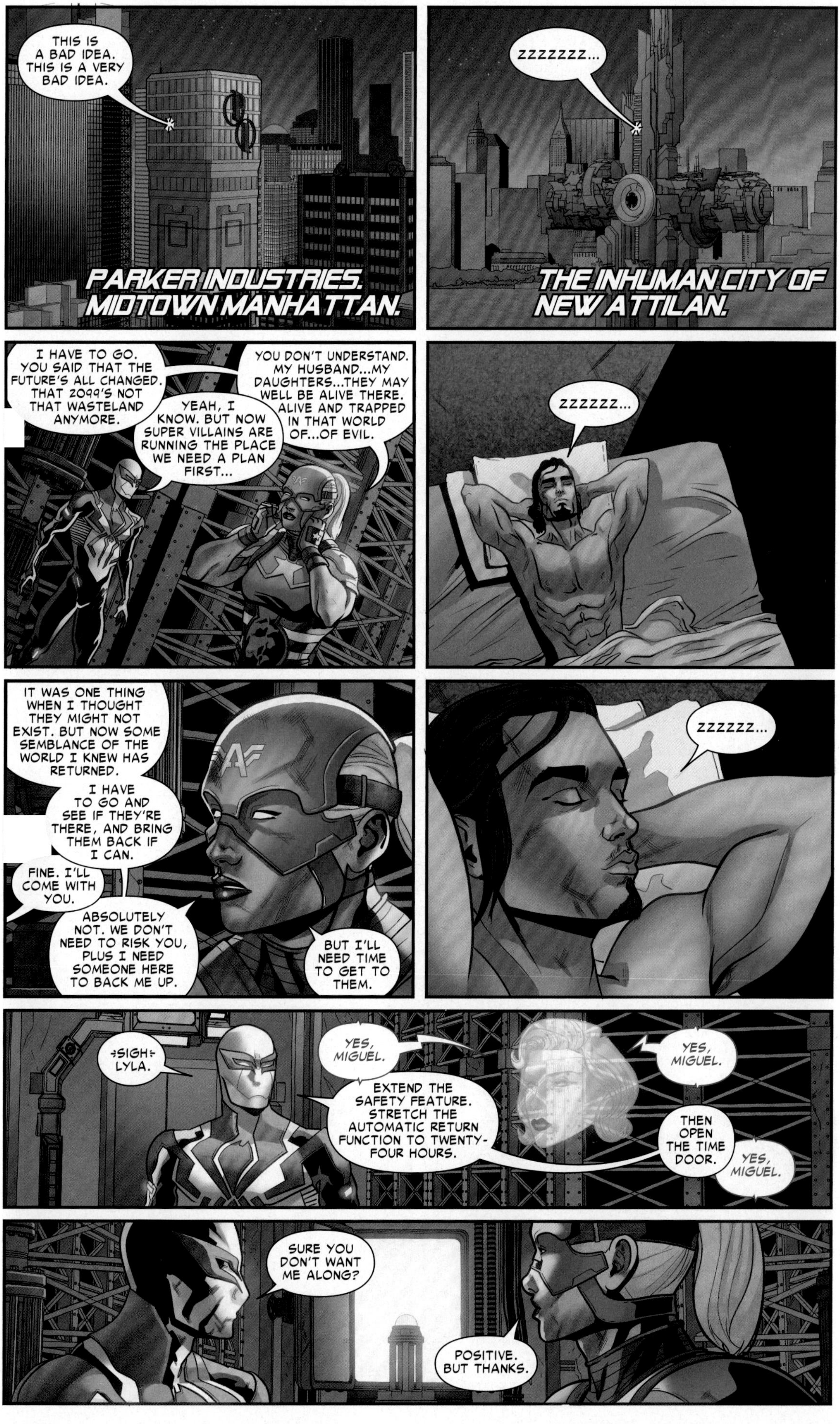
THIS IS A BAD IDEA. THIS IS A VERY BAD IDEA.
PARKER INDUSTRIES. MIDTOWN MANHATTAN.
ZZZZZZZ...
THE INHUMAN CITY OF NEW ATTILAN.
I HAVE TO GO. YOU SAID THAT THE FUTURE'S ALL CHANGED. THAT 2099'S NOT THAT WASTELAND ANYMORE.
YEAH, I KNOW. BUT NOW SUPER VILLAINS ARE RUNNING THE PLACE WE NEED A PLAN FIRST...
YOU DON'T UNDERSTAND. MY HUSBAND...MY DAUGHTERS...THEY MAY WELL BE ALIVE THERE. ALIVE AND TRAPPED IN THAT WORLD OF...OF EVIL.
ZZZZZZ...
IT WAS ONE THING WHEN I THOUGHT THEY MIGHT NOT EXIST. BUT NOW SOME SEMBLANCE OF THE WORLD I KNEW HAS RETURNED.
I HAVE TO GO AND SEE IF THEY'RE THERE, AND BRING THEM BACK IF I CAN.
FINE. I'LL COME WITH YOU.
ABSOLUTELY NOT. WE DON'T NEED TO RISK YOU, PLUS I NEED SOMEONE HERE TO BACK ME UP.
BUT I'LL NEED TIME TO GET TO THEM.
ZZZZZZ...
-SIGH- LYLA.
YES, MIGUEL.
EXTEND THE SAFETY FEATURE. STRETCH THE AUTOMATIC RETURN FUNCTION TO TWENTY-FOUR HOURS.
YES, MIGUEL.
THEN OPEN THE TIME DOOR.
YES, MIGUEL.
SURE YOU DON'T WANT ME ALONG?
POSITIVE. BUT THANKS.

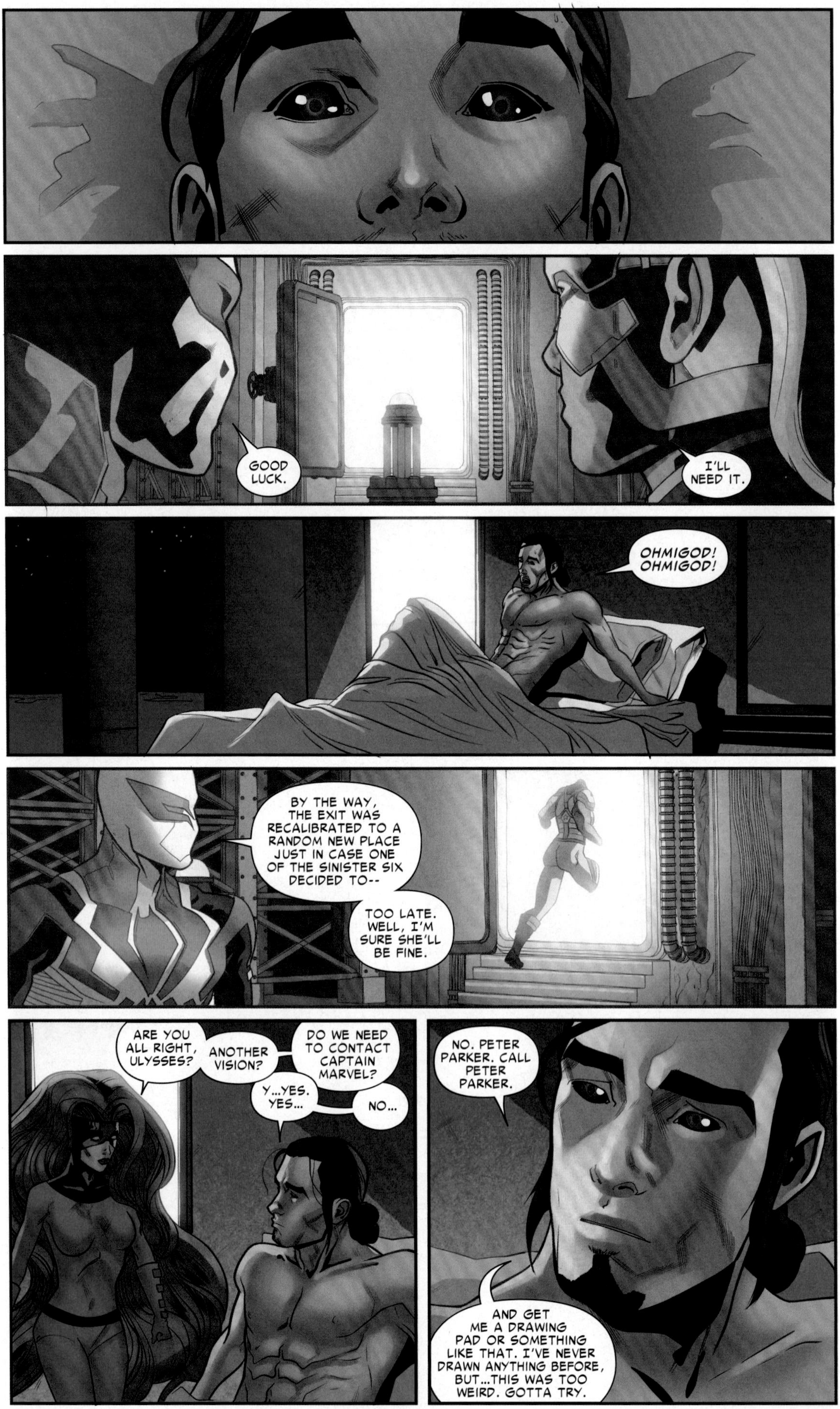
GOOD LUCK.
I'LL NEED IT.
OHMIGOD! OHMIGOD!
BY THE WAY, THE EXIT WAS RECALIBRATED TO A RANDOM NEW PLACE JUST IN CASE ONE OF THE SINISTER SIX DECIDED TO--
TOO LATE. WELL, I'M SURE SHE'LL BE FINE.
ARE YOU ALL RIGHT, ULYSSES?
ANOTHER VISION?
DO WE NEED TO CONTACT CAPTAIN MARVEL?
Y...YES. YES...
NO...
NO. PETER PARKER. CALL PETER PARKER.
AND GET ME A DRAWING PAD OR SOMETHING LIKE THAT. I'VE NEVER DRAWN ANYTHING BEFORE, BUT...THIS WAS TOO WEIRD. GOTTA TRY.

MIGUEL O'HARA WAS A YOUNG GENETICS GENIUS EMPLOYED AT THE MEGACORPORATION ALCHEMAX IN THE FUTURE CITY OF NUEVA YORK! ONE OF HIS EXPERIMENTS–TO REPLICATE THE POWERS OF THE PRESENT-DAY SPIDER-MAN–WAS TURNED AGAINST HIM AND REWROTE HIS DNA TO MAKE IT 50 PERCENT SPIDER! AFTER LEARNING HOW TO USE HIS AMAZING NEW ABILITIES, MIGUEL BECAME...

SPIDER-MAN 2099

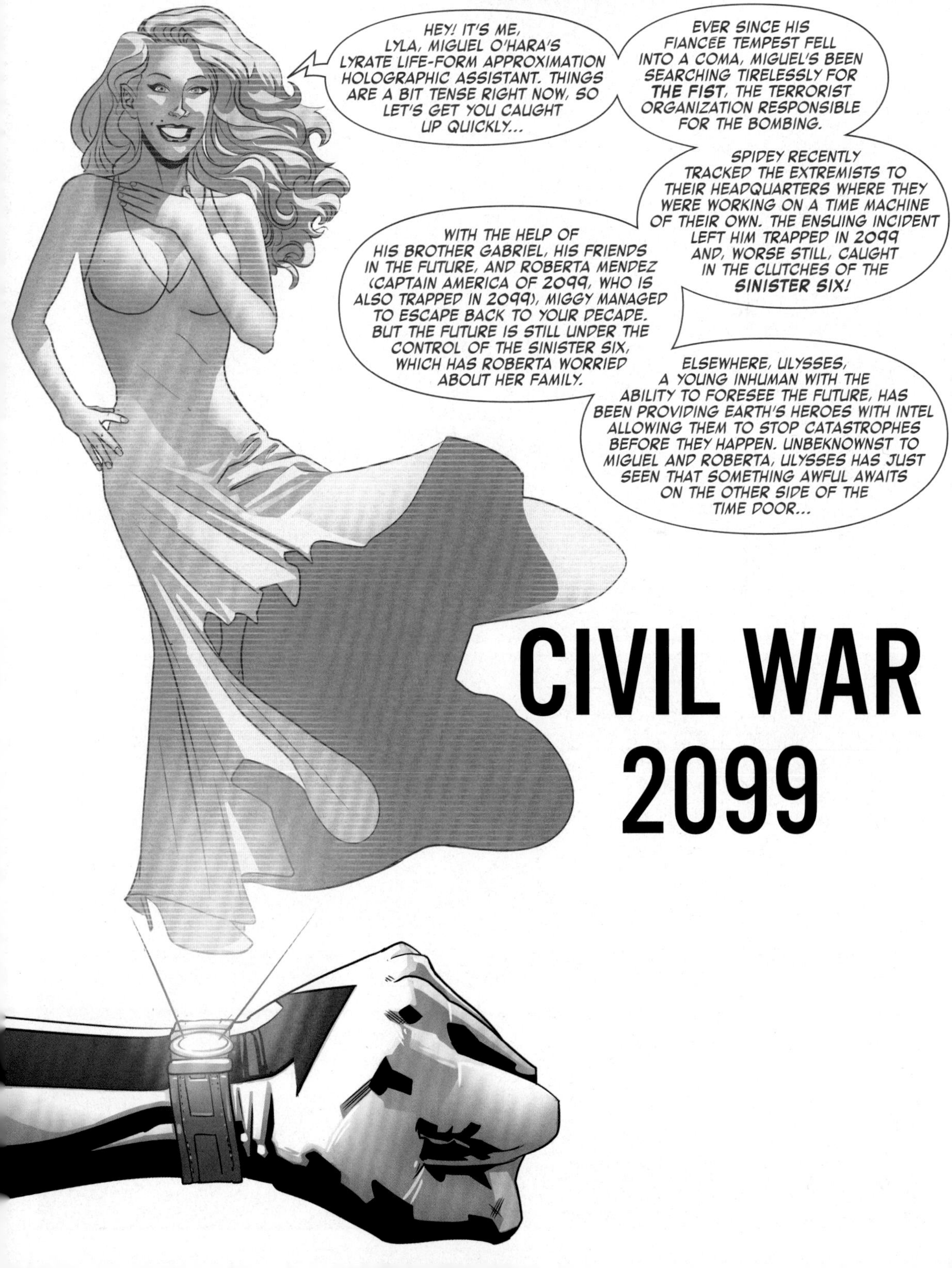
HEY! IT'S ME, LYLA, MIGUEL O'HARA'S LYRATE LIFE-FORM APPROXIMATION HOLOGRAPHIC ASSISTANT. THINGS ARE A BIT TENSE RIGHT NOW, SO LET'S GET YOU CAUGHT UP QUICKLY...
EVER SINCE HIS FIANCÉE TEMPEST FELL INTO A COMA, MIGUEL'S BEEN SEARCHING TIRELESSLY FOR **THE FIST**, THE TERRORIST ORGANIZATION RESPONSIBLE FOR THE BOMBING.
SPIDEY RECENTLY TRACKED THE EXTREMISTS TO THEIR HEADQUARTERS WHERE THEY WERE WORKING ON A TIME MACHINE OF THEIR OWN. THE ENSUING INCIDENT LEFT HIM TRAPPED IN 2099 AND, WORSE STILL, CAUGHT IN THE CLUTCHES OF THE **SINISTER SIX!**
WITH THE HELP OF HIS BROTHER GABRIEL, HIS FRIENDS IN THE FUTURE, AND ROBERTA MENDEZ (CAPTAIN AMERICA OF 2099, WHO IS ALSO TRAPPED IN 2099), MIGGY MANAGED TO ESCAPE BACK TO YOUR DECADE. BUT THE FUTURE IS STILL UNDER THE CONTROL OF THE SINISTER SIX, WHICH HAS ROBERTA WORRIED ABOUT HER FAMILY.
ELSEWHERE, ULYSSES, A YOUNG INHUMAN WITH THE ABILITY TO FORESEE THE FUTURE, HAS BEEN PROVIDING EARTH'S HEROES WITH INTEL ALLOWING THEM TO STOP CATASTROPHES BEFORE THEY HAPPEN. UNBEKNOWNST TO MIGUEL AND ROBERTA, ULYSSES HAS JUST SEEN THAT SOMETHING AWFUL AWAITS ON THE OTHER SIDE OF THE TIME DOOR...

CIVIL WAR 2099

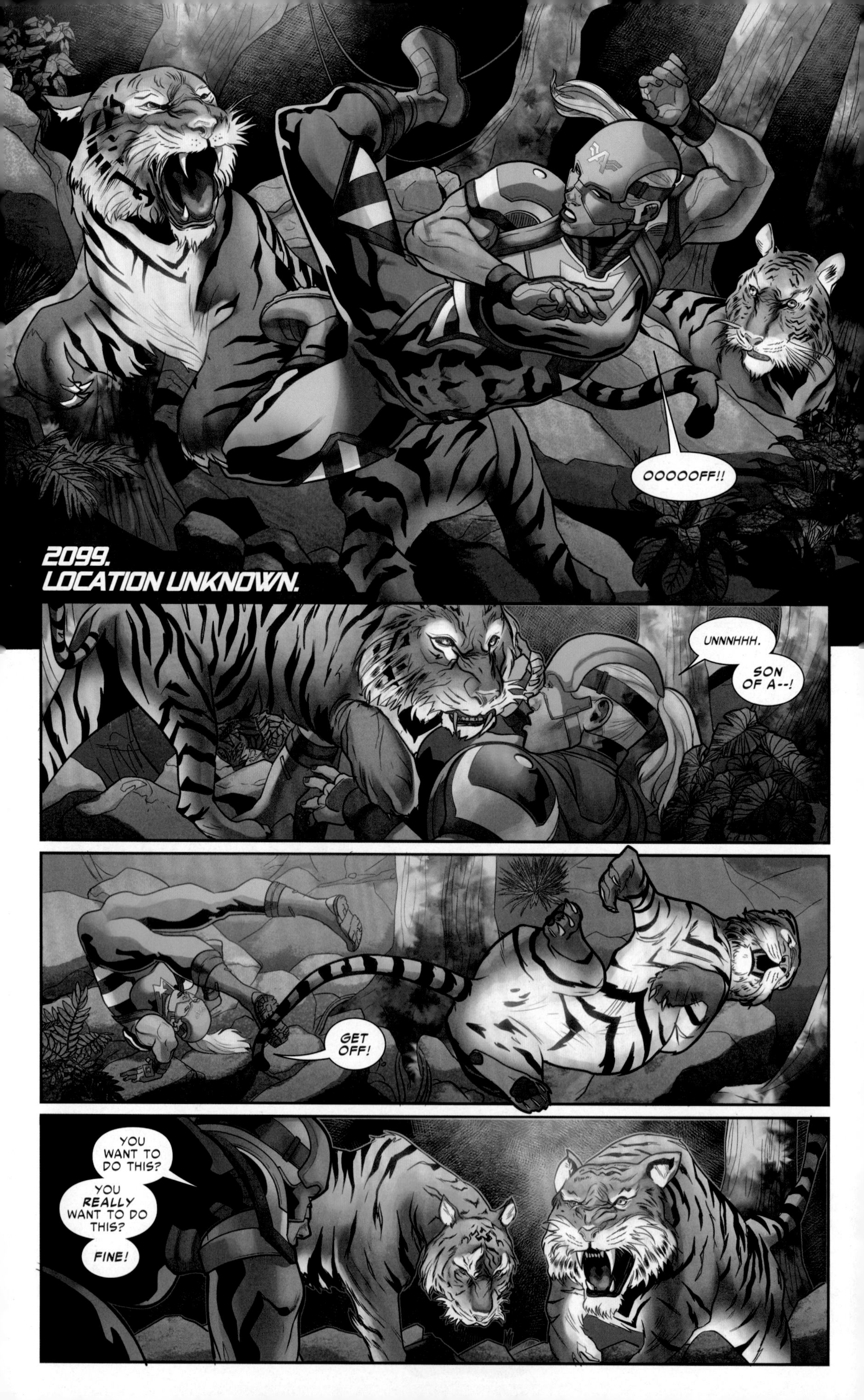
OOOOOFF!!
2099.
LOCATION UNKNOWN.
UNNHHH.
SON OF A--!
GET OFF!
YOU WANT TO DO THIS?
YOU REALLY WANT TO DO THIS?
FINE!

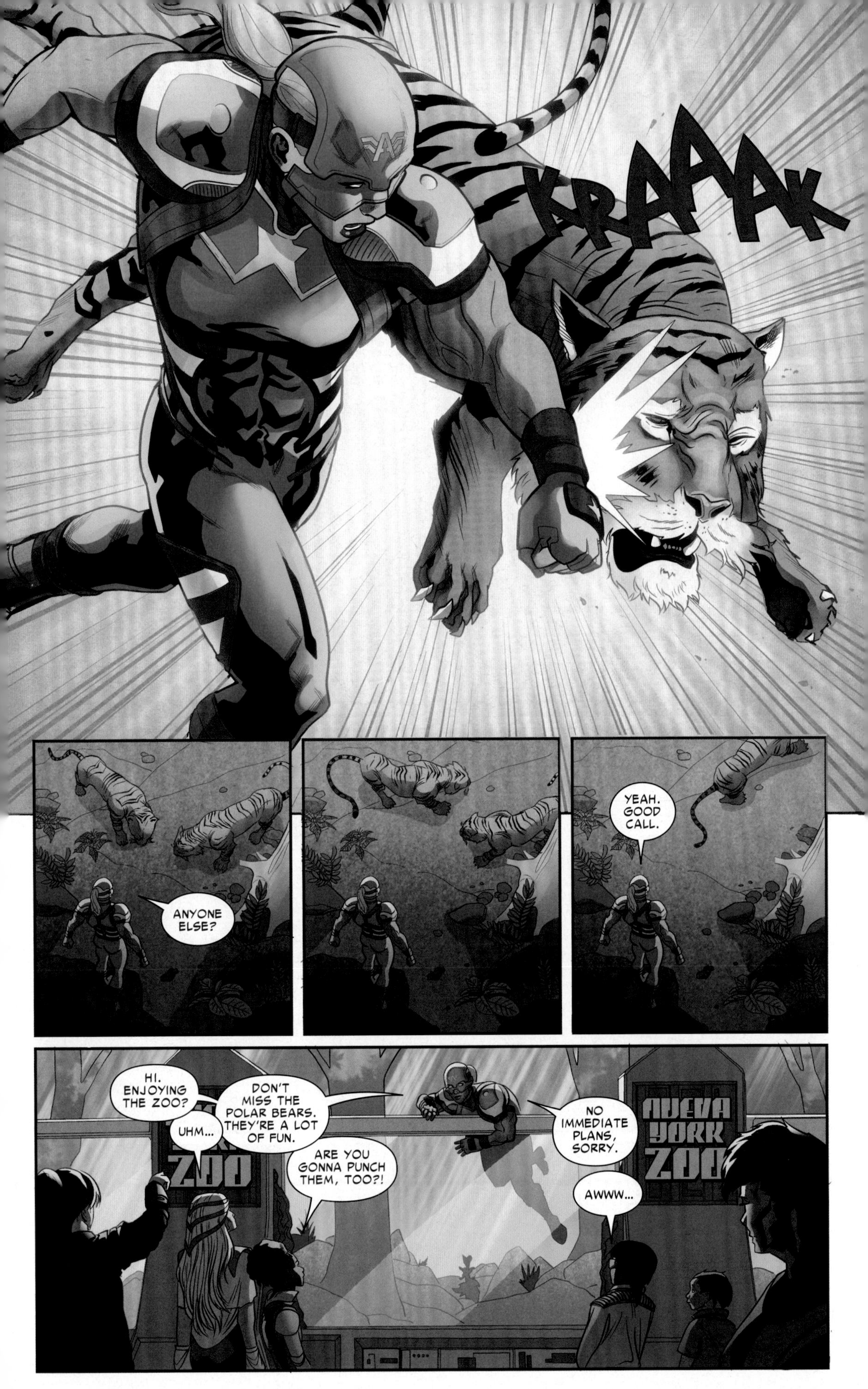
KRAAAAK
ANYONE ELSE?
YEAH. GOOD CALL.
HI. ENJOYING THE ZOO?
UHM...
DON'T MISS THE POLAR BEARS. THEY'RE A LOT OF FUN.
ARE YOU GONNA PUNCH THEM, TOO?!
NO IMMEDIATE PLANS, SORRY.
AWWW...
NEW YORK ZOO
ZOO

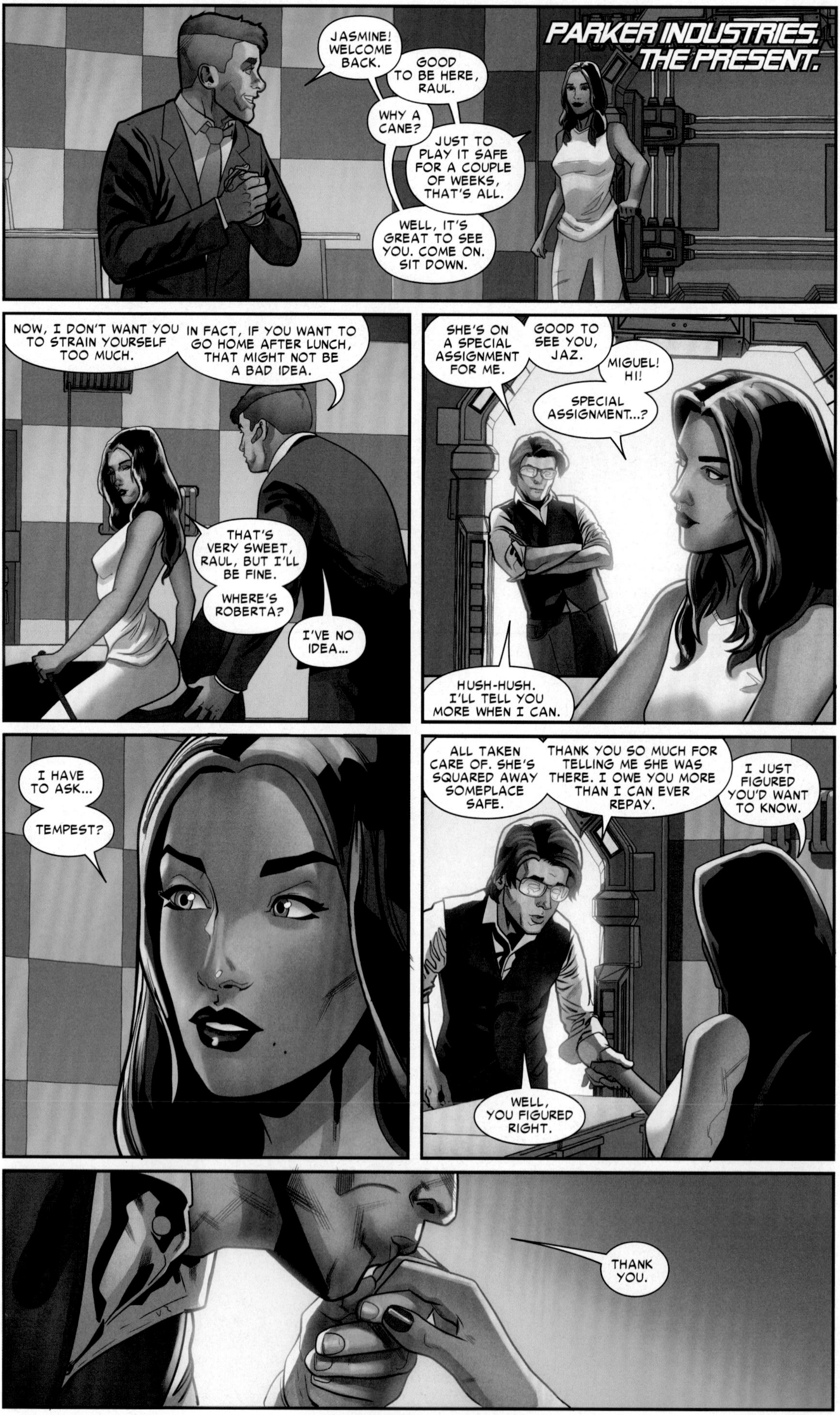
PARKER INDUSTRIES. THE PRESENT.
JASMINE! WELCOME BACK.
GOOD TO BE HERE, RAUL.
WHY A CANE?
JUST TO PLAY IT SAFE FOR A COUPLE OF WEEKS, THAT'S ALL.
WELL, IT'S GREAT TO SEE YOU. COME ON. SIT DOWN.
NOW, I DON'T WANT YOU TO STRAIN YOURSELF TOO MUCH.
IN FACT, IF YOU WANT TO GO HOME AFTER LUNCH, THAT MIGHT NOT BE A BAD IDEA.
THAT'S VERY SWEET, RAUL, BUT I'LL BE FINE.
WHERE'S ROBERTA?
I'VE NO IDEA...
SHE'S ON A SPECIAL ASSIGNMENT FOR ME.
GOOD TO SEE YOU, JAZ.
MIGUEL! HI!
SPECIAL ASSIGNMENT...?
HUSH-HUSH. I'LL TELL YOU MORE WHEN I CAN.
I HAVE TO ASK...
TEMPEST?
ALL TAKEN CARE OF. SHE'S SQUARED AWAY SOMEPLACE SAFE.
THANK YOU SO MUCH FOR TELLING ME SHE WAS THERE. I OWE YOU MORE THAN I CAN EVER REPAY.
I JUST FIGURED YOU'D WANT TO KNOW.
WELL, YOU FIGURED RIGHT.
THANK YOU.

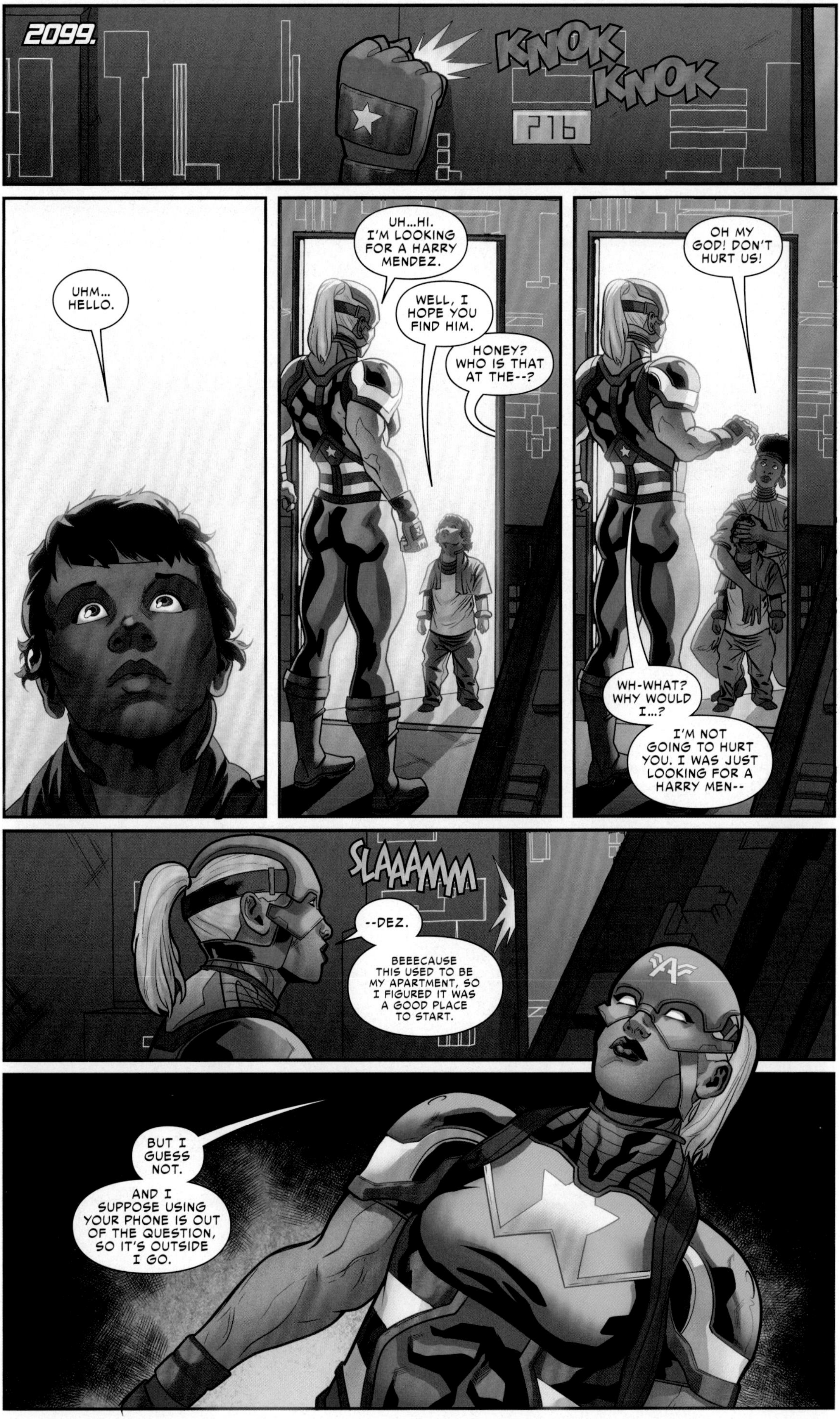
2099.
KNOK KNOK
216
UHM... HELLO.
UH...HI. I'M LOOKING FOR A HARRY MENDEZ.
WELL, I HOPE YOU FIND HIM.
HONEY? WHO IS THAT AT THE--?
OH MY GOD! DON'T HURT US!
WH-WHAT? WHY WOULD I...?
I'M NOT GOING TO HURT YOU. I WAS JUST LOOKING FOR A HARRY MEN--
SLAAAMM
--DEZ.
BEEECAUSE THIS USED TO BE MY APARTMENT, SO I FIGURED IT WAS A GOOD PLACE TO START.
BUT I GUESS NOT.
AND I SUPPOSE USING YOUR PHONE IS OUT OF THE QUESTION, SO IT'S OUTSIDE I GO.

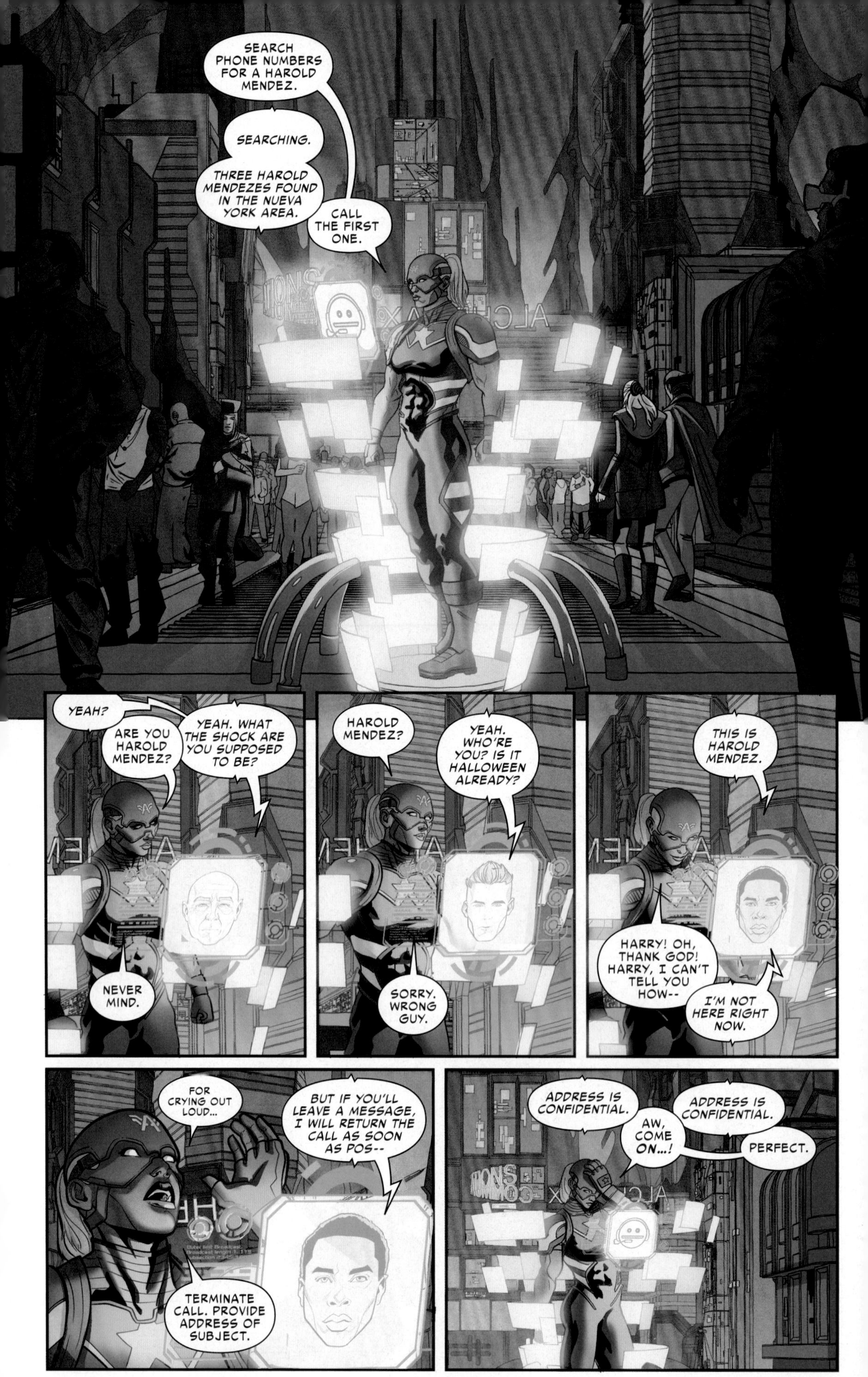
SEARCH PHONE NUMBERS FOR A HAROLD MENDEZ.
SEARCHING.
THREE HAROLD MENDEZES FOUND IN THE NUEVA YORK AREA.
CALL THE FIRST ONE.
YEAH?
ARE YOU HAROLD MENDEZ?
YEAH. WHAT THE SHOCK ARE YOU SUPPOSED TO BE?
NEVER MIND.
HAROLD MENDEZ?
YEAH. WHO'RE YOU? IS IT HALLOWEEN ALREADY?
SORRY. WRONG GUY.
THIS IS HAROLD MENDEZ.
HARRY! OH, THANK GOD! HARRY, I CAN'T TELL YOU HOW--
I'M NOT HERE RIGHT NOW.
FOR CRYING OUT LOUD...
BUT IF YOU'LL LEAVE A MESSAGE, I WILL RETURN THE CALL AS SOON AS POS--
TERMINATE CALL. PROVIDE ADDRESS OF SUBJECT.
ADDRESS IS CONFIDENTIAL.
AW, COME ON...!
ADDRESS IS CONFIDENTIAL.
PERFECT.

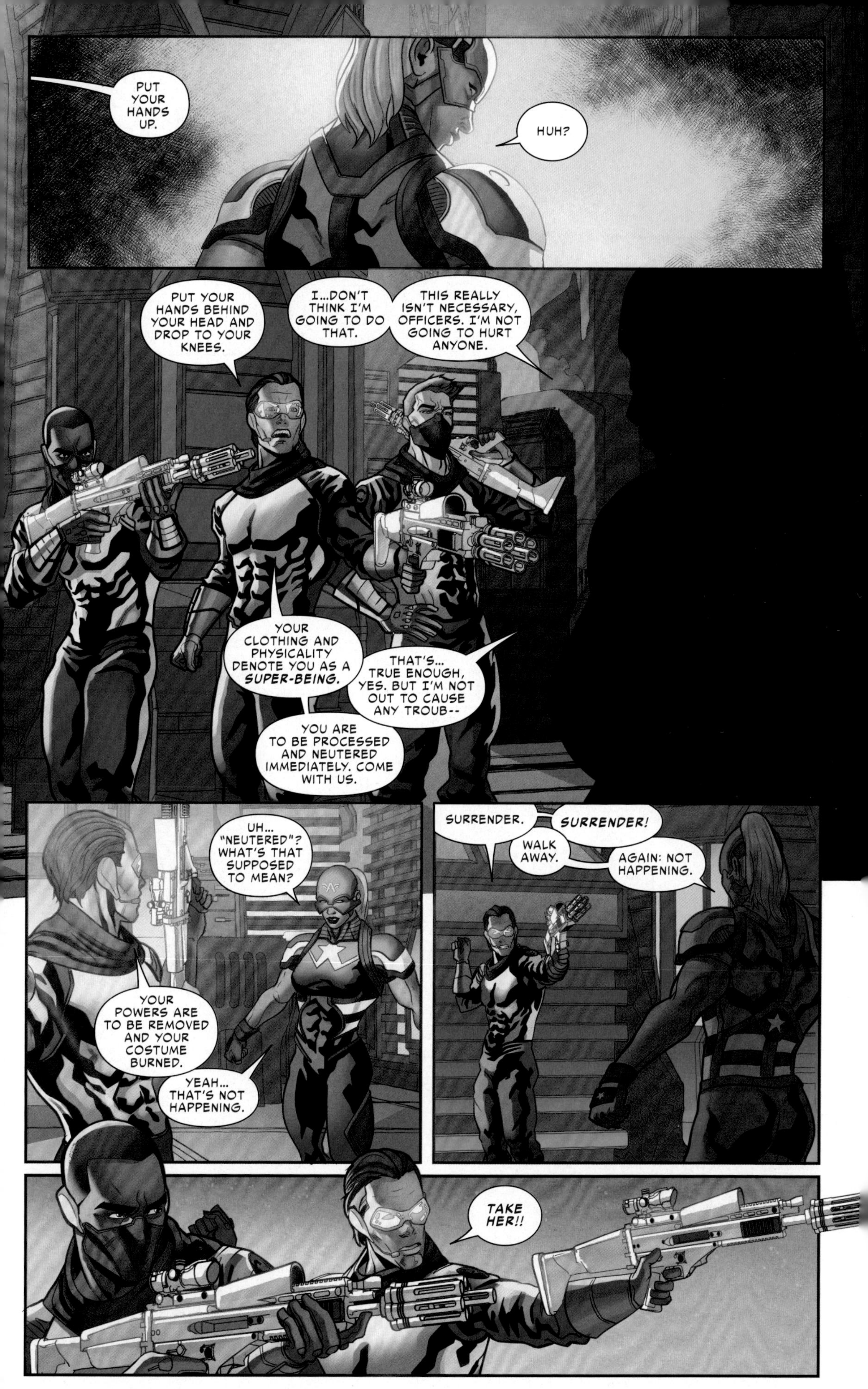
PUT YOUR HANDS UP.
HUH?
PUT YOUR HANDS BEHIND YOUR HEAD AND DROP TO YOUR KNEES.
I...DON'T THINK I'M GOING TO DO THAT.
THIS REALLY ISN'T NECESSARY, OFFICERS. I'M NOT GOING TO HURT ANYONE.
YOUR CLOTHING AND PHYSICALITY DENOTE YOU AS A SUPER-BEING.
THAT'S... TRUE ENOUGH, YES. BUT I'M NOT OUT TO CAUSE ANY TROUB--
YOU ARE TO BE PROCESSED AND NEUTERED IMMEDIATELY. COME WITH US.
UH... "NEUTERED"? WHAT'S THAT SUPPOSED TO MEAN?
YOUR POWERS ARE TO BE REMOVED AND YOUR COSTUME BURNED.
YEAH... THAT'S NOT HAPPENING.
SURRENDER.
SURRENDER!
WALK AWAY.
AGAIN: NOT HAPPENING.
TAKE HER!!

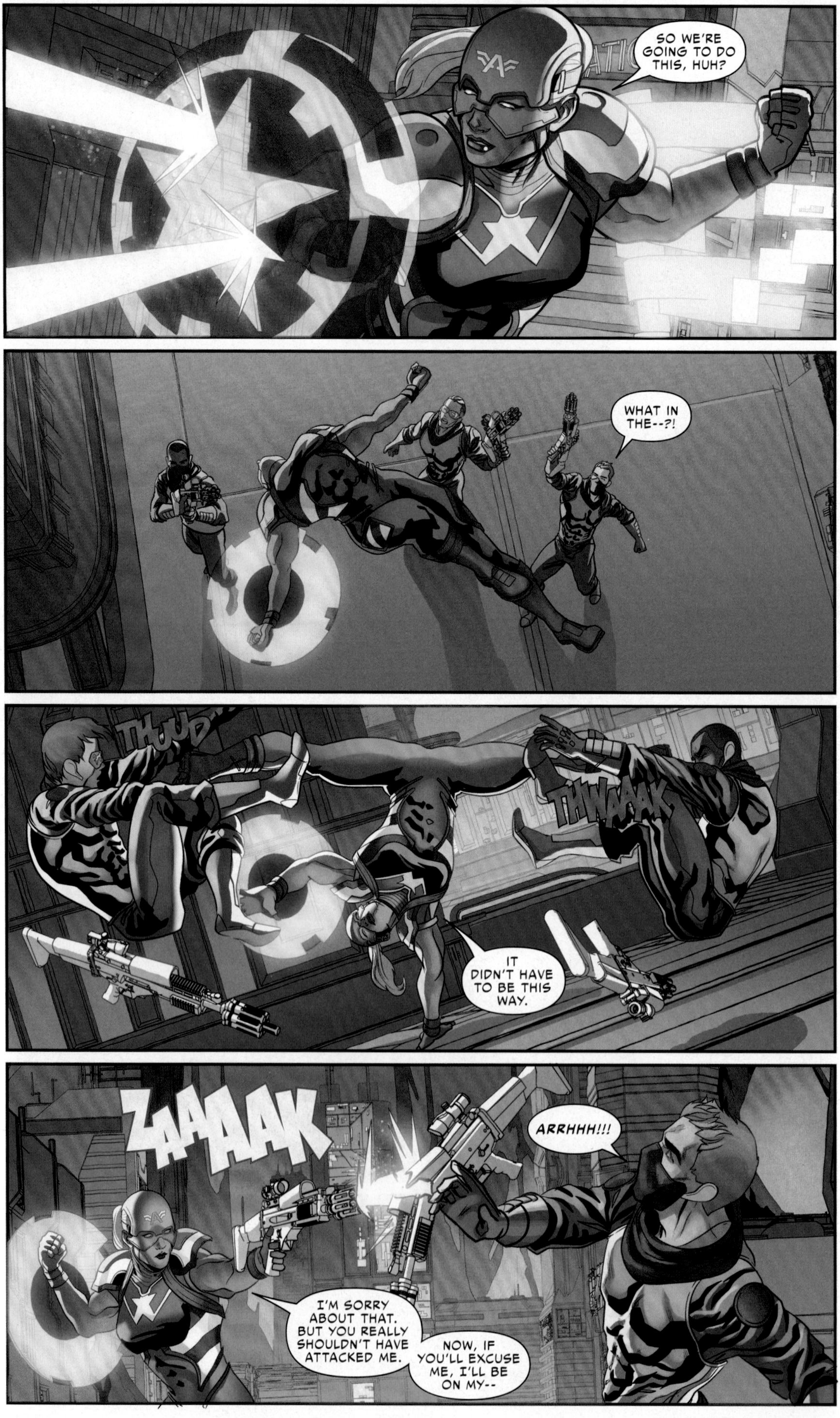
SO WE'RE GOING TO DO THIS, HUH?
WHAT IN THE--?!
THUD
THWAAAK
IT DIDN'T HAVE TO BE THIS WAY.
ZAAAAK
ARRHHH!!!
I'M SORRY ABOUT THAT. BUT YOU REALLY SHOULDN'T HAVE ATTACKED ME.
NOW, IF YOU'LL EXCUSE ME, I'LL BE ON MY--

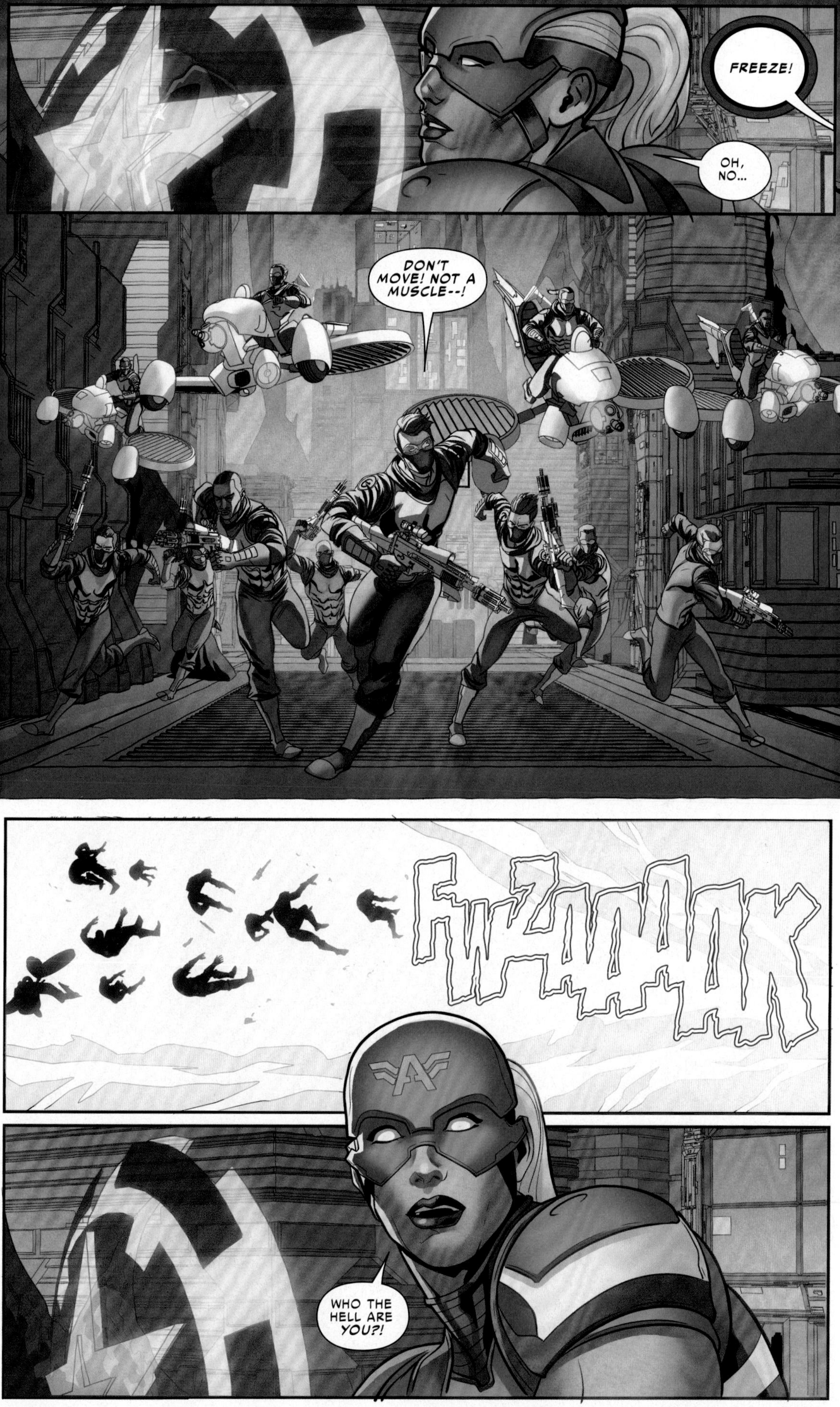
FREEZE!
OH, NO...
DON'T MOVE! NOT A MUSCLE--!
FWZAAAAK
WHO THE HELL ARE YOU?!

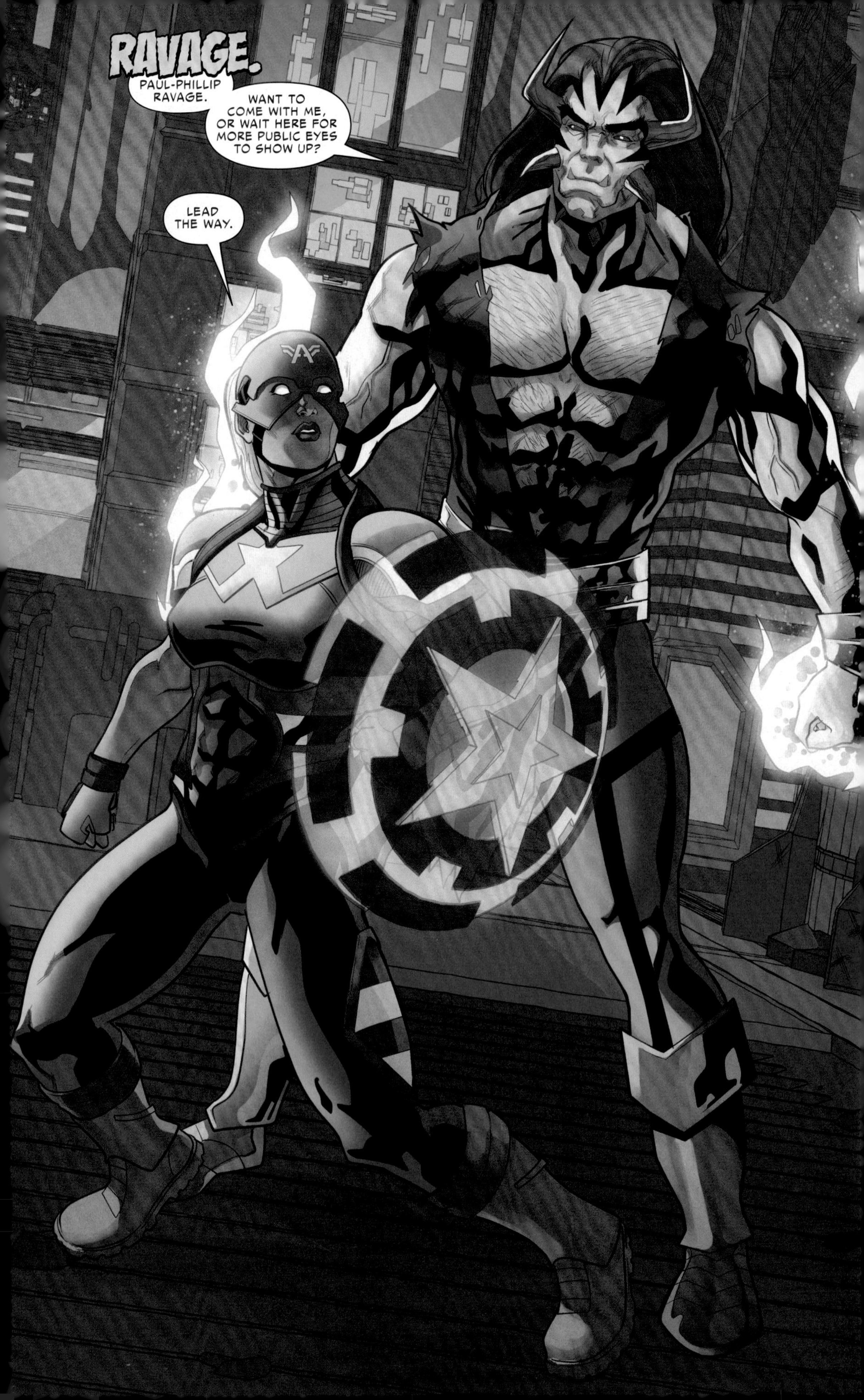
RAVAGE.
PAUL-PHILLIP RAVAGE.
WANT TO COME WITH ME, OR WAIT HERE FOR MORE PUBLIC EYES TO SHOW UP?
LEAD THE WAY.

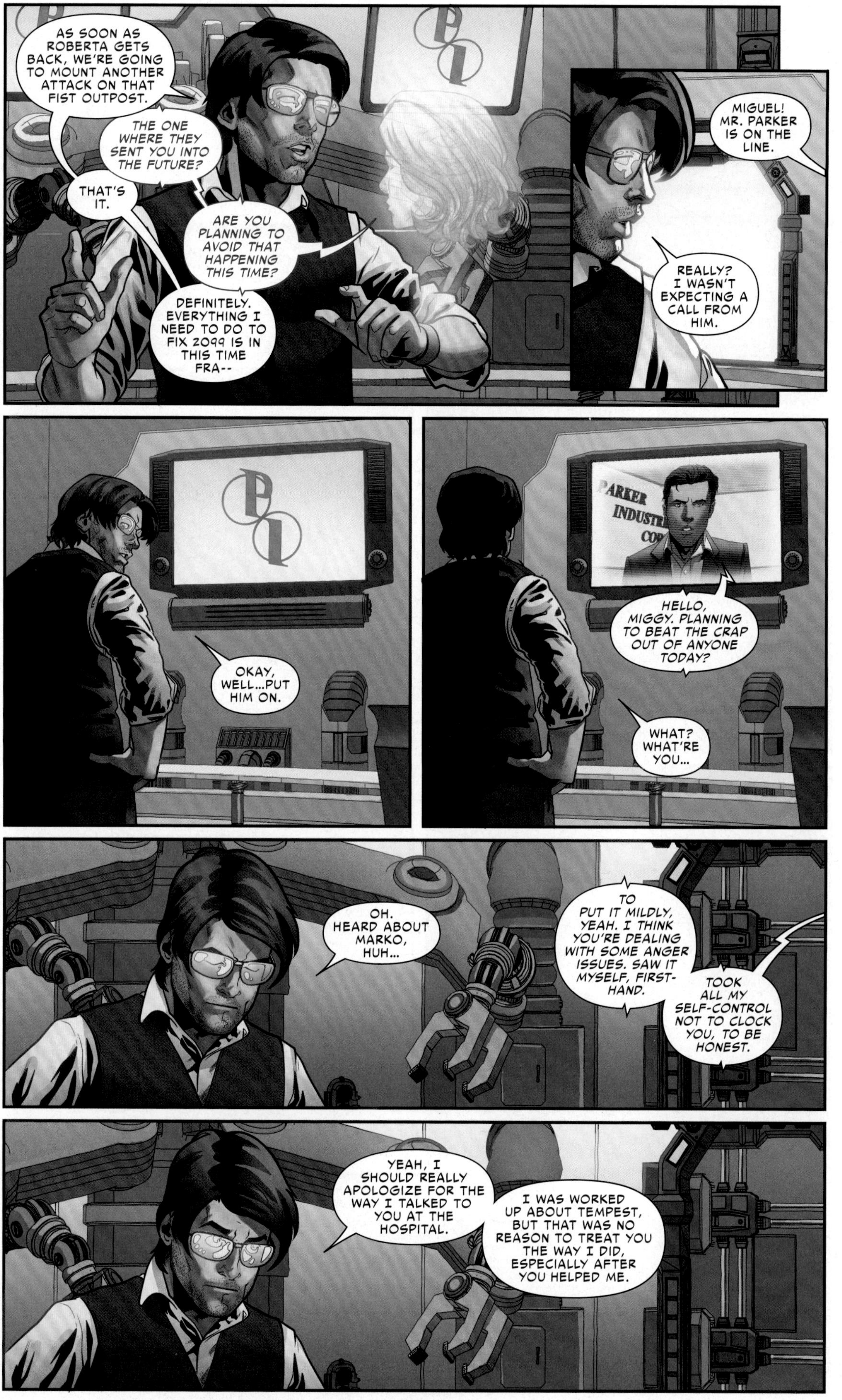
AS SOON AS ROBERTA GETS BACK, WE'RE GOING TO MOUNT ANOTHER ATTACK ON THAT FIST OUTPOST.
THE ONE WHERE THEY SENT YOU INTO THE FUTURE?
THAT'S IT.
ARE YOU PLANNING TO AVOID THAT HAPPENING THIS TIME?
DEFINITELY. EVERYTHING I NEED TO DO TO FIX 2099 IS IN THIS TIME FRA--
MIGUEL! MR. PARKER IS ON THE LINE.
REALLY? I WASN'T EXPECTING A CALL FROM HIM.
OKAY, WELL...PUT HIM ON.
PARKER INDUSTR
HELLO, MIGGY. PLANNING TO BEAT THE CRAP OUT OF ANYONE TODAY?
WHAT? WHAT'RE YOU...
OH. HEARD ABOUT MARKO, HUH...
TO PUT IT MILDLY, YEAH. I THINK YOU'RE DEALING WITH SOME ANGER ISSUES. SAW IT MYSELF, FIRST-HAND.
TOOK ALL MY SELF-CONTROL NOT TO CLOCK YOU, TO BE HONEST.
YEAH, I SHOULD REALLY APOLOGIZE FOR THE WAY I TALKED TO YOU AT THE HOSPITAL.
I WAS WORKED UP ABOUT TEMPEST, BUT THAT WAS NO REASON TO TREAT YOU THE WAY I DID, ESPECIALLY AFTER YOU HELPED ME.

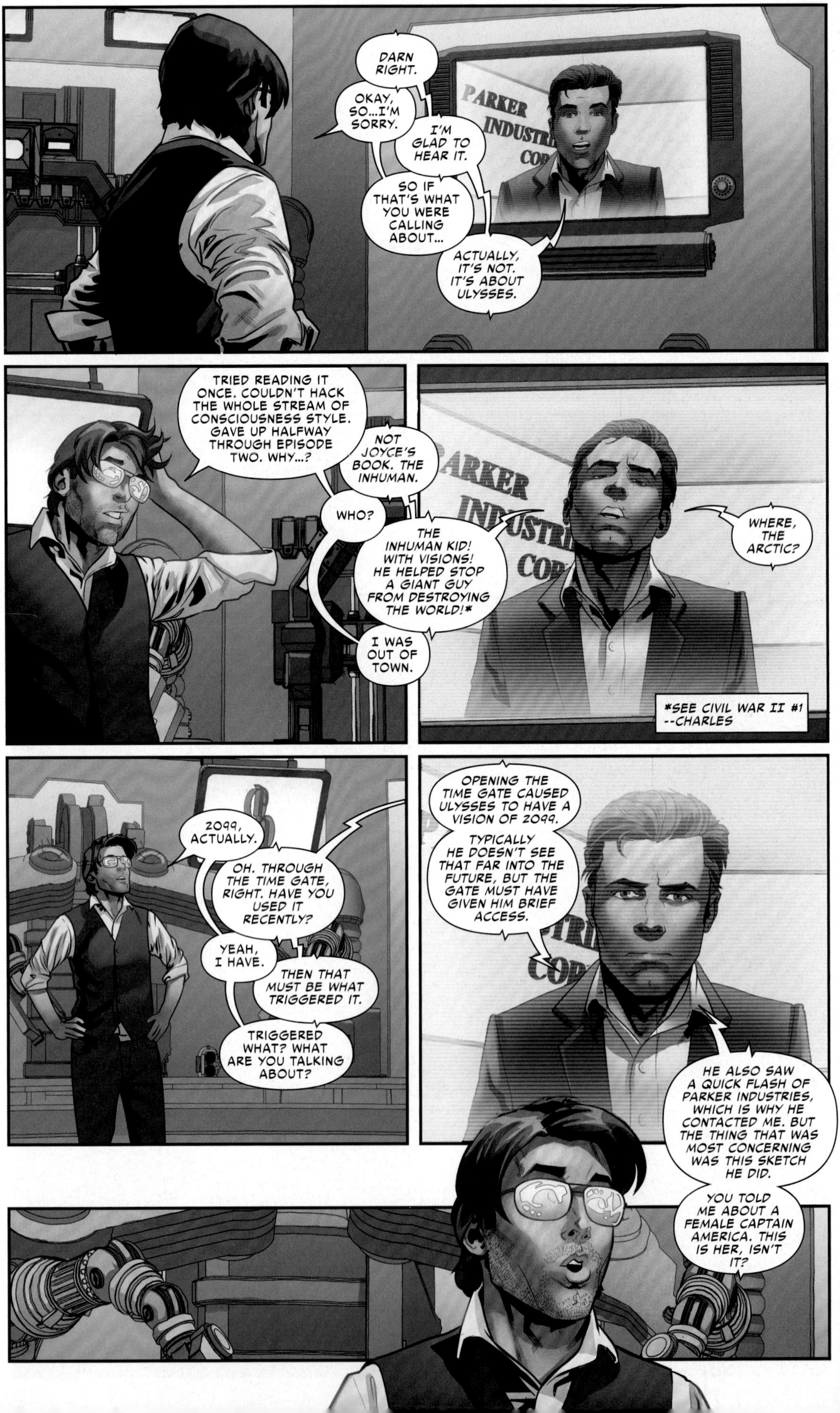
DARN RIGHT.
OKAY, SO...I'M SORRY.
I'M GLAD TO HEAR IT.
SO IF THAT'S WHAT YOU WERE CALLING ABOUT...
ACTUALLY, IT'S NOT. IT'S ABOUT ULYSSES.
TRIED READING IT ONCE. COULDN'T HACK THE WHOLE STREAM OF CONSCIOUSNESS STYLE. GAVE UP HALFWAY THROUGH EPISODE TWO. WHY...?
NOT JOYCE'S BOOK. THE INHUMAN.
WHO?
THE INHUMAN KID! WITH VISIONS! HE HELPED STOP A GIANT GUY FROM DESTROYING THE WORLD!*
I WAS OUT OF TOWN.
WHERE, THE ARCTIC?
*SEE CIVIL WAR II #1 --CHARLES
2099, ACTUALLY.
OH. THROUGH THE TIME GATE, RIGHT. HAVE YOU USED IT RECENTLY?
YEAH, I HAVE.
THEN THAT MUST BE WHAT TRIGGERED IT.
TRIGGERED WHAT? WHAT ARE YOU TALKING ABOUT?
OPENING THE TIME GATE CAUSED ULYSSES TO HAVE A VISION OF 2099.
TYPICALLY HE DOESN'T SEE THAT FAR INTO THE FUTURE, BUT THE GATE MUST HAVE GIVEN HIM BRIEF ACCESS.
HE ALSO SAW A QUICK FLASH OF PARKER INDUSTRIES, WHICH IS WHY HE CONTACTED ME. BUT THE THING THAT WAS MOST CONCERNING WAS THIS SKETCH HE DID.
YOU TOLD ME ABOUT A FEMALE CAPTAIN AMERICA. THIS IS HER, ISN'T IT?

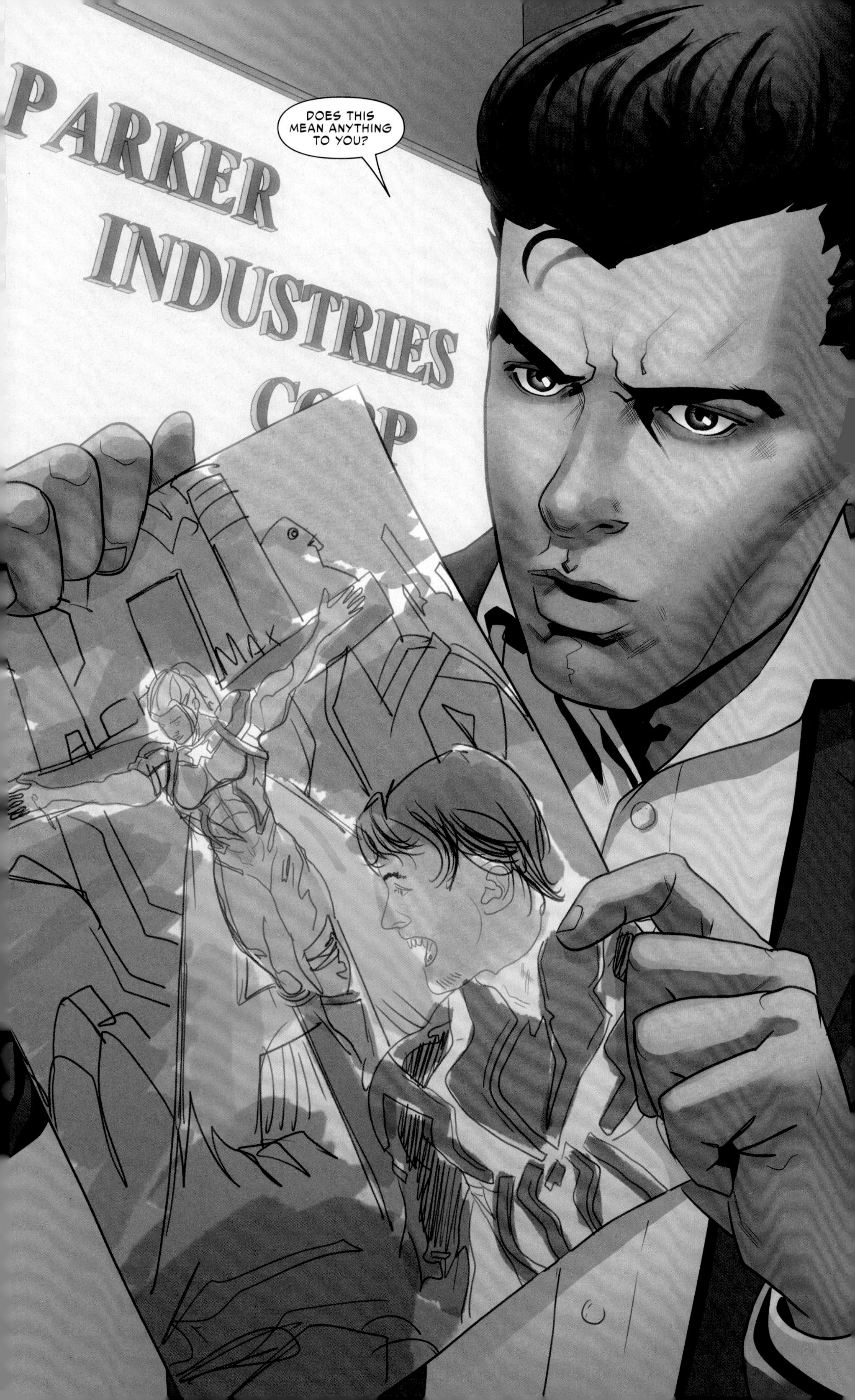
PARKER INDUSTRIES
DOES THIS MEAN ANYTHING TO YOU?
MAX

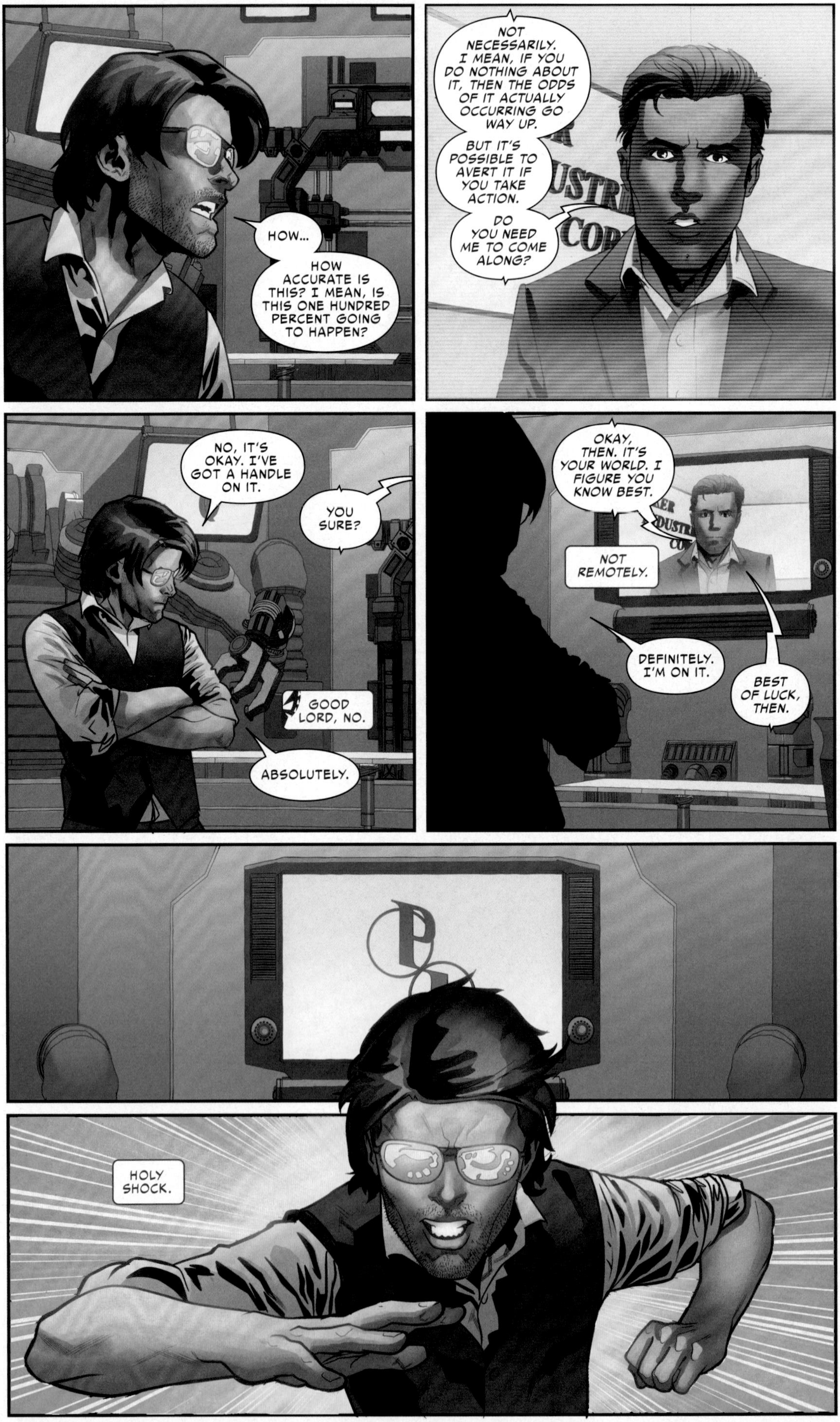
HOW...
HOW ACCURATE IS THIS? I MEAN, IS THIS ONE HUNDRED PERCENT GOING TO HAPPEN?
NOT NECESSARILY. I MEAN, IF YOU DO NOTHING ABOUT IT, THEN THE ODDS OF IT ACTUALLY OCCURRING GO WAY UP.
BUT IT'S POSSIBLE TO AVERT IT IF YOU TAKE ACTION.
DO YOU NEED ME TO COME ALONG?
NO, IT'S OKAY. I'VE GOT A HANDLE ON IT.
YOU SURE?
GOOD LORD, NO.
ABSOLUTELY.
OKAY, THEN. IT'S YOUR WORLD. I FIGURE YOU KNOW BEST.
NOT REMOTELY.
DEFINITELY. I'M ON IT.
BEST OF LUCK, THEN.
HOLY SHOCK.

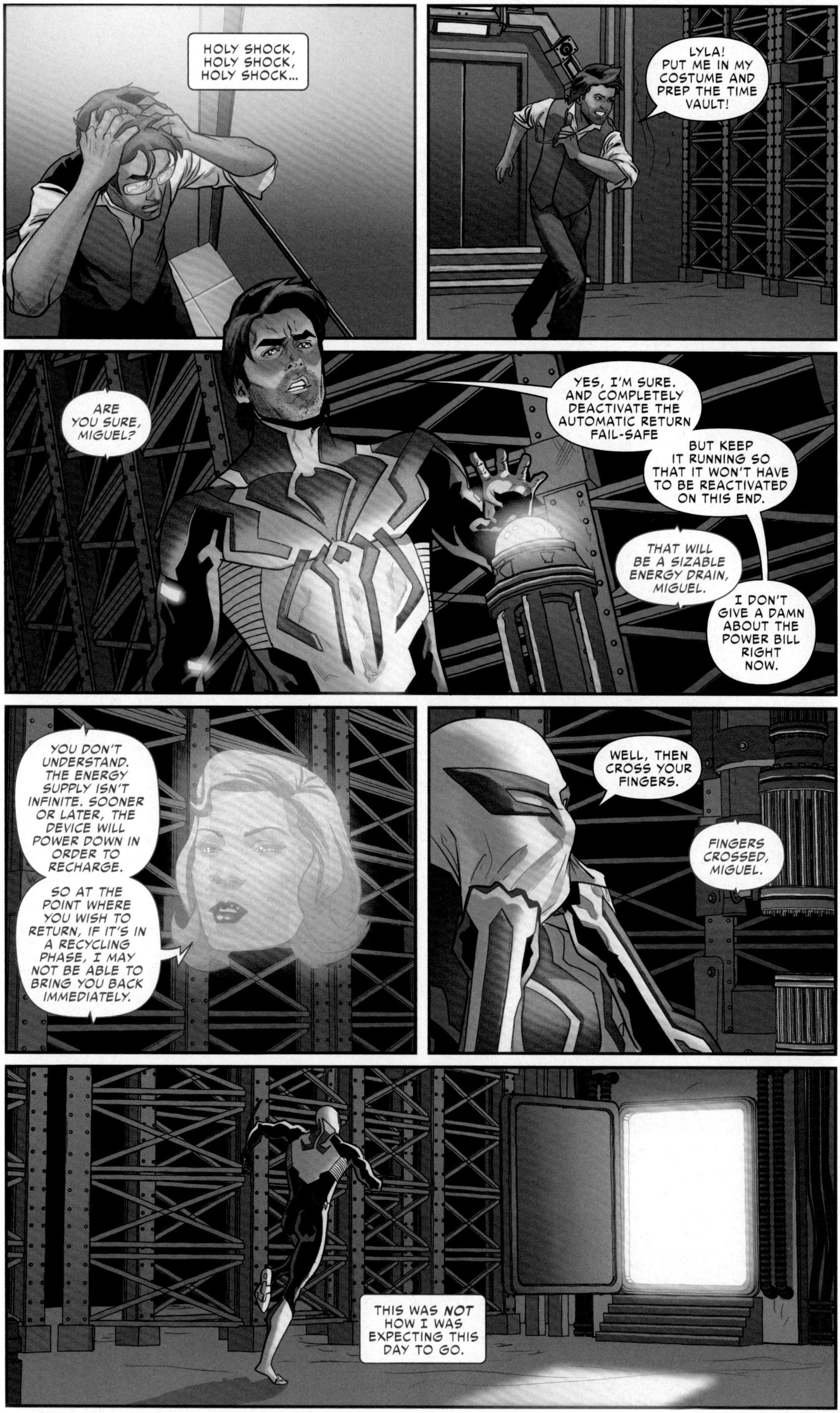
HOLY SHOCK, HOLY SHOCK, HOLY SHOCK...
LYLA! PUT ME IN MY COSTUME AND PREP THE TIME VAULT!
ARE YOU SURE, MIGUEL?
YES, I'M SURE. AND COMPLETELY DEACTIVATE THE AUTOMATIC RETURN FAIL-SAFE
BUT KEEP IT RUNNING SO THAT IT WON'T HAVE TO BE REACTIVATED ON THIS END.
THAT WILL BE A SIZABLE ENERGY DRAIN, MIGUEL.
I DON'T GIVE A DAMN ABOUT THE POWER BILL RIGHT NOW.
YOU DON'T UNDERSTAND. THE ENERGY SUPPLY ISN'T INFINITE. SOONER OR LATER, THE DEVICE WILL POWER DOWN IN ORDER TO RECHARGE.
SO AT THE POINT WHERE YOU WISH TO RETURN, IF IT'S IN A RECYCLING PHASE, I MAY NOT BE ABLE TO BRING YOU BACK IMMEDIATELY.
WELL, THEN CROSS YOUR FINGERS.
FINGERS CROSSED, MIGUEL.
THIS WAS *NOT* HOW I WAS EXPECTING THIS DAY TO GO.

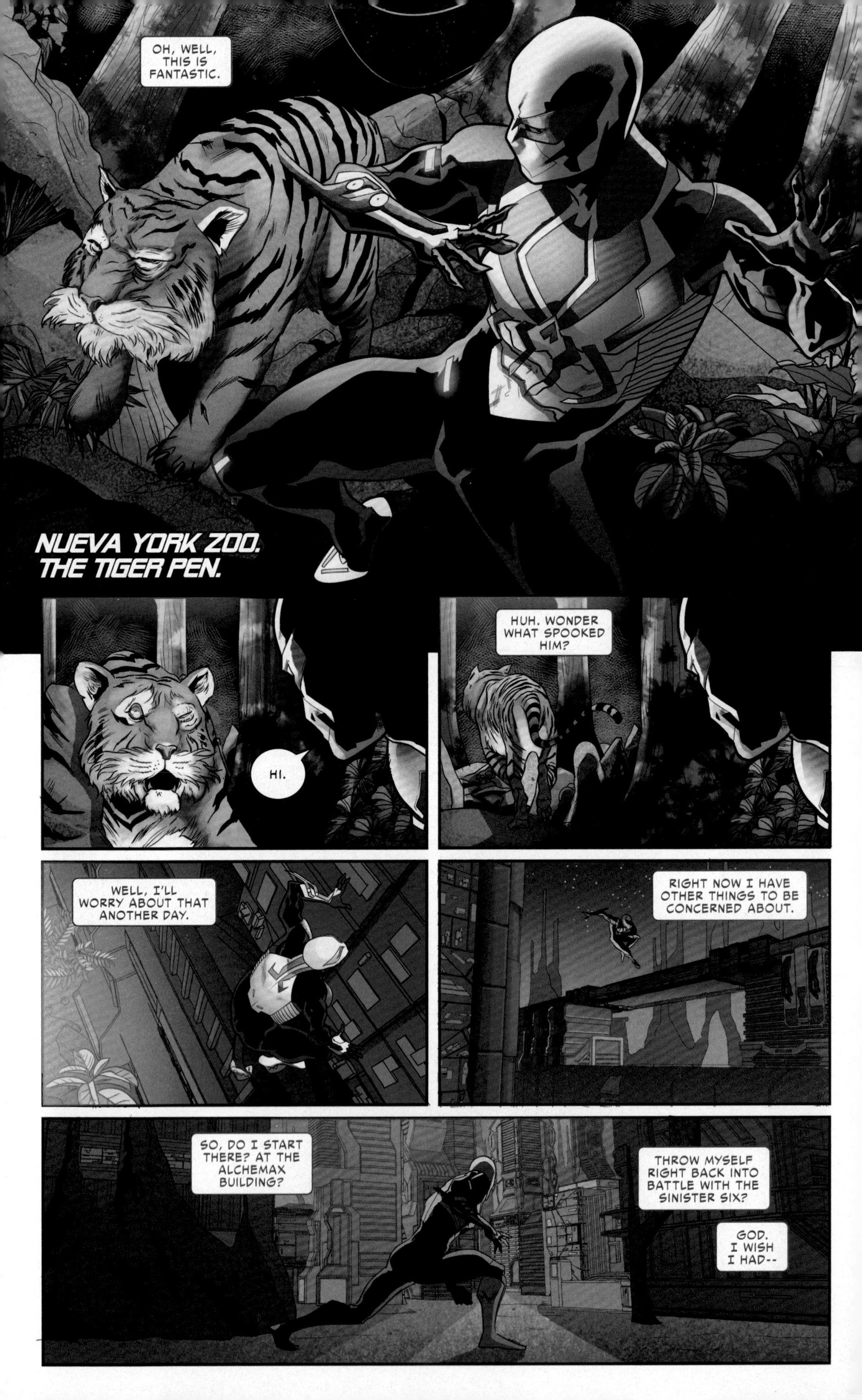
OH, WELL, THIS IS FANTASTIC.
NUEVA YORK ZOO. THE TIGER PEN.
HI.
HUH. WONDER WHAT SPOOKED HIM?
WELL, I'LL WORRY ABOUT THAT ANOTHER DAY.
RIGHT NOW I HAVE OTHER THINGS TO BE CONCERNED ABOUT.
SO, DO I START THERE? AT THE ALCHEMAX BUILDING?
THROW MYSELF RIGHT BACK INTO BATTLE WITH THE SINISTER SIX?
GOD. I WISH I HAD--

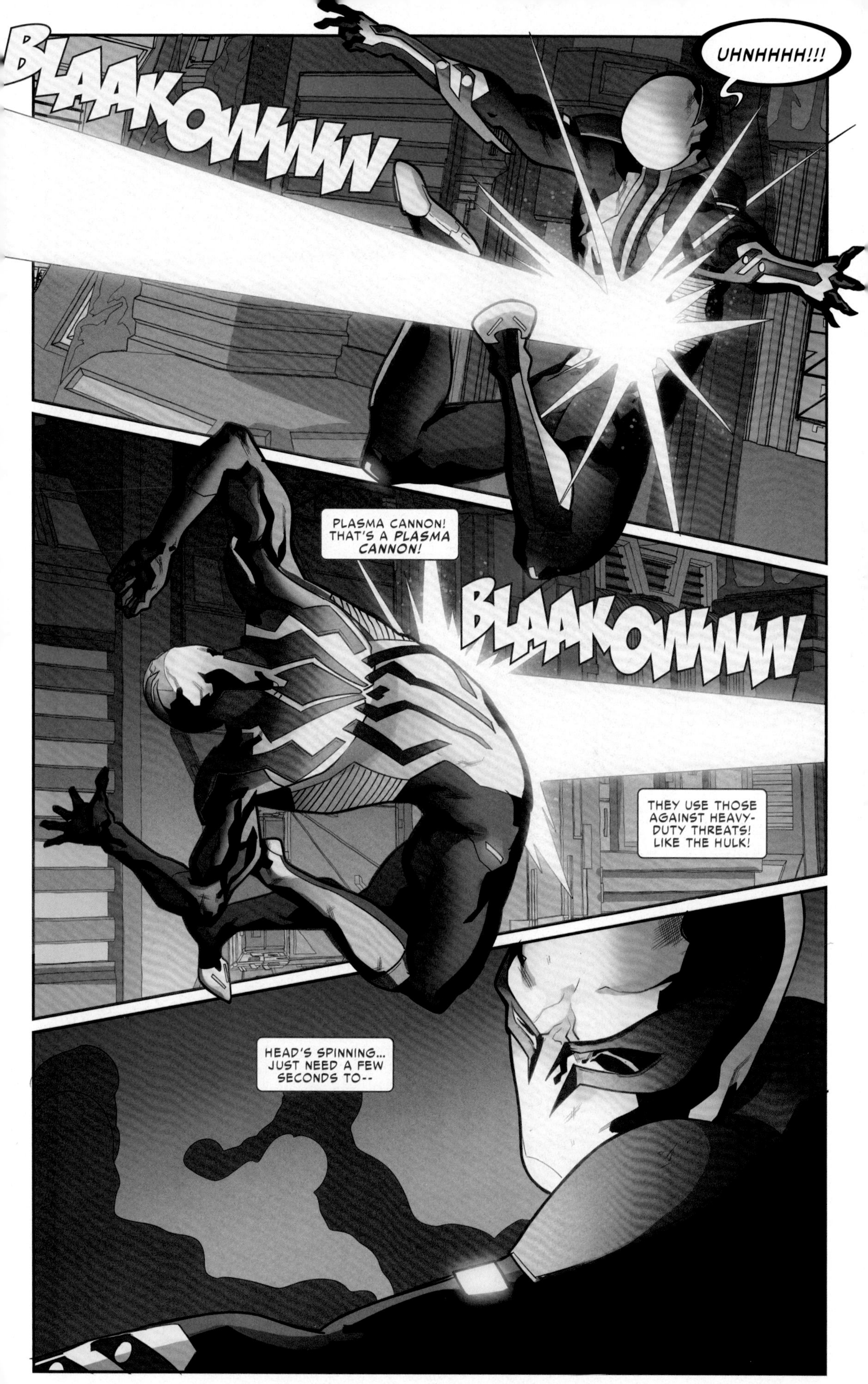
BLAAKOWWW
UHNHHHH!!!
PLASMA CANNON! THAT'S A PLASMA CANNON!
BLAAKOWWW
THEY USE THOSE AGAINST HEAVY-DUTY THREATS! LIKE THE HULK!
HEAD'S SPINNING... JUST NEED A FEW SECONDS TO--

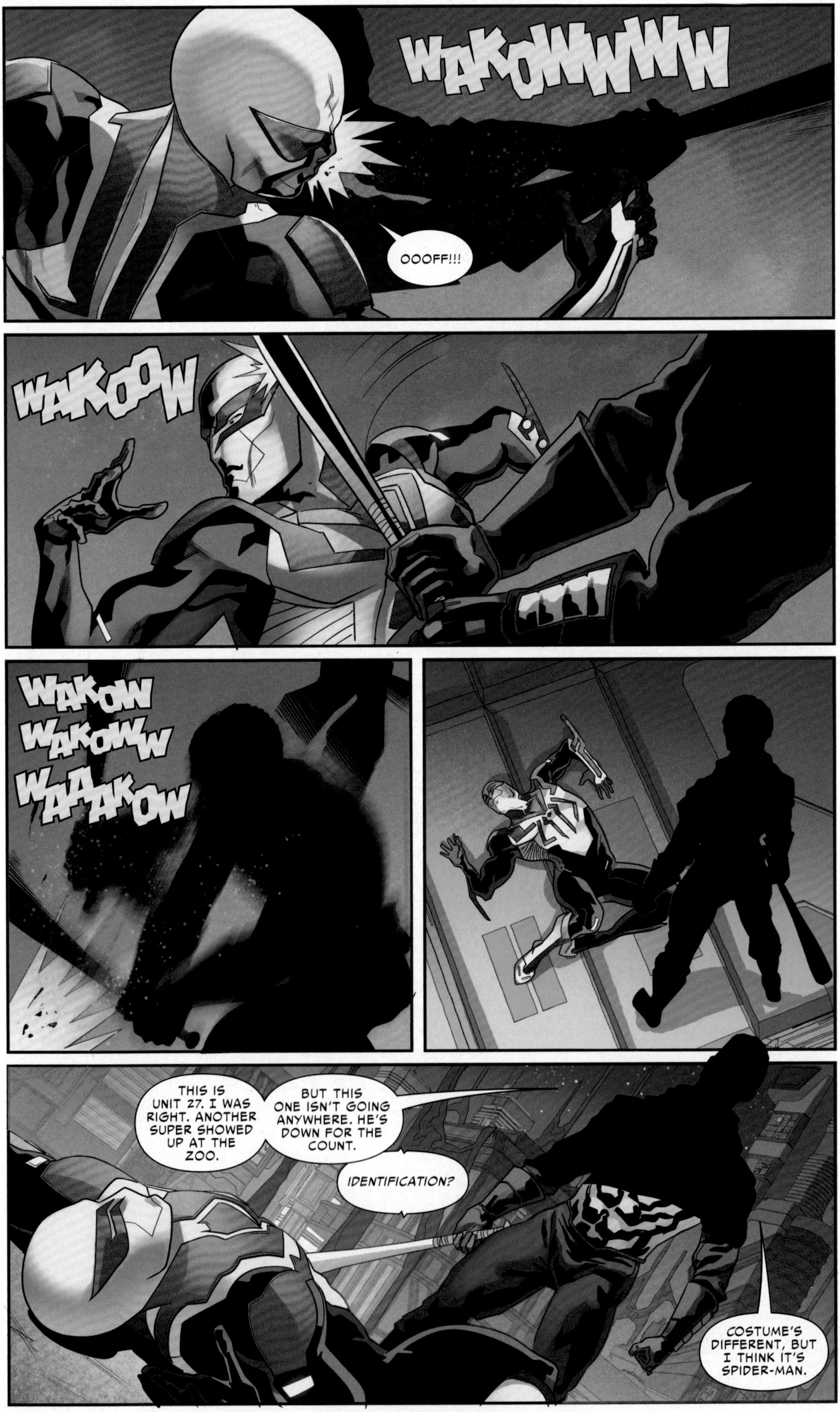
WAKOWWWWW
OOOFF!!!
WAKOOW
WAKOW
WAKOWW
WAAAKOW
THIS IS UNIT 27. I WAS RIGHT. ANOTHER SUPER SHOWED UP AT THE ZOO.
BUT THIS ONE ISN'T GOING ANYWHERE. HE'S DOWN FOR THE COUNT.
IDENTIFICATION?
COSTUME'S DIFFERENT, BUT I THINK IT'S SPIDER-MAN.

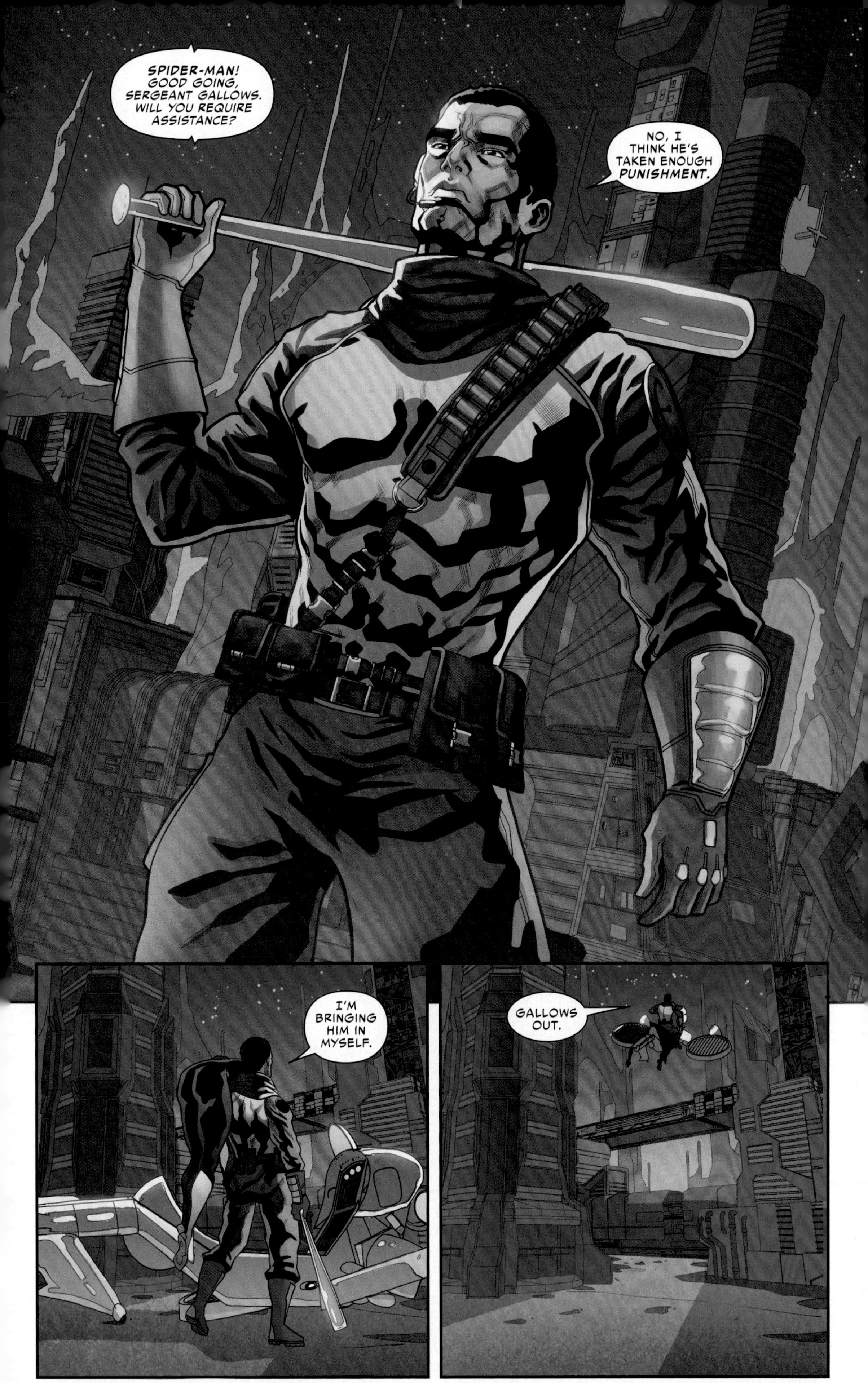
SPIDER-MAN! GOOD GOING, SERGEANT GALLOWS. WILL YOU REQUIRE ASSISTANCE?
NO, I THINK HE'S TAKEN ENOUGH PUNISHMENT.
I'M BRINGING HIM IN MYSELF.
GALLOWS OUT.

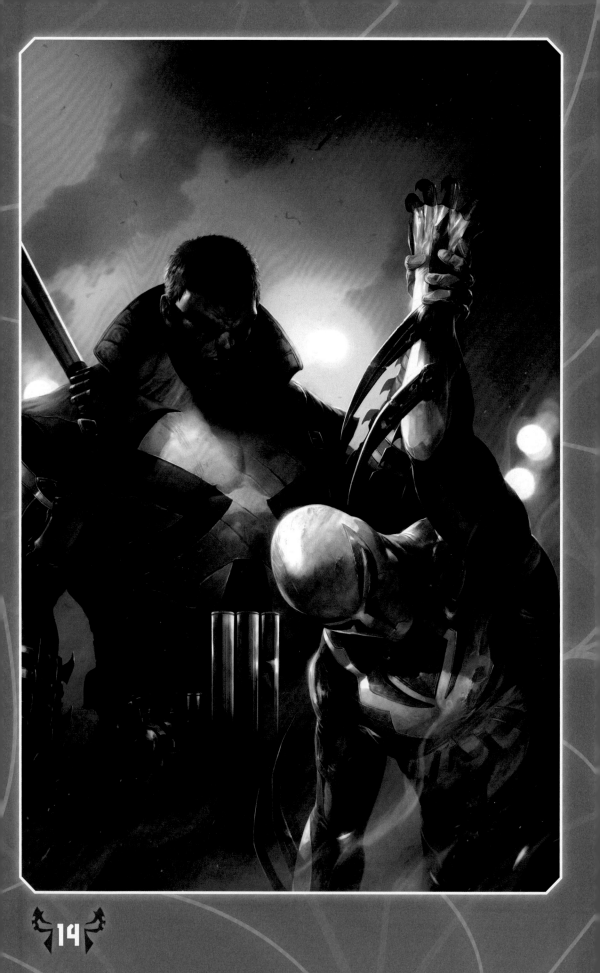

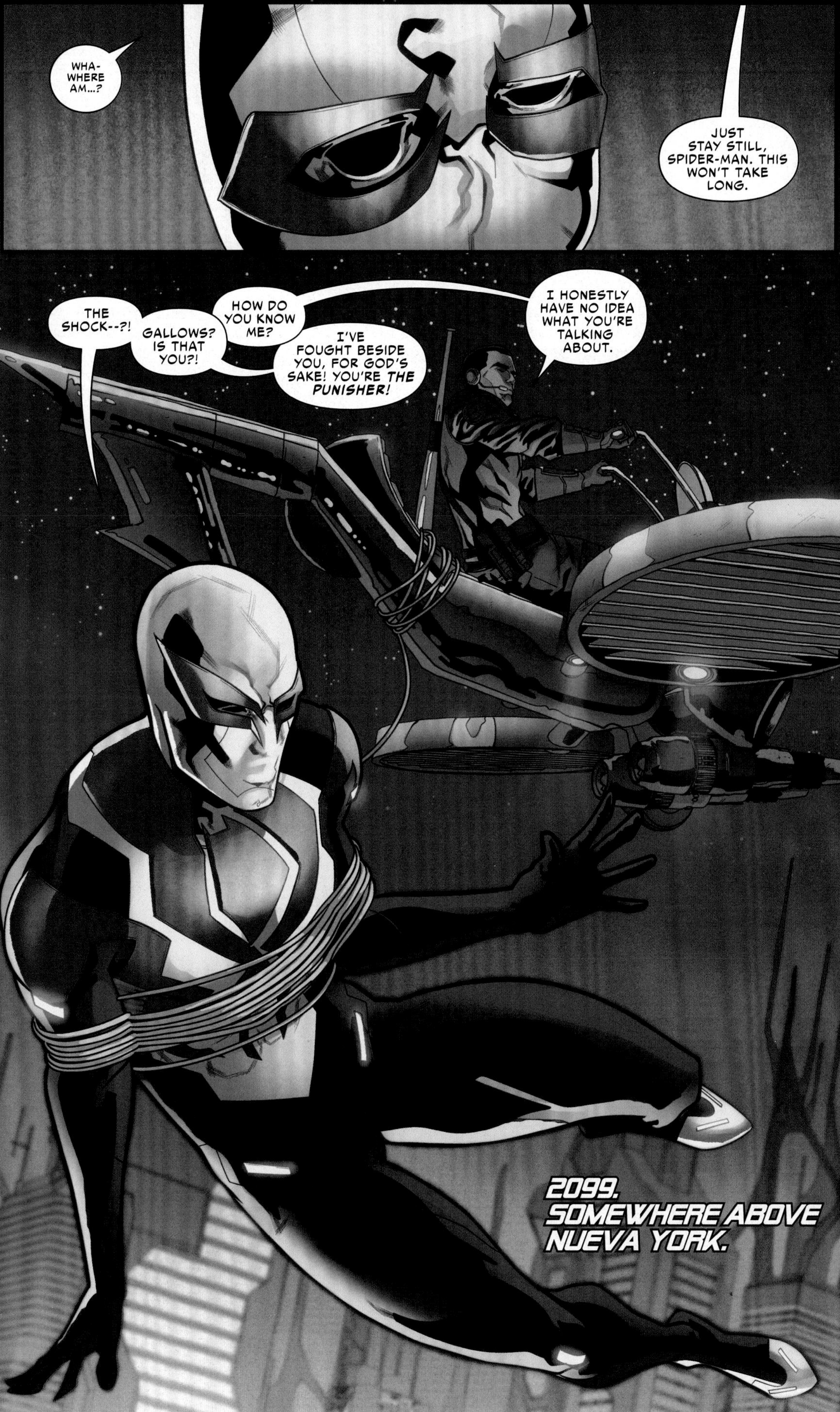
WHA-WHERE AM...?
JUST STAY STILL, SPIDER-MAN. THIS WON'T TAKE LONG.
THE SHOCK--?!
GALLOWS? IS THAT YOU?!
HOW DO YOU KNOW ME?
I'VE FOUGHT BESIDE YOU, FOR GOD'S SAKE! YOU'RE THE PUNISHER!
I HONESTLY HAVE NO IDEA WHAT YOU'RE TALKING ABOUT.
2099. SOMEWHERE ABOVE NUEVA YORK.

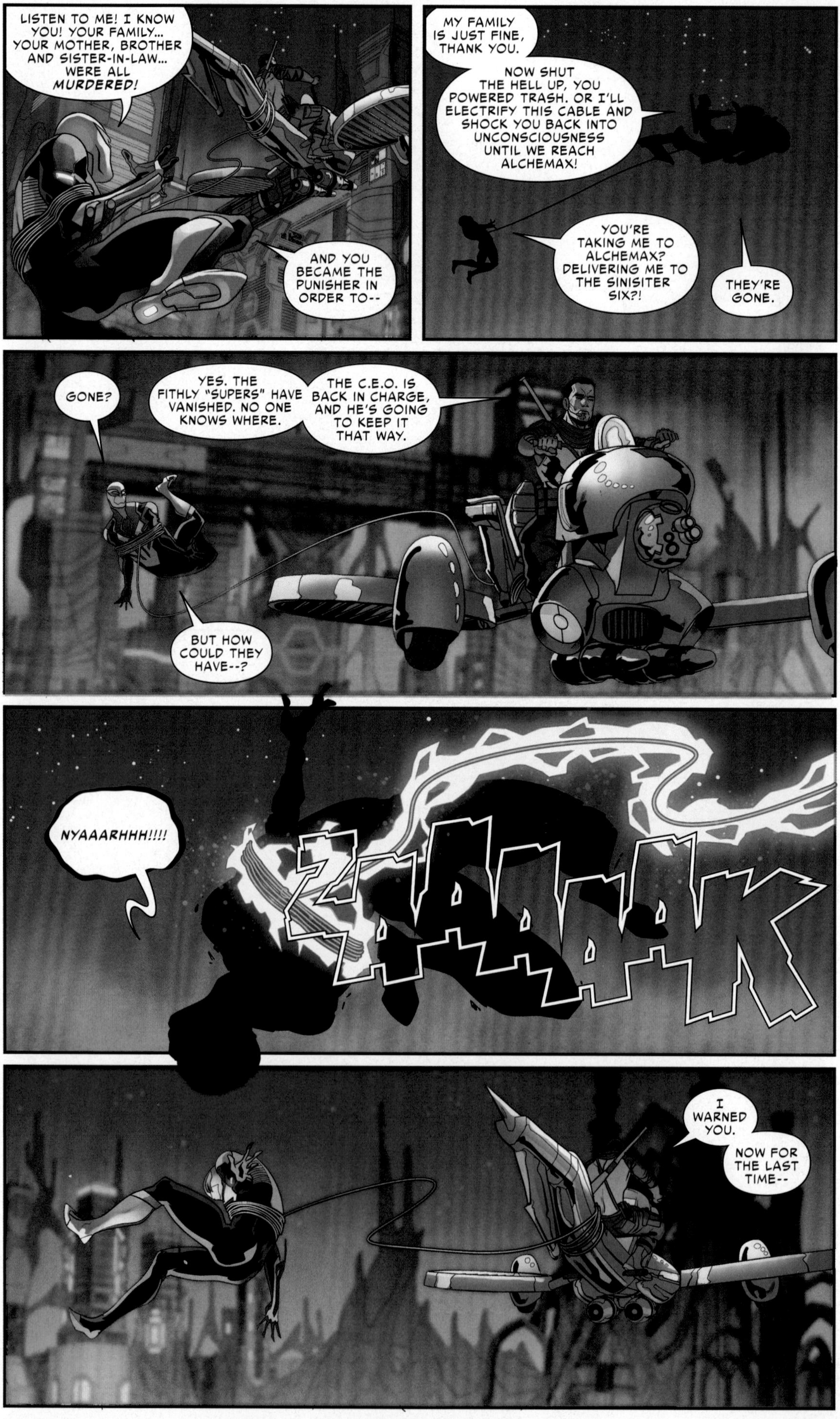

LISTEN TO ME! I KNOW YOU! YOUR FAMILY... YOUR MOTHER, BROTHER AND SISTER-IN-LAW... WERE ALL *MURDERED!*
AND YOU BECAME THE PUNISHER IN ORDER TO--
MY FAMILY IS JUST FINE, THANK YOU.
NOW SHUT THE HELL UP, YOU POWERED TRASH. OR I'LL ELECTRIFY THIS CABLE AND SHOCK YOU BACK INTO UNCONSCIOUSNESS UNTIL WE REACH ALCHEMAX!
YOU'RE TAKING ME TO ALCHEMAX? DELIVERING ME TO THE SINISITER SIX?!
THEY'RE GONE.
GONE?
YES. THE FITHLY "SUPERS" HAVE VANISHED. NO ONE KNOWS WHERE.
THE C.E.O. IS BACK IN CHARGE, AND HE'S GOING TO KEEP IT THAT WAY.
BUT HOW COULD THEY HAVE--?
NYAAARHHH!!!!
ZZAAAK
I WARNED YOU.
NOW FOR THE LAST TIME--

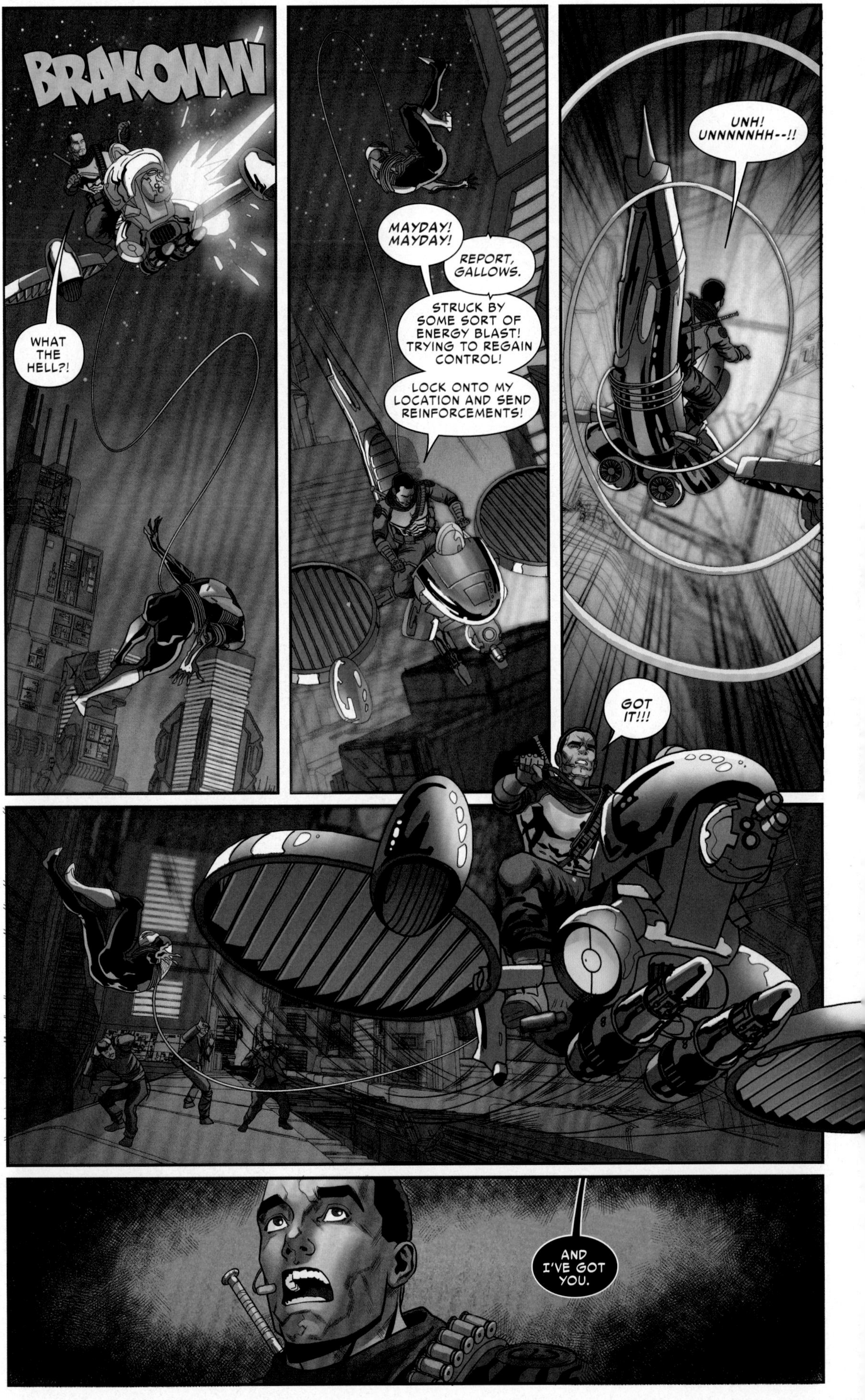
BRAKOWW
WHAT THE HELL?!
MAYDAY! MAYDAY!
REPORT, GALLOWS.
STRUCK BY SOME SORT OF ENERGY BLAST! TRYING TO REGAIN CONTROL!
LOCK ONTO MY LOCATION AND SEND REINFORCEMENTS!
UNH! UNNNNNHH--!!
GOT IT!!!
AND I'VE GOT YOU.

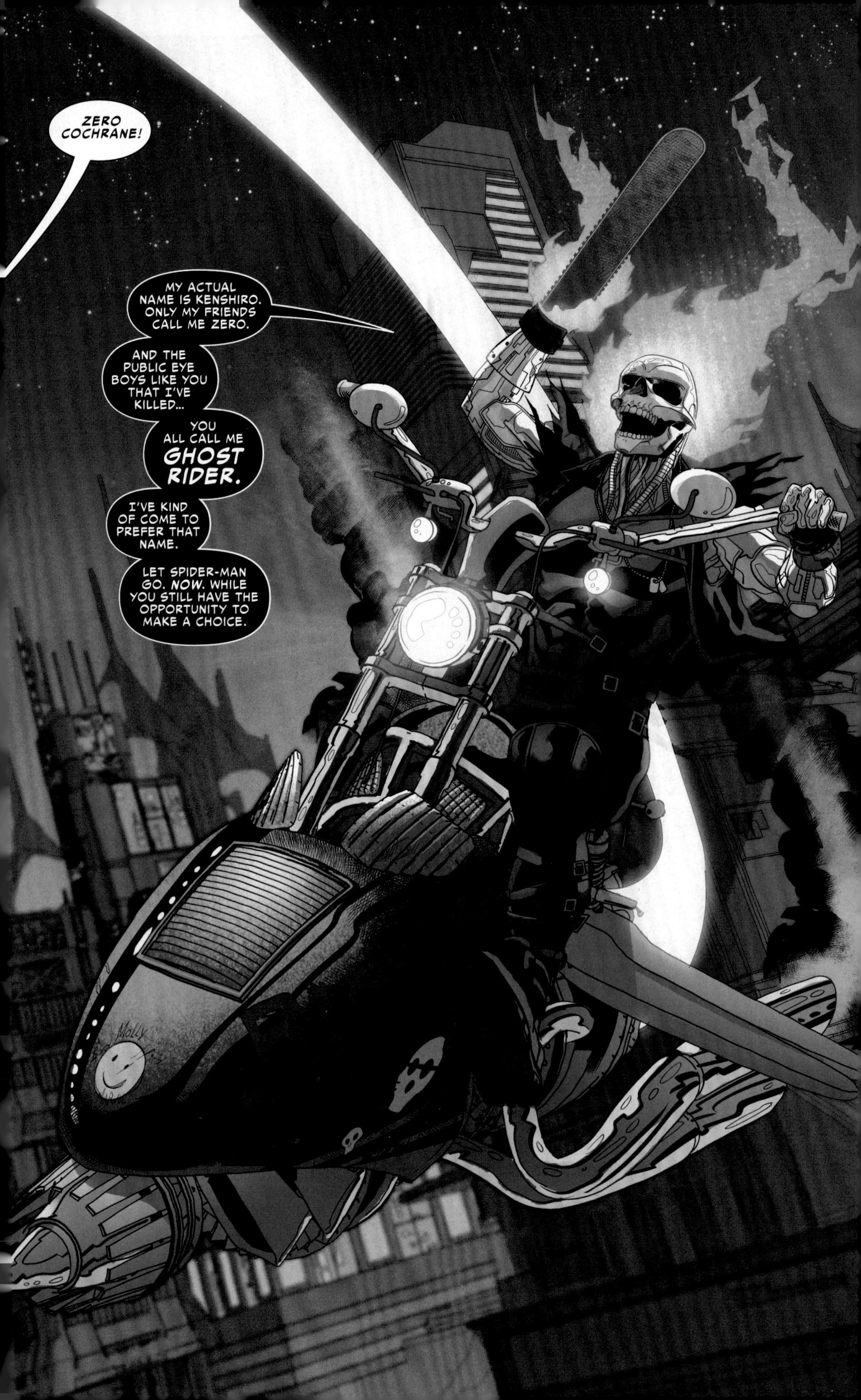
ZERO COCHRANE!
MY ACTUAL NAME IS KENSHIRO. ONLY MY FRIENDS CALL ME ZERO.
AND THE PUBLIC EYE BOYS LIKE YOU THAT I'VE KILLED...
YOU ALL CALL ME GHOST RIDER.
I'VE KIND OF COME TO PREFER THAT NAME.
LET SPIDER-MAN GO. NOW. WHILE YOU STILL HAVE THE OPPORTUNITY TO MAKE A CHOICE.

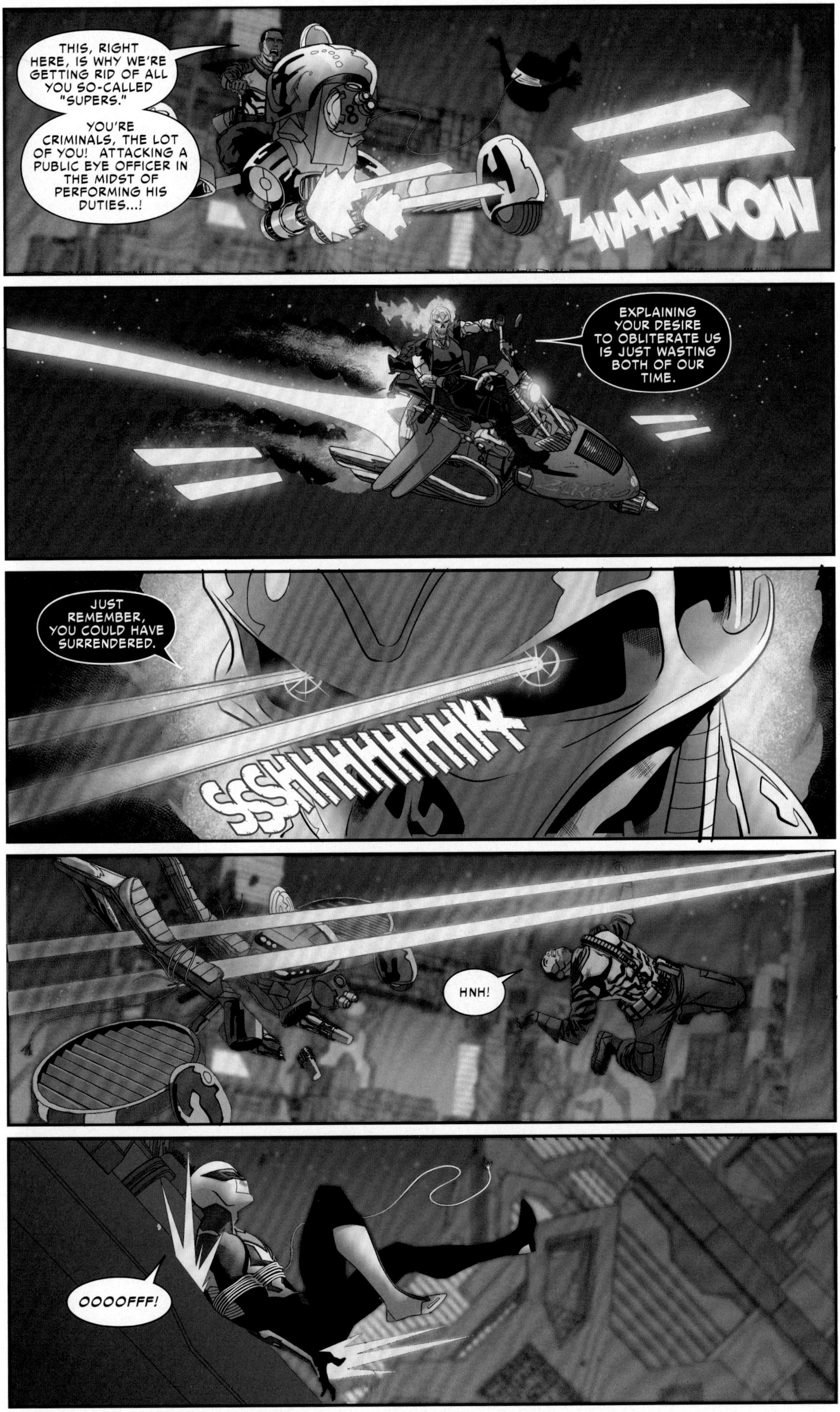
THIS, RIGHT HERE, IS WHY WE'RE GETTING RID OF ALL YOU SO-CALLED "SUPERS."
YOU'RE CRIMINALS, THE LOT OF YOU! ATTACKING A PUBLIC EYE OFFICER IN THE MIDST OF PERFORMING HIS DUTIES...!
ZWAAAKOW
EXPLAINING YOUR DESIRE TO OBLITERATE US IS JUST WASTING BOTH OF OUR TIME.
JUST REMEMBER, YOU COULD HAVE SURRENDERED.
SSSHHHHHHHKK
HNH!
OOOOFFF!

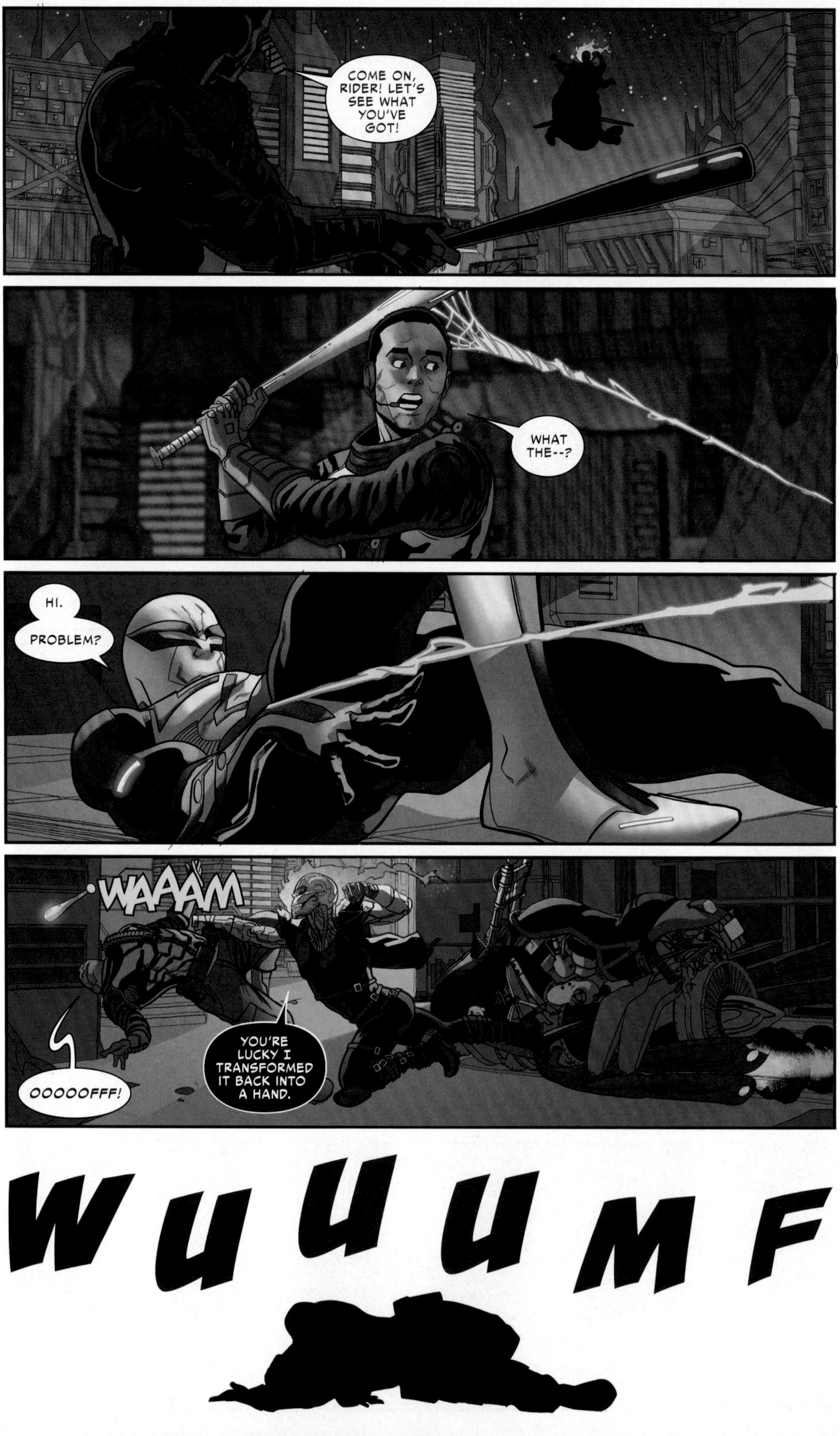
COME ON, RIDER! LET'S SEE WHAT YOU'VE GOT!
WHAT THE--?
HI.
PROBLEM?
WAAAM
OOOOOFFF!
YOU'RE LUCKY I TRANSFORMED IT BACK INTO A HAND.
WUUUMF

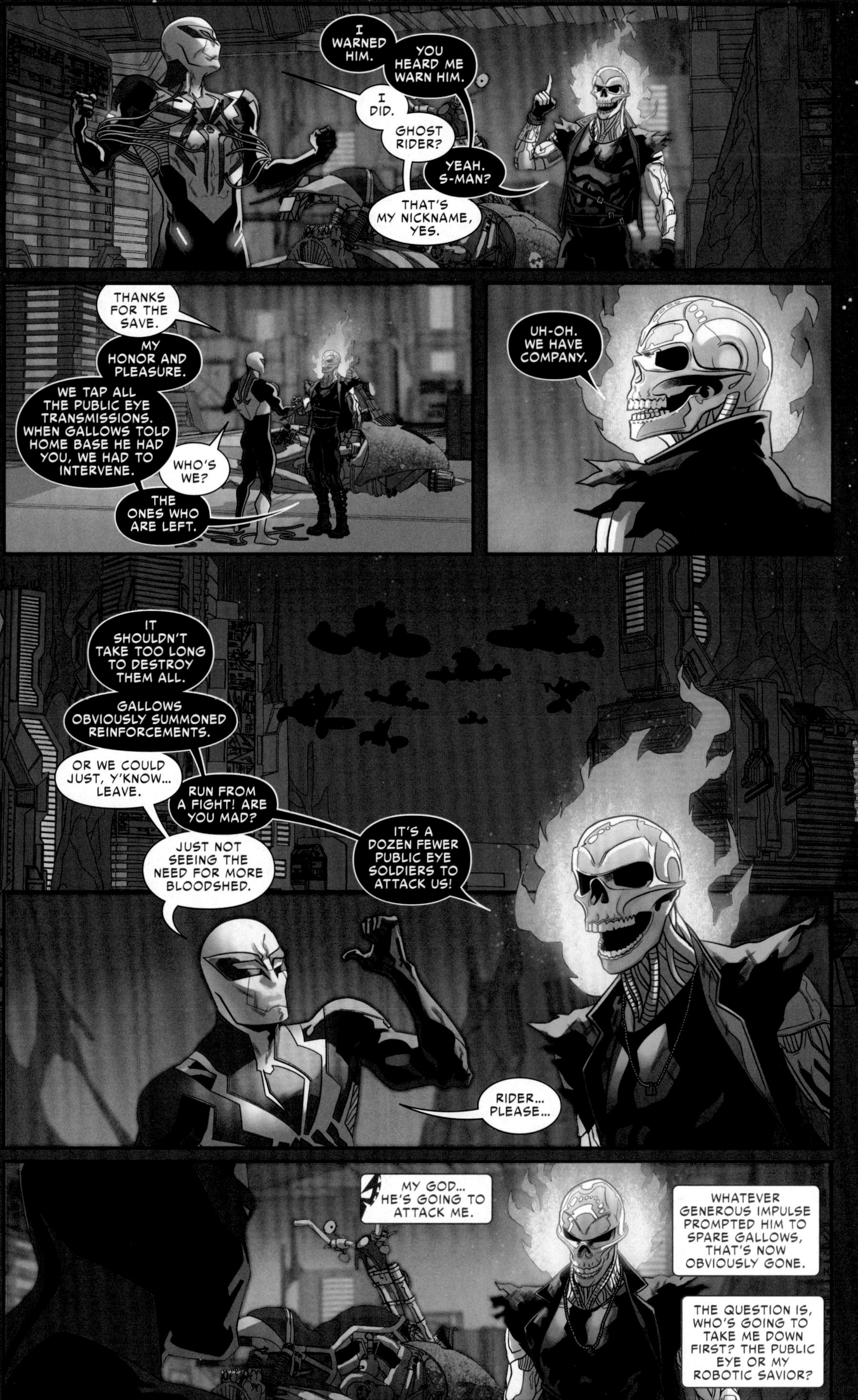
I WARNED HIM.
YOU HEARD ME WARN HIM.
I DID.
GHOST RIDER?
YEAH. S-MAN?
THAT'S MY NICKNAME, YES.
THANKS FOR THE SAVE.
MY HONOR AND PLEASURE.
WE TAP ALL THE PUBLIC EYE TRANSMISSIONS. WHEN GALLOWS TOLD HOME BASE HE HAD YOU, WE HAD TO INTERVENE.
WHO'S WE?
THE ONES WHO ARE LEFT.
UH-OH. WE HAVE COMPANY.
IT SHOULDN'T TAKE TOO LONG TO DESTROY THEM ALL.
GALLOWS OBVIOUSLY SUMMONED REINFORCEMENTS.
OR WE COULD JUST, Y'KNOW... LEAVE.
RUN FROM A FIGHT! ARE YOU MAD?
JUST NOT SEEING THE NEED FOR MORE BLOODSHED.
IT'S A DOZEN FEWER PUBLIC EYE SOLDIERS TO ATTACK US!
RIDER... PLEASE...
MY GOD... HE'S GOING TO ATTACK ME.
WHATEVER GENEROUS IMPULSE PROMPTED HIM TO SPARE GALLOWS, THAT'S NOW OBVIOUSLY GONE.
THE QUESTION IS, WHO'S GOING TO TAKE ME DOWN FIRST? THE PUBLIC EYE OR MY ROBOTIC SAVIOR?

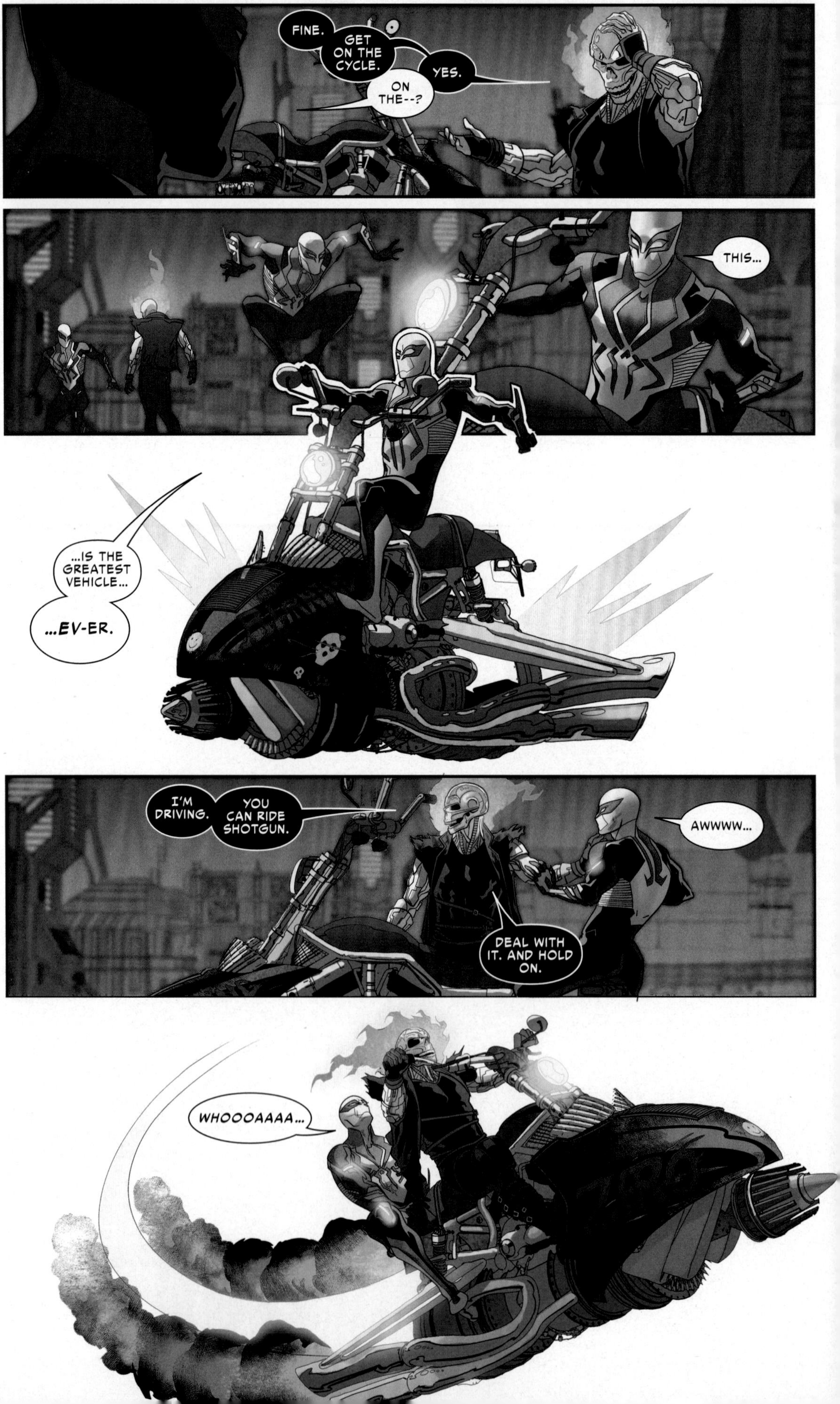
FINE.
GET ON THE CYCLE.
ON THE--?
YES.
THIS...
...IS THE GREATEST VEHICLE...
...EV-ER.
I'M DRIVING.
YOU CAN RIDE SHOTGUN.
AWWWW...
DEAL WITH IT. AND HOLD ON.
WHOOOAAAA...

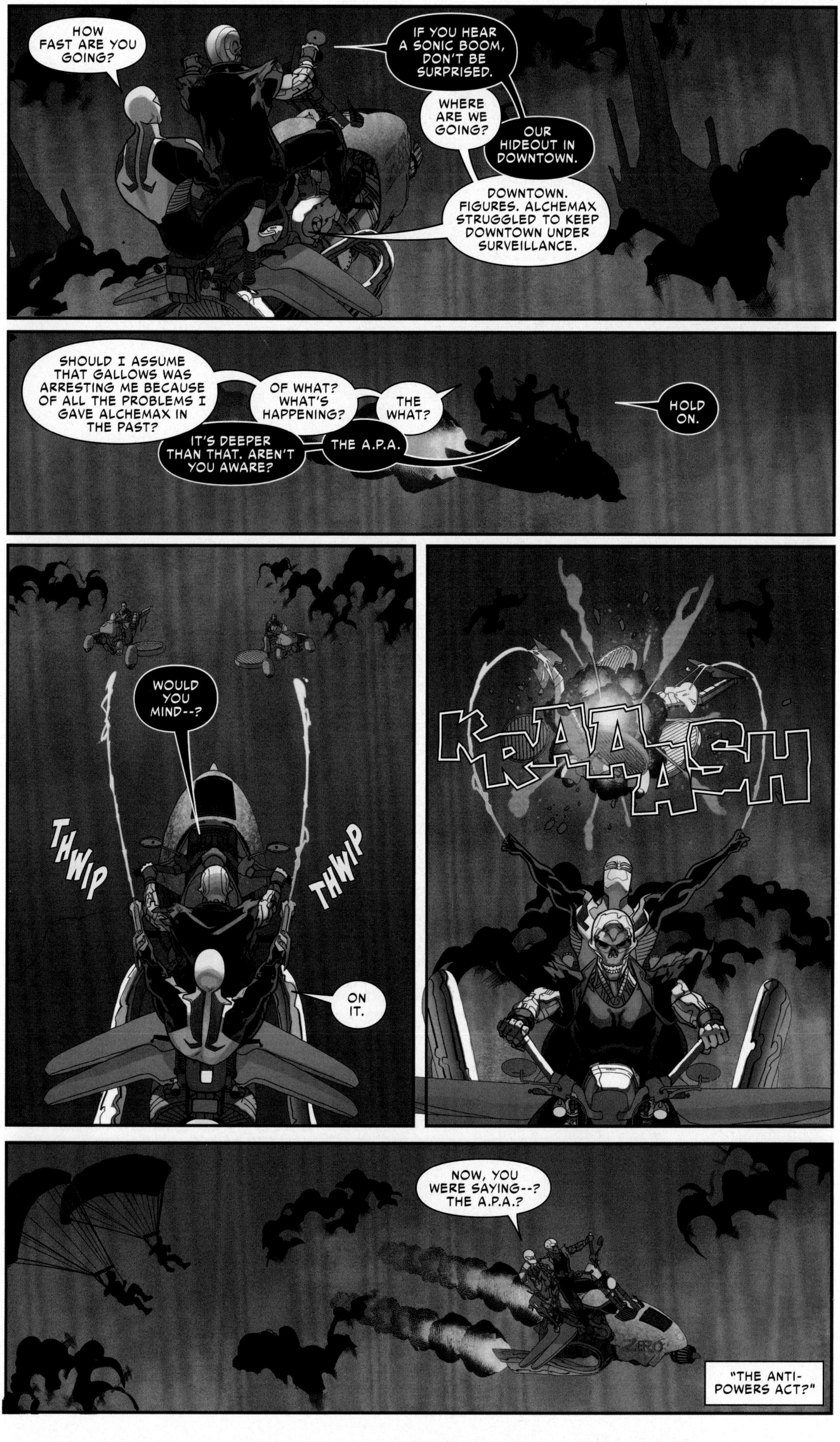
HOW FAST ARE YOU GOING?
IF YOU HEAR A SONIC BOOM, DON'T BE SURPRISED.
WHERE ARE WE GOING?
OUR HIDEOUT IN DOWNTOWN.
DOWNTOWN. FIGURES. ALCHEMAX STRUGGLED TO KEEP DOWNTOWN UNDER SURVEILLANCE.
SHOULD I ASSUME THAT GALLOWS WAS ARRESTING ME BECAUSE OF ALL THE PROBLEMS I GAVE ALCHEMAX IN THE PAST?
IT'S DEEPER THAN THAT. AREN'T YOU AWARE?
OF WHAT? WHAT'S HAPPENING?
THE A.P.A.
THE WHAT?
HOLD ON.
WOULD YOU MIND--?
THWIP
THWIP
ON IT.
KRAAASH
NOW, YOU WERE SAYING--? THE A.P.A.?
ZERO
"THE ANTI-POWERS ACT?"

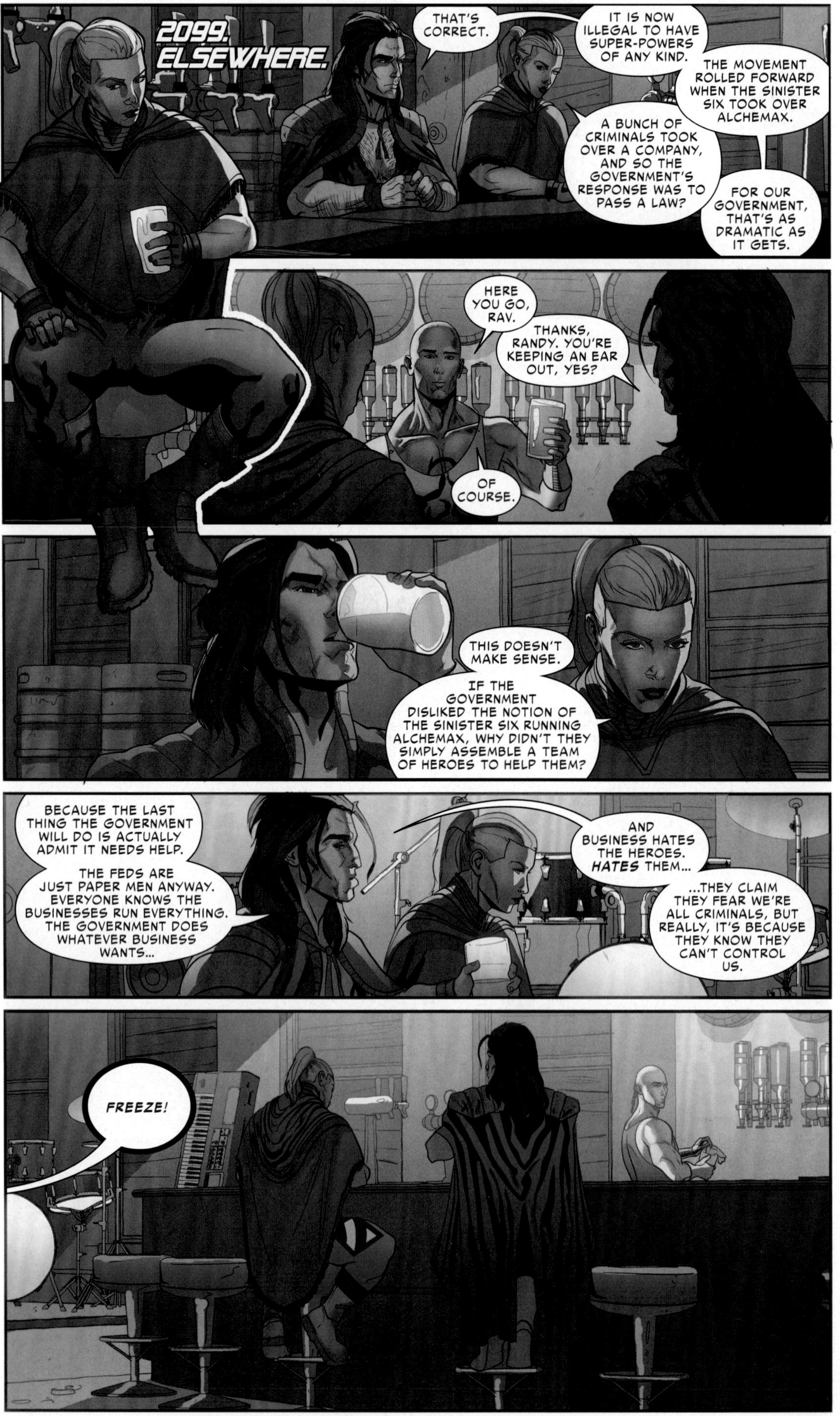
2099. ELSEWHERE.
THAT'S CORRECT.
IT IS NOW ILLEGAL TO HAVE SUPER-POWERS OF ANY KIND.
THE MOVEMENT ROLLED FORWARD WHEN THE SINISTER SIX TOOK OVER ALCHEMAX.
A BUNCH OF CRIMINALS TOOK OVER A COMPANY, AND SO THE GOVERNMENT'S RESPONSE WAS TO PASS A LAW?
FOR OUR GOVERNMENT, THAT'S AS DRAMATIC AS IT GETS.
HERE YOU GO, RAV.
THANKS, RANDY. YOU'RE KEEPING AN EAR OUT, YES?
OF COURSE.
THIS DOESN'T MAKE SENSE.
IF THE GOVERNMENT DISLIKED THE NOTION OF THE SINISTER SIX RUNNING ALCHEMAX, WHY DIDN'T THEY SIMPLY ASSEMBLE A TEAM OF HEROES TO HELP THEM?
BECAUSE THE LAST THING THE GOVERNMENT WILL DO IS ACTUALLY ADMIT IT NEEDS HELP.
THE FEDS ARE JUST PAPER MEN ANYWAY. EVERYONE KNOWS THE BUSINESSES RUN EVERYTHING. THE GOVERNMENT DOES WHATEVER BUSINESS WANTS...
AND BUSINESS HATES THE HEROES. HATES THEM...
...THEY CLAIM THEY FEAR WE'RE ALL CRIMINALS, BUT REALLY, IT'S BECAUSE THEY KNOW THEY CAN'T CONTROL US.
FREEZE!

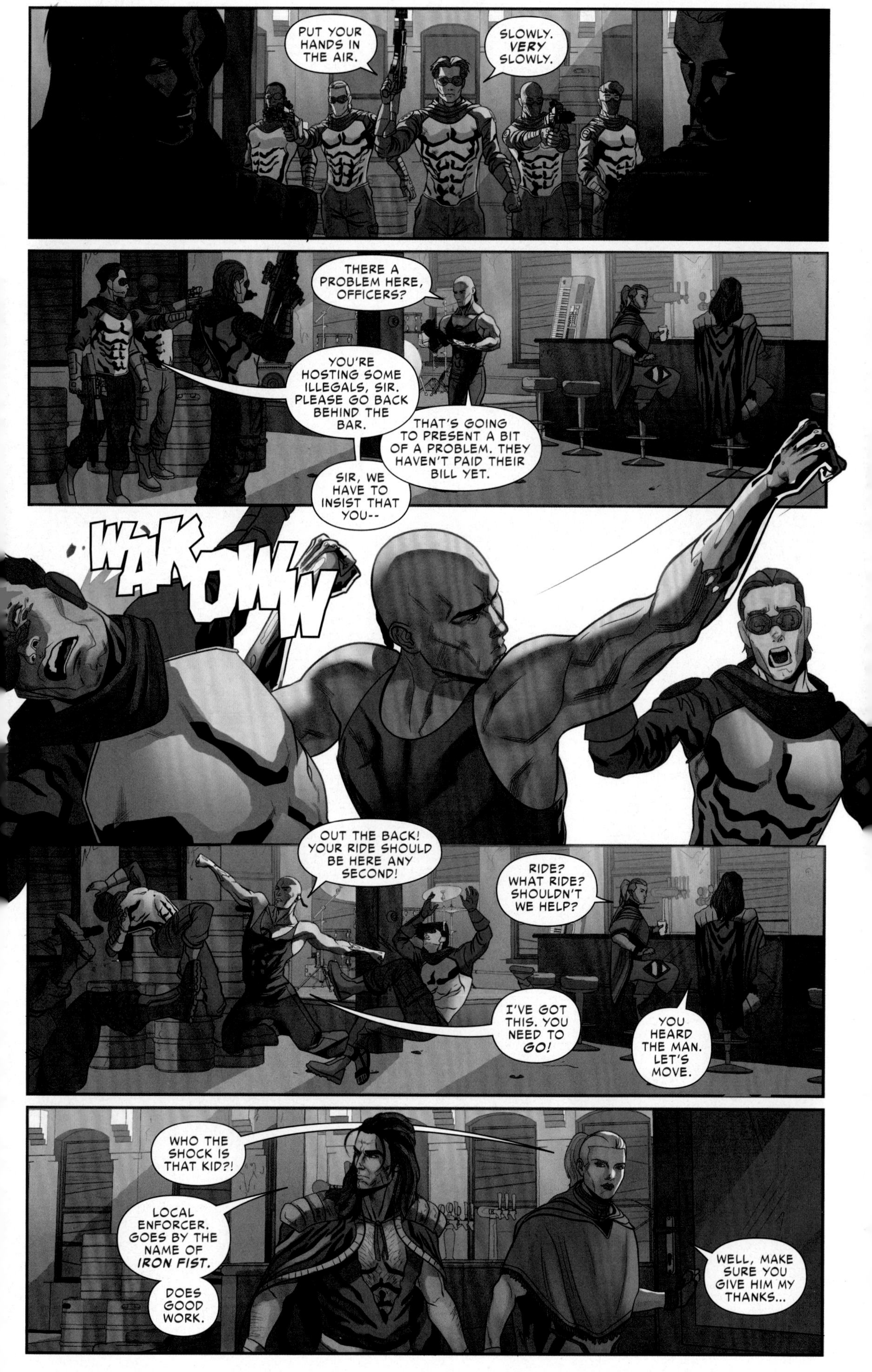
PUT YOUR HANDS IN THE AIR.
SLOWLY. VERY SLOWLY.
THERE A PROBLEM HERE, OFFICERS?
YOU'RE HOSTING SOME ILLEGALS, SIR. PLEASE GO BACK BEHIND THE BAR.
THAT'S GOING TO PRESENT A BIT OF A PROBLEM. THEY HAVEN'T PAID THEIR BILL YET.
SIR, WE HAVE TO INSIST THAT YOU--
WAKOWW
OUT THE BACK! YOUR RIDE SHOULD BE HERE ANY SECOND!
RIDE? WHAT RIDE? SHOULDN'T WE HELP?
I'VE GOT THIS. YOU NEED TO GO!
YOU HEARD THE MAN. LET'S MOVE.
WHO THE SHOCK IS THAT KID?!
LOCAL ENFORCER. GOES BY THE NAME OF IRON FIST.
DOES GOOD WORK.
WELL, MAKE SURE YOU GIVE HIM MY THANKS...

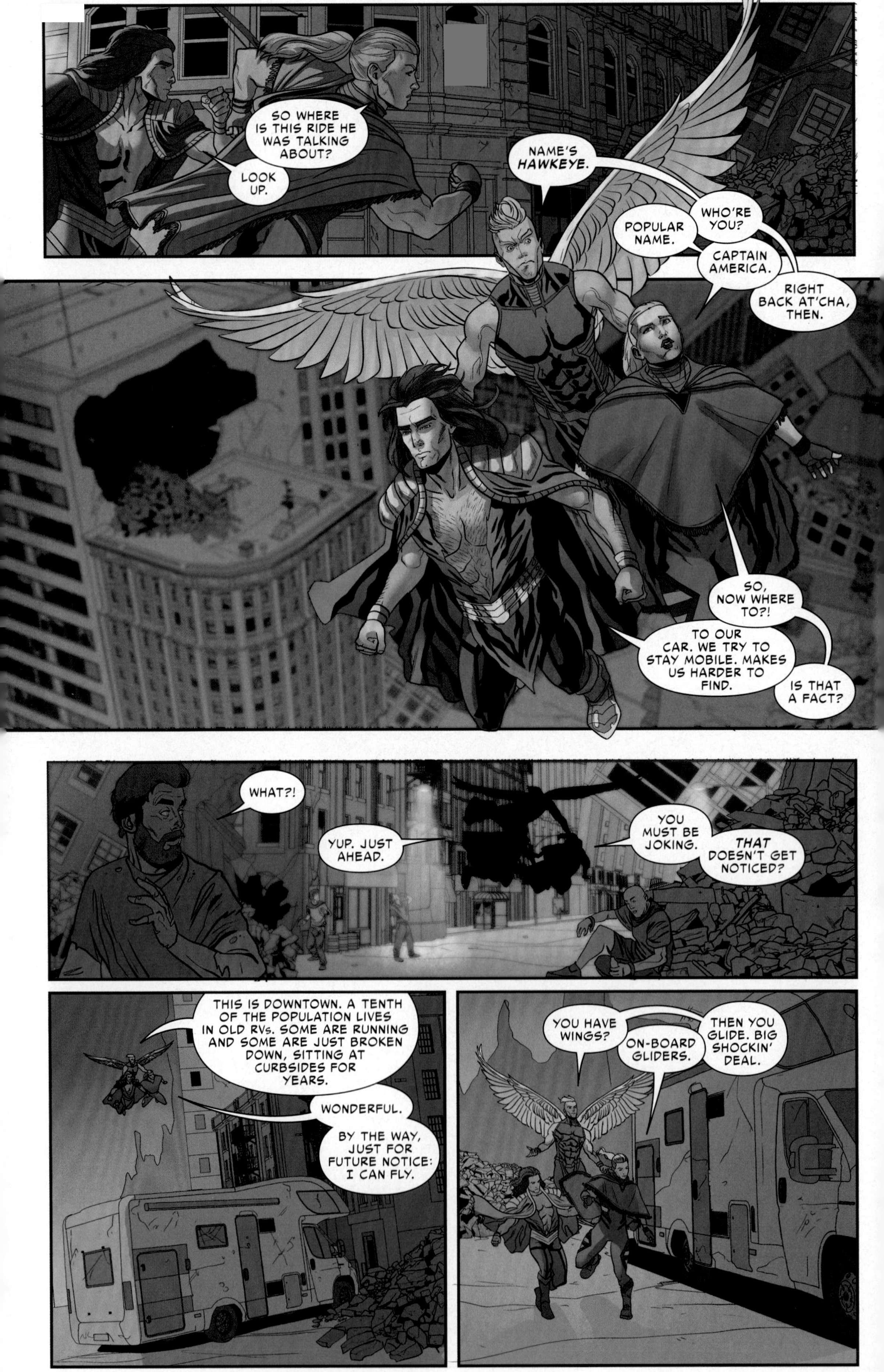

SO WHERE IS THIS RIDE HE WAS TALKING ABOUT?
LOOK UP.
NAME'S *HAWKEYE.*
WHO'RE YOU?
POPULAR NAME.
CAPTAIN AMERICA.
RIGHT BACK AT'CHA, THEN.
SO, NOW WHERE TO?!
TO OUR CAR. WE TRY TO STAY MOBILE. MAKES US HARDER TO FIND.
IS THAT A FACT?
WHAT?!
YUP. JUST AHEAD.
YOU MUST BE JOKING.
THAT DOESN'T GET NOTICED?
THIS IS DOWNTOWN. A TENTH OF THE POPULATION LIVES IN OLD RVs. SOME ARE RUNNING AND SOME ARE JUST BROKEN DOWN, SITTING AT CURBSIDES FOR YEARS.
WONDERFUL.
BY THE WAY, JUST FOR FUTURE NOTICE: I CAN FLY.
YOU HAVE WINGS?
ON-BOARD GLIDERS.
THEN YOU GLIDE. BIG SHOCKIN' DEAL.

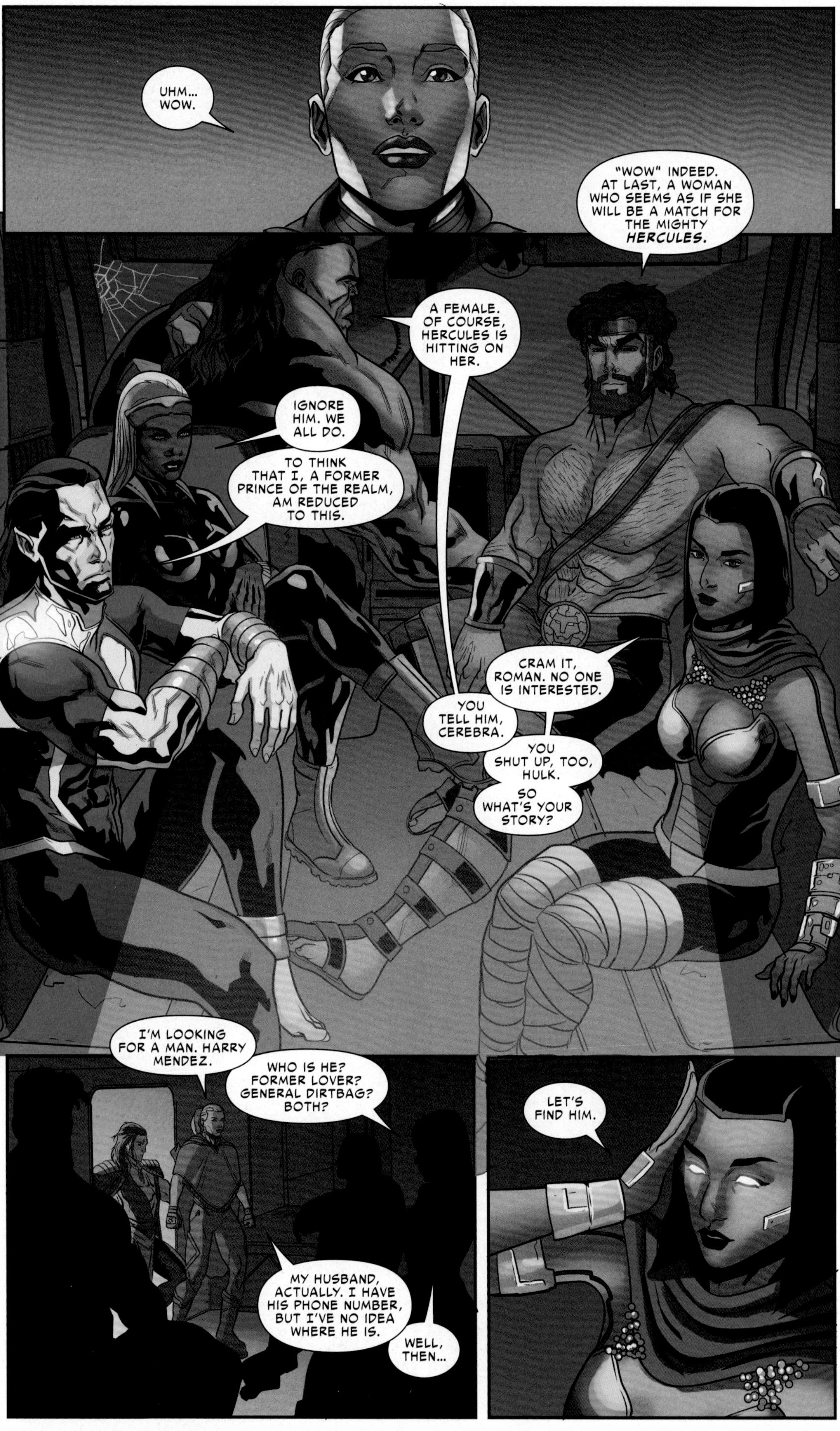
UHM... WOW.
"WOW" INDEED. AT LAST, A WOMAN WHO SEEMS AS IF SHE WILL BE A MATCH FOR THE MIGHTY *HERCULES.*
A FEMALE. OF COURSE, HERCULES IS HITTING ON HER.
IGNORE HIM. WE ALL DO.
TO THINK THAT I, A FORMER PRINCE OF THE REALM, AM REDUCED TO THIS.
CRAM IT, ROMAN. NO ONE IS INTERESTED.
YOU TELL HIM, CEREBRA.
YOU SHUT UP, TOO, HULK.
SO WHAT'S YOUR STORY?
I'M LOOKING FOR A MAN. HARRY MENDEZ.
WHO IS HE? FORMER LOVER? GENERAL DIRTBAG? BOTH?
MY HUSBAND, ACTUALLY. I HAVE HIS PHONE NUMBER, BUT I'VE NO IDEA WHERE HE IS.
WELL, THEN...
LET'S FIND HIM.

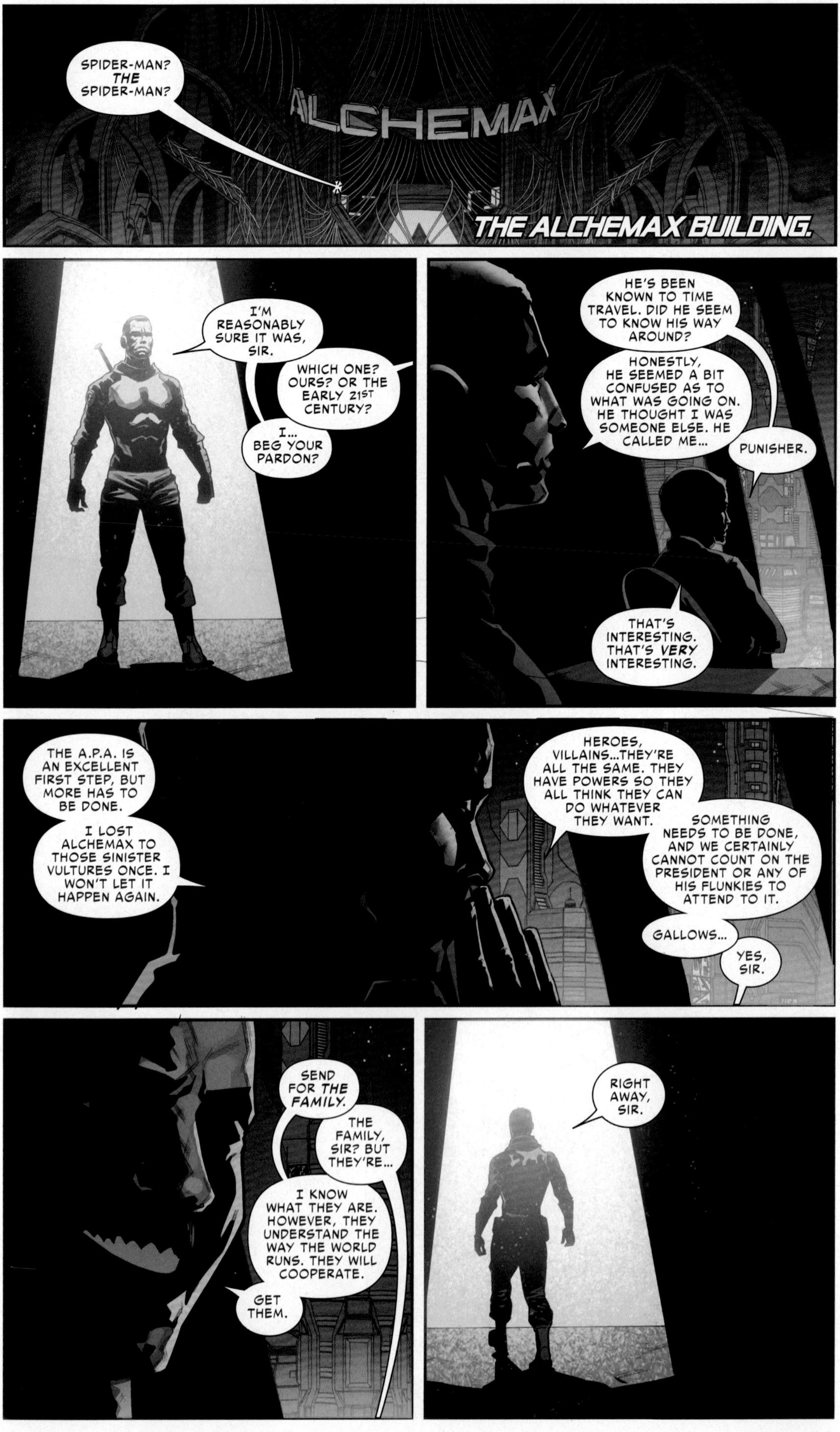
SPIDER-MAN? THE SPIDER-MAN?
ALCHEMAX
THE ALCHEMAX BUILDING.
I'M REASONABLY SURE IT WAS, SIR.
WHICH ONE? OURS? OR THE EARLY 21ST CENTURY?
I... BEG YOUR PARDON?
HE'S BEEN KNOWN TO TIME TRAVEL. DID HE SEEM TO KNOW HIS WAY AROUND?
HONESTLY, HE SEEMED A BIT CONFUSED AS TO WHAT WAS GOING ON. HE THOUGHT I WAS SOMEONE ELSE. HE CALLED ME...
PUNISHER.
THAT'S INTERESTING. THAT'S VERY INTERESTING.
THE A.P.A. IS AN EXCELLENT FIRST STEP, BUT MORE HAS TO BE DONE.
I LOST ALCHEMAX TO THOSE SINISTER VULTURES ONCE. I WON'T LET IT HAPPEN AGAIN.
HEROES, VILLAINS...THEY'RE ALL THE SAME. THEY HAVE POWERS SO THEY ALL THINK THEY CAN DO WHATEVER THEY WANT.
SOMETHING NEEDS TO BE DONE, AND WE CERTAINLY CANNOT COUNT ON THE PRESIDENT OR ANY OF HIS FLUNKIES TO ATTEND TO IT.
GALLOWS...
YES, SIR.
SEND FOR THE FAMILY.
THE FAMILY, SIR? BUT THEY'RE...
I KNOW WHAT THEY ARE. HOWEVER, THEY UNDERSTAND THE WAY THE WORLD RUNS. THEY WILL COOPERATE.
GET THEM.
RIGHT AWAY, SIR.

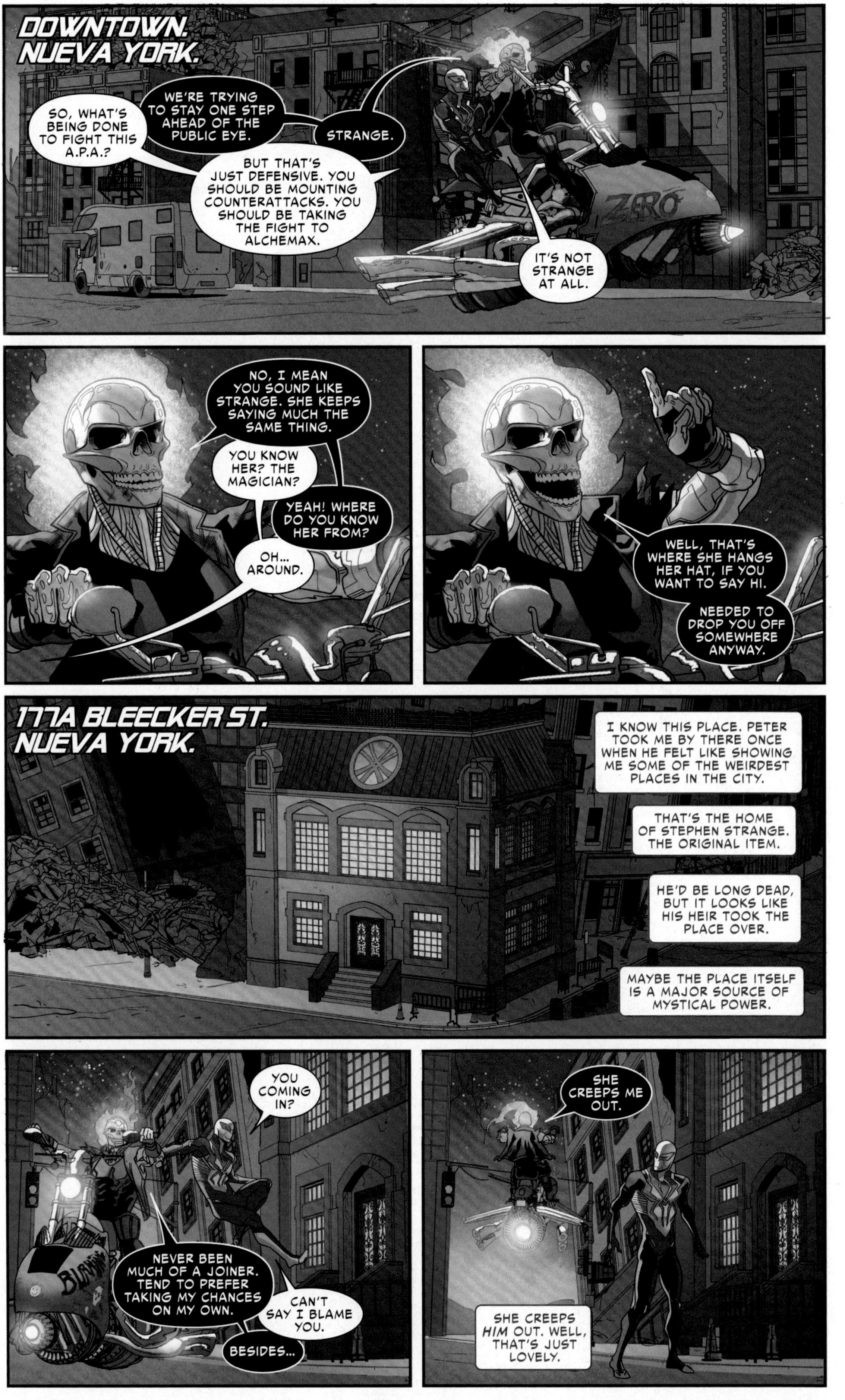
DOWNTOWN. NUEVA YORK.
SO, WHAT'S BEING DONE TO FIGHT THIS A.P.A.?
WE'RE TRYING TO STAY ONE STEP AHEAD OF THE PUBLIC EYE.
BUT THAT'S JUST DEFENSIVE. YOU SHOULD BE MOUNTING COUNTERATTACKS. YOU SHOULD BE TAKING THE FIGHT TO ALCHEMAX.
STRANGE.
IT'S NOT STRANGE AT ALL.
ZERO
NO, I MEAN YOU SOUND LIKE STRANGE. SHE KEEPS SAYING MUCH THE SAME THING.
YOU KNOW HER? THE MAGICIAN?
YEAH! WHERE DO YOU KNOW HER FROM?
OH... AROUND.
WELL, THAT'S WHERE SHE HANGS HER HAT, IF YOU WANT TO SAY HI.
NEEDED TO DROP YOU OFF SOMEWHERE ANYWAY.
177A BLEECKER ST. NUEVA YORK.
I KNOW THIS PLACE. PETER TOOK ME BY THERE ONCE WHEN HE FELT LIKE SHOWING ME SOME OF THE WEIRDEST PLACES IN THE CITY.
THAT'S THE HOME OF STEPHEN STRANGE. THE ORIGINAL ITEM.
HE'D BE LONG DEAD, BUT IT LOOKS LIKE HIS HEIR TOOK THE PLACE OVER.
MAYBE THE PLACE ITSELF IS A MAJOR SOURCE OF MYSTICAL POWER.
YOU COMING IN?
NEVER BEEN MUCH OF A JOINER. TEND TO PREFER TAKING MY CHANCES ON MY OWN.
CAN'T SAY I BLAME YOU.
BESIDES...
SHE CREEPS ME OUT.
SHE CREEPS *HIM* OUT. WELL, THAT'S JUST LOVELY.

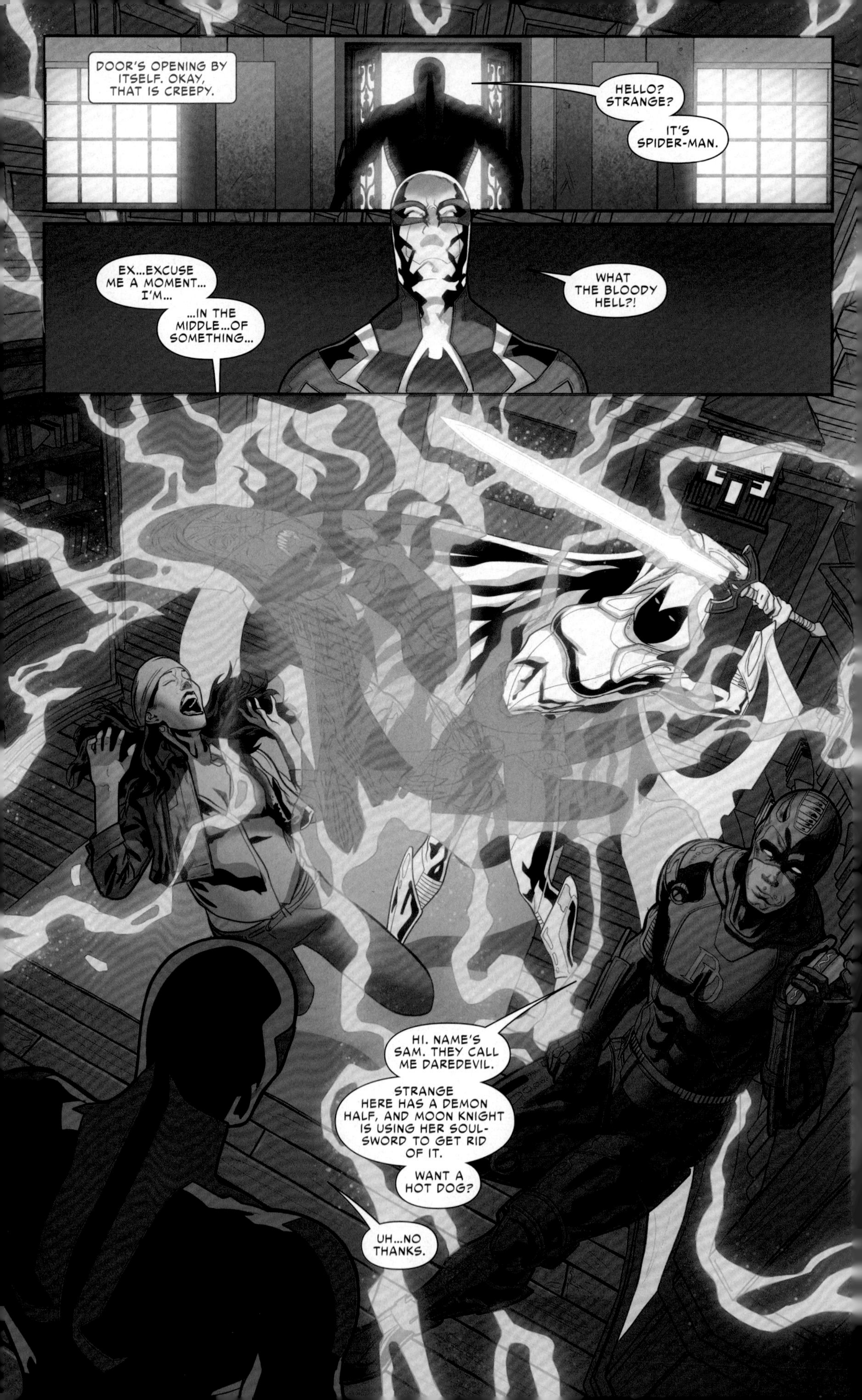
DOOR'S OPENING BY ITSELF. OKAY, THAT IS CREEPY.
HELLO? STRANGE?
IT'S SPIDER-MAN.
EX...EXCUSE ME A MOMENT... I'M...
...IN THE MIDDLE...OF SOMETHING...
WHAT THE BLOODY HELL?!
HI. NAME'S SAM. THEY CALL ME DAREDEVIL.
STRANGE HERE HAS A DEMON HALF, AND MOON KNIGHT IS USING HER SOUL-SWORD TO GET RID OF IT.
WANT A HOT DOG?
UH...NO THANKS.

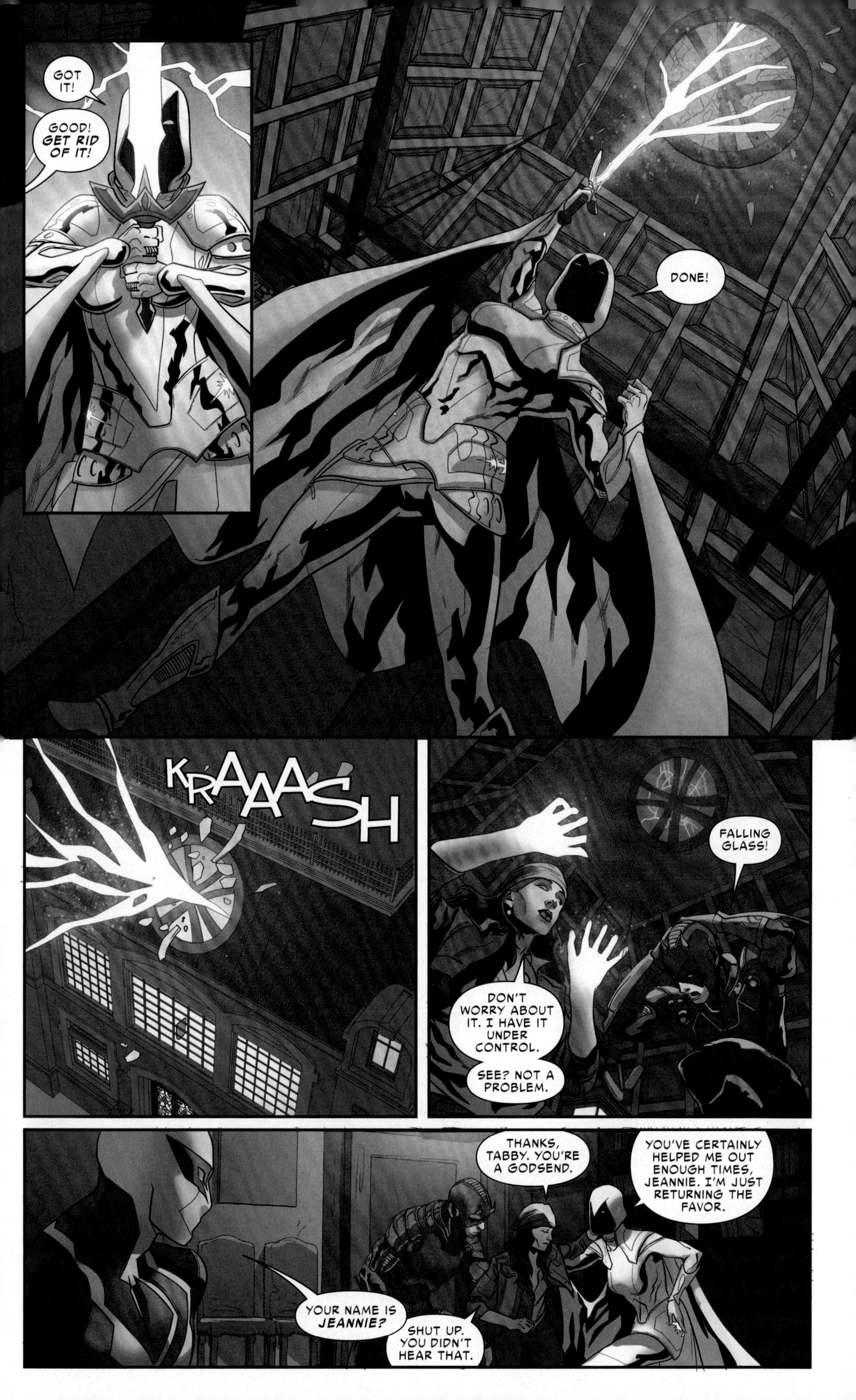
GOT IT!
GOOD! GET RID OF IT!
DONE!
KRAAASH
FALLING GLASS!
DON'T WORRY ABOUT IT. I HAVE IT UNDER CONTROL.
SEE? NOT A PROBLEM.
THANKS, TABBY. YOU'RE A GODSEND.
YOU'VE CERTAINLY HELPED ME OUT ENOUGH TIMES, JEANNIE. I'M JUST RETURNING THE FAVOR.
YOUR NAME IS JEANNIE?
SHUT UP. YOU DIDN'T HEAR THAT.

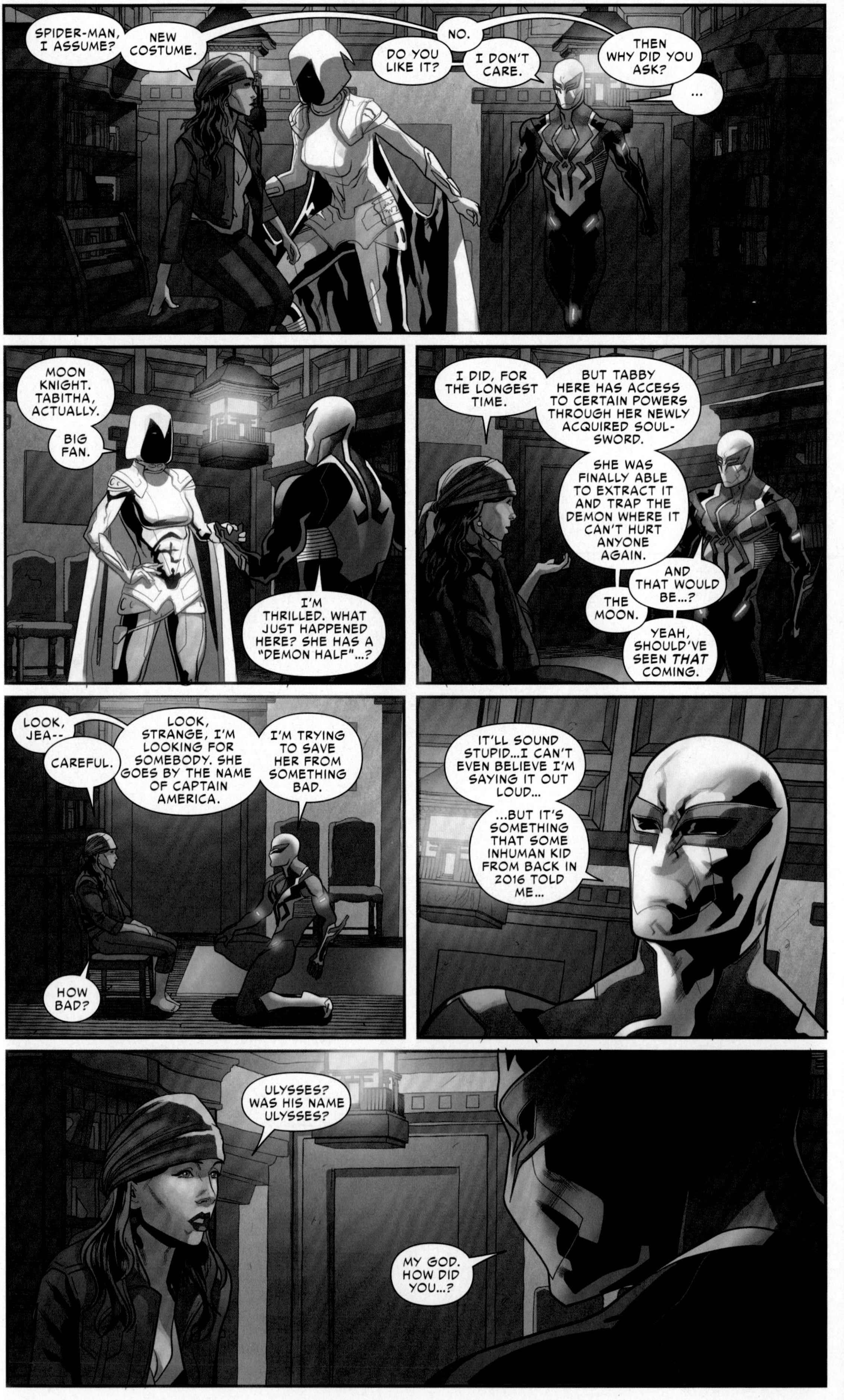
SPIDER-MAN, I ASSUME?
NEW COSTUME.
NO.
DO YOU LIKE IT?
I DON'T CARE.
THEN WHY DID YOU ASK?
...
MOON KNIGHT. TABITHA, ACTUALLY.
BIG FAN.
I'M THRILLED. WHAT JUST HAPPENED HERE? SHE HAS A "DEMON HALF"...?
I DID, FOR THE LONGEST TIME.
BUT TABBY HERE HAS ACCESS TO CERTAIN POWERS THROUGH HER NEWLY ACQUIRED SOUL-SWORD.
SHE WAS FINALLY ABLE TO EXTRACT IT AND TRAP THE DEMON WHERE IT CAN'T HURT ANYONE AGAIN.
AND THAT WOULD BE...?
THE MOON.
YEAH, SHOULD'VE SEEN *THAT* COMING.
LOOK, JEA--
CAREFUL.
LOOK, STRANGE, I'M LOOKING FOR SOMEBODY. SHE GOES BY THE NAME OF CAPTAIN AMERICA.
I'M TRYING TO SAVE HER FROM SOMETHING BAD.
HOW BAD?
IT'LL SOUND STUPID...I CAN'T EVEN BELIEVE I'M SAYING IT OUT LOUD...
...BUT IT'S SOMETHING THAT SOME INHUMAN KID FROM BACK IN 2016 TOLD ME...
ULYSSES? WAS HIS NAME ULYSSES?
MY GOD. HOW DID YOU...?

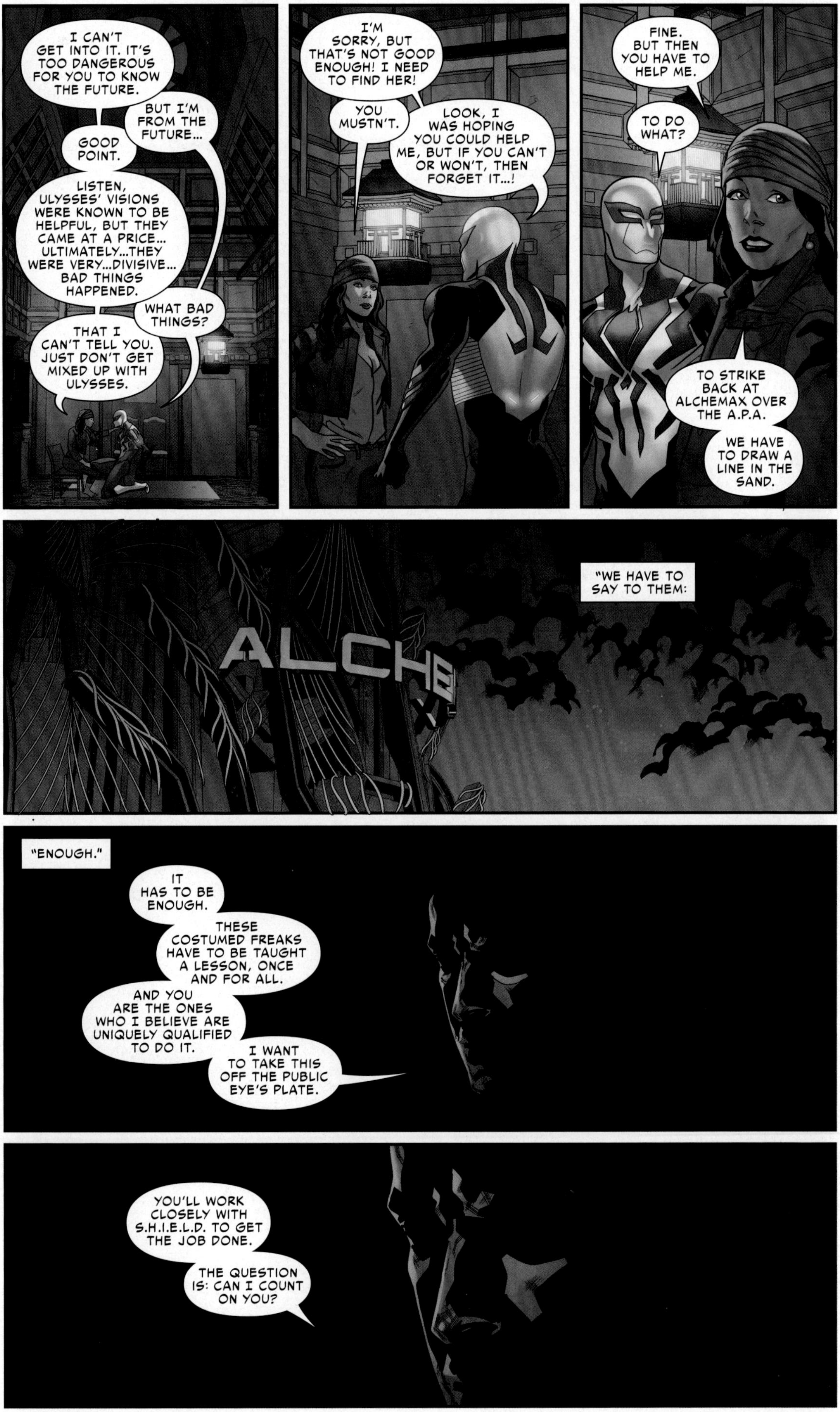
I CAN'T GET INTO IT. IT'S TOO DANGEROUS FOR YOU TO KNOW THE FUTURE.
BUT I'M FROM THE FUTURE...
GOOD POINT.
LISTEN, ULYSSES' VISIONS WERE KNOWN TO BE HELPFUL, BUT THEY CAME AT A PRICE... ULTIMATELY...THEY WERE VERY...DIVISIVE... BAD THINGS HAPPENED.
WHAT BAD THINGS?
THAT I CAN'T TELL YOU. JUST DON'T GET MIXED UP WITH ULYSSES.
I'M SORRY, BUT THAT'S NOT GOOD ENOUGH! I NEED TO FIND HER!
YOU MUSTN'T.
LOOK, I WAS HOPING YOU COULD HELP ME, BUT IF YOU CAN'T OR WON'T, THEN FORGET IT...!
FINE. BUT THEN YOU HAVE TO HELP ME.
TO DO WHAT?
TO STRIKE BACK AT ALCHEMAX OVER THE A.P.A.
WE HAVE TO DRAW A LINE IN THE SAND.
"WE HAVE TO SAY TO THEM:
ALCHE
"ENOUGH."
IT HAS TO BE ENOUGH.
THESE COSTUMED FREAKS HAVE TO BE TAUGHT A LESSON, ONCE AND FOR ALL.
AND YOU ARE THE ONES WHO I BELIEVE ARE UNIQUELY QUALIFIED TO DO IT.
I WANT TO TAKE THIS OFF THE PUBLIC EYE'S PLATE.
YOU'LL WORK CLOSELY WITH S.H.I.E.L.D. TO GET THE JOB DONE.
THE QUESTION IS: CAN I COUNT ON YOU?

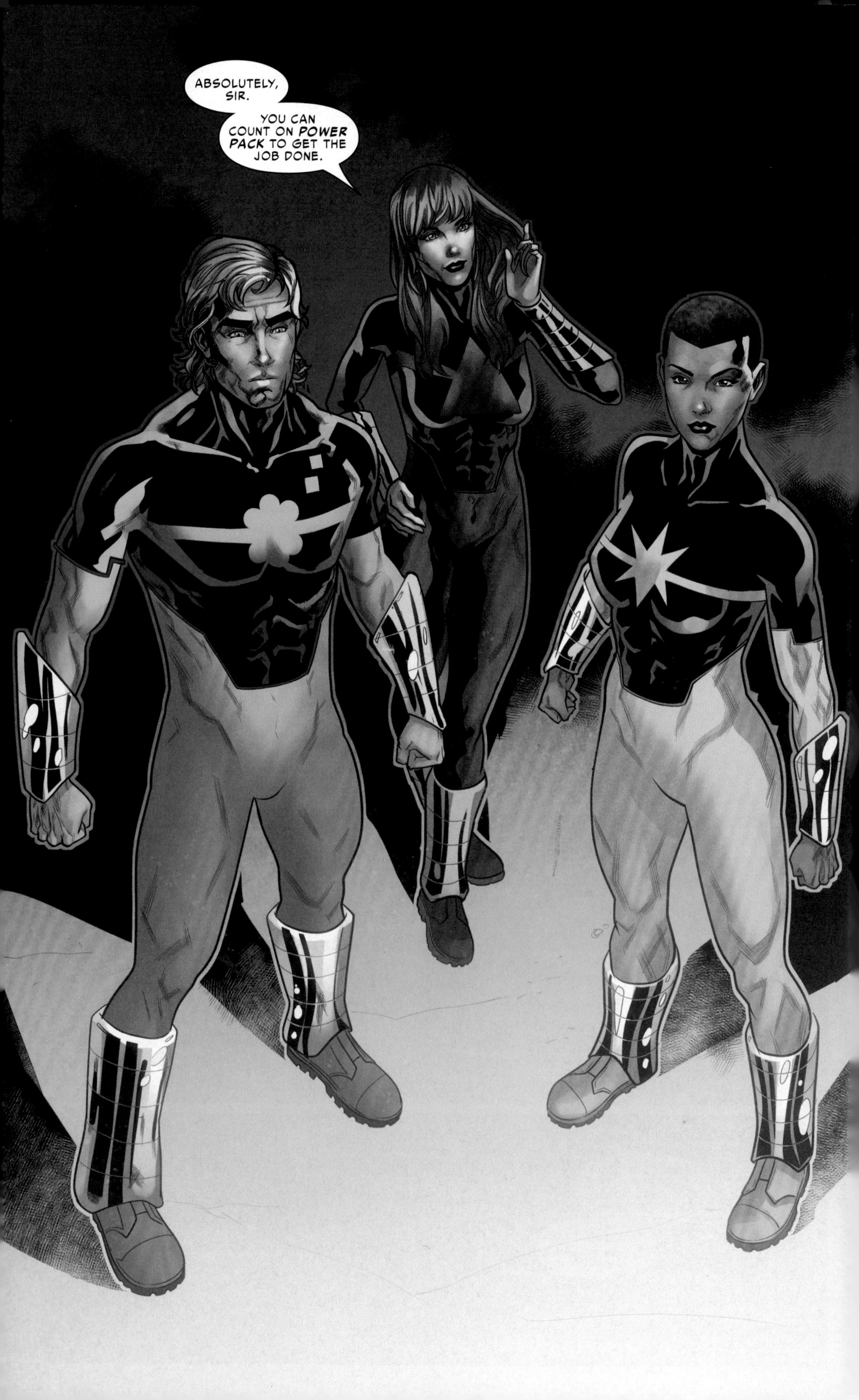
ABSOLUTELY, SIR.
YOU CAN COUNT ON **POWER PACK** TO GET THE JOB DONE.

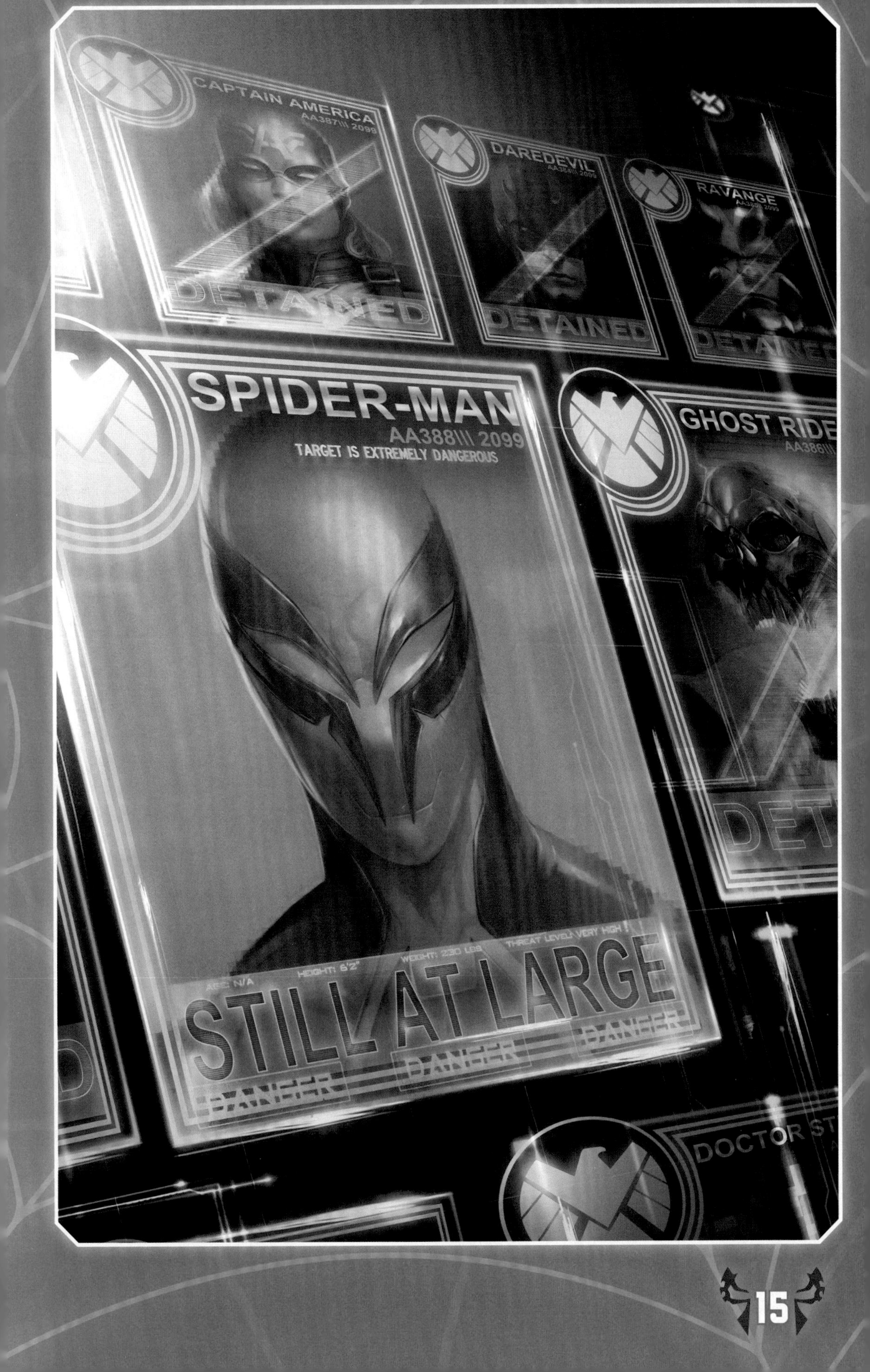
CAPTAIN AMERICA
AA387\\\ 2099
DETAINED
DAREDEVIL
DETAINED
RAVANGE
DETAINED
SPIDER-MAN
AA388\\\ 2099
TARGET IS EXTREMELY DANGEROUS
HEIGHT: 6'2"
WEIGHT: 230 LBS
STILL AT LARGE
GHOST RIDE
AA386\\\
DOCTOR ST

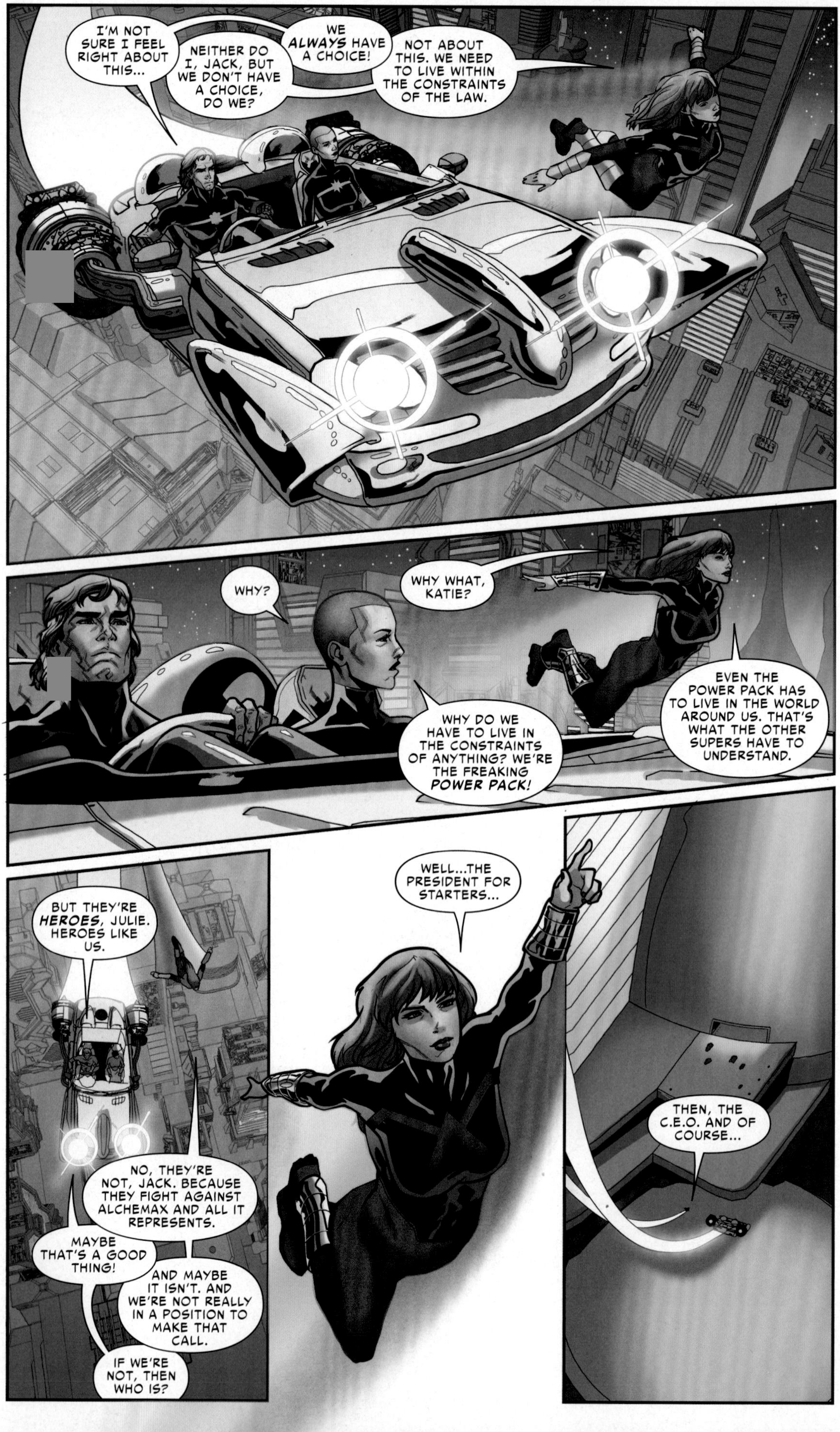
I'M NOT SURE I FEEL RIGHT ABOUT THIS...
NEITHER DO I, JACK, BUT WE DON'T HAVE A CHOICE, DO WE?
WE *ALWAYS* HAVE A CHOICE!
NOT ABOUT THIS. WE NEED TO LIVE WITHIN THE CONSTRAINTS OF THE LAW.
WHY?
WHY WHAT, KATIE?
WHY DO WE HAVE TO LIVE IN THE CONSTRAINTS OF ANYTHING? WE'RE THE FREAKING *POWER PACK!*
EVEN THE POWER PACK HAS TO LIVE IN THE WORLD AROUND US. THAT'S WHAT THE OTHER SUPERS HAVE TO UNDERSTAND.
BUT THEY'RE *HEROES*, JULIE. HEROES LIKE US.
NO, THEY'RE NOT, JACK. BECAUSE THEY FIGHT AGAINST ALCHEMAX AND ALL IT REPRESENTS.
MAYBE THAT'S A GOOD THING!
AND MAYBE IT ISN'T. AND WE'RE NOT REALLY IN A POSITION TO MAKE THAT CALL.
IF WE'RE NOT, THEN WHO IS?
WELL...THE PRESIDENT FOR STARTERS...
THEN, THE C.E.O. AND OF COURSE...

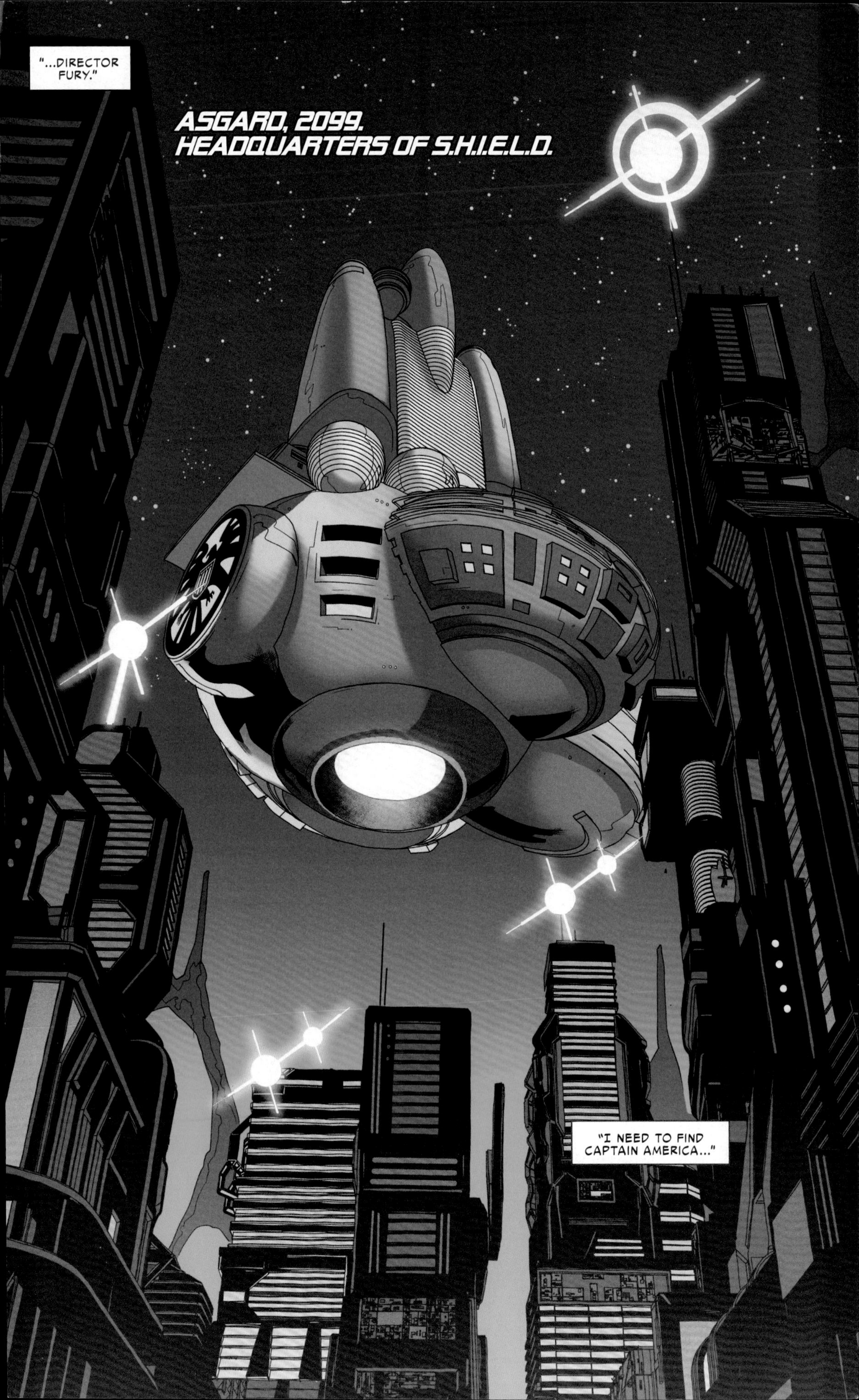
"...DIRECTOR FURY."
ASGARD, 2099.
HEADQUARTERS OF S.H.I.E.L.D.
"I NEED TO FIND CAPTAIN AMERICA..."

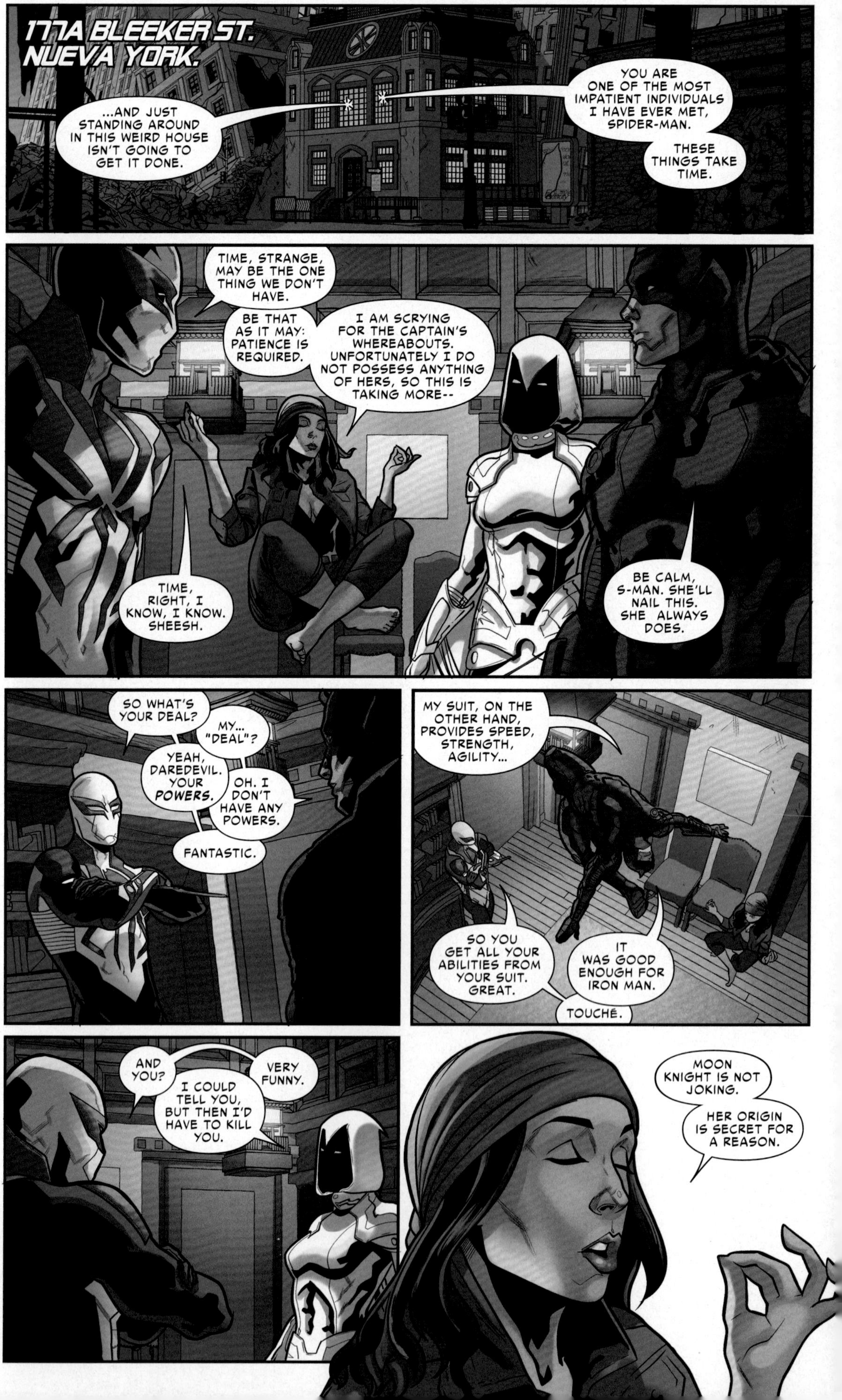
177A BLEEKER ST. NUEVA YORK.
...AND JUST STANDING AROUND IN THIS WEIRD HOUSE ISN'T GOING TO GET IT DONE.
YOU ARE ONE OF THE MOST IMPATIENT INDIVIDUALS I HAVE EVER MET, SPIDER-MAN.
THESE THINGS TAKE TIME.
TIME, STRANGE, MAY BE THE ONE THING WE DON'T HAVE.
BE THAT AS IT MAY: PATIENCE IS REQUIRED.
I AM SCRYING FOR THE CAPTAIN'S WHEREABOUTS. UNFORTUNATELY I DO NOT POSSESS ANYTHING OF HERS, SO THIS IS TAKING MORE--
TIME, RIGHT, I KNOW, I KNOW. SHEESH.
BE CALM, S-MAN. SHE'LL NAIL THIS. SHE ALWAYS DOES.
SO WHAT'S YOUR DEAL?
MY... "DEAL"?
YEAH, DAREDEVIL. YOUR POWERS.
OH. I DON'T HAVE ANY POWERS.
FANTASTIC.
MY SUIT, ON THE OTHER HAND, PROVIDES SPEED, STRENGTH, AGILITY...
SO YOU GET ALL YOUR ABILITIES FROM YOUR SUIT. GREAT.
IT WAS GOOD ENOUGH FOR IRON MAN.
TOUCHÉ.
AND YOU?
VERY FUNNY.
I COULD TELL YOU, BUT THEN I'D HAVE TO KILL YOU.
MOON KNIGHT IS NOT JOKING.
HER ORIGIN IS SECRET FOR A REASON.

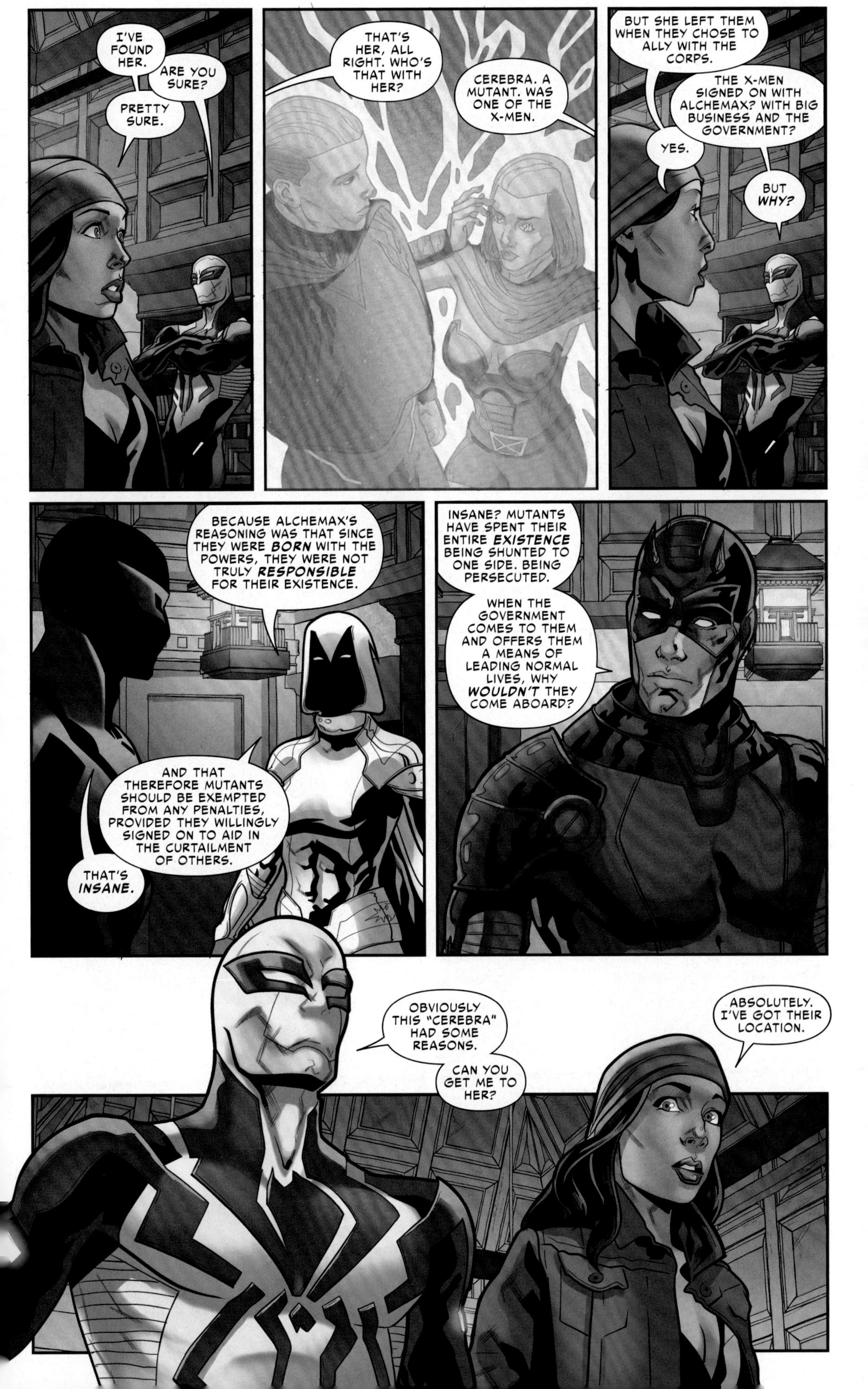
I'VE FOUND HER.
ARE YOU SURE?
PRETTY SURE.
THAT'S HER, ALL RIGHT. WHO'S THAT WITH HER?
CEREBRA. A MUTANT. WAS ONE OF THE X-MEN.
BUT SHE LEFT THEM WHEN THEY CHOSE TO ALLY WITH THE CORPS.
THE X-MEN SIGNED ON WITH ALCHEMAX? WITH BIG BUSINESS AND THE GOVERNMENT?
YES.
BUT WHY?
BECAUSE ALCHEMAX'S REASONING WAS THAT SINCE THEY WERE BORN WITH THE POWERS, THEY WERE NOT TRULY RESPONSIBLE FOR THEIR EXISTENCE.
AND THAT THEREFORE MUTANTS SHOULD BE EXEMPTED FROM ANY PENALTIES, PROVIDED THEY WILLINGLY SIGNED ON TO AID IN THE CURTAILMENT OF OTHERS.
THAT'S INSANE.
INSANE? MUTANTS HAVE SPENT THEIR ENTIRE EXISTENCE BEING SHUNTED TO ONE SIDE. BEING PERSECUTED.
WHEN THE GOVERNMENT COMES TO THEM AND OFFERS THEM A MEANS OF LEADING NORMAL LIVES, WHY WOULDN'T THEY COME ABOARD?
OBVIOUSLY THIS "CEREBRA" HAD SOME REASONS.
CAN YOU GET ME TO HER?
ABSOLUTELY. I'VE GOT THEIR LOCATION.

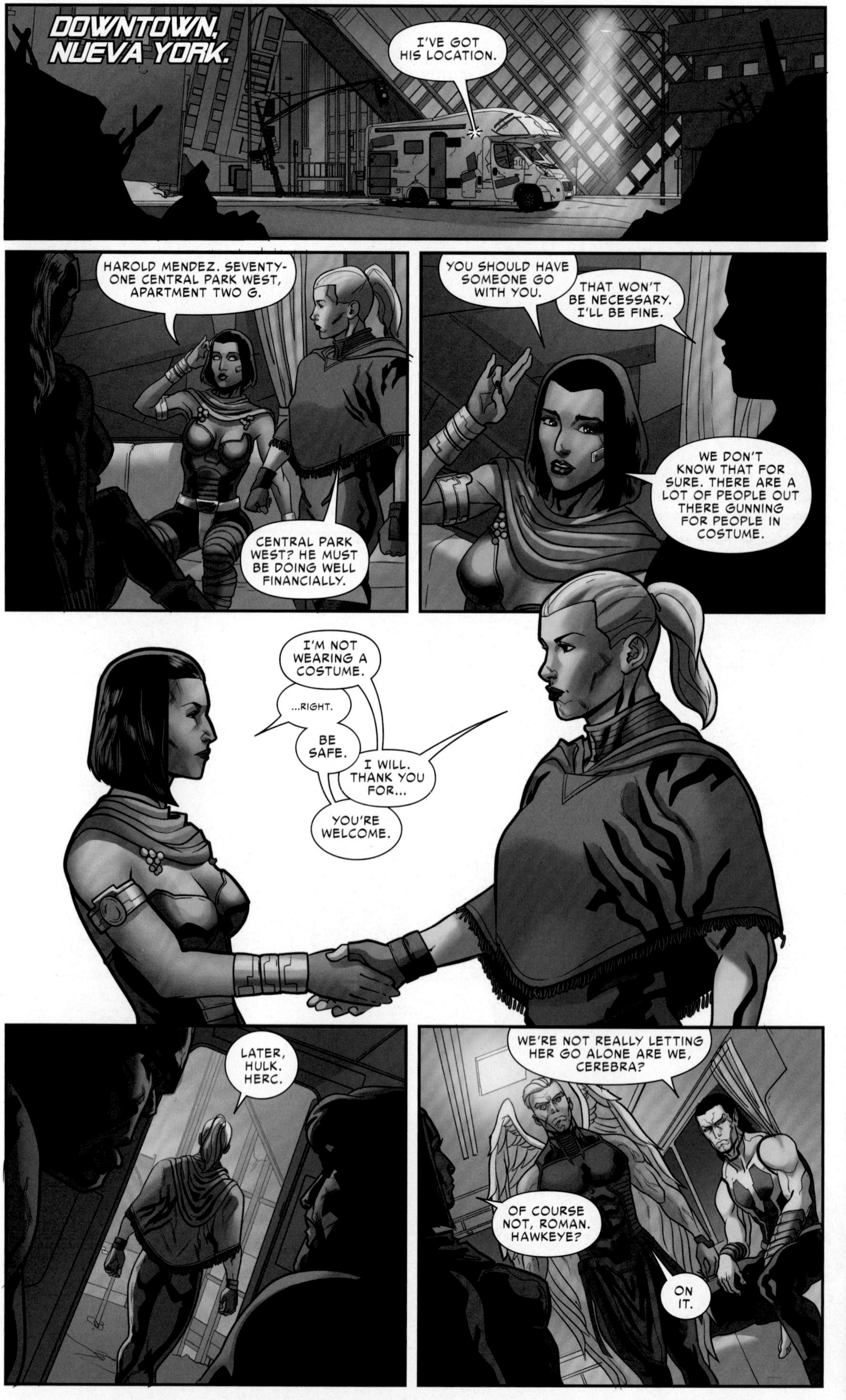
DOWNTOWN, NUEVA YORK.
I'VE GOT HIS LOCATION.
HAROLD MENDEZ. SEVENTY-ONE CENTRAL PARK WEST, APARTMENT TWO G.
CENTRAL PARK WEST? HE MUST BE DOING WELL FINANCIALLY.
YOU SHOULD HAVE SOMEONE GO WITH YOU.
THAT WON'T BE NECESSARY. I'LL BE FINE.
WE DON'T KNOW THAT FOR SURE. THERE ARE A LOT OF PEOPLE OUT THERE GUNNING FOR PEOPLE IN COSTUME.
I'M NOT WEARING A COSTUME.
...RIGHT.
BE SAFE.
I WILL. THANK YOU FOR...
YOU'RE WELCOME.
LATER, HULK. HERC.
WE'RE NOT REALLY LETTING HER GO ALONE ARE WE, CEREBRA?
OF COURSE NOT, ROMAN. HAWKEYE?
ON IT.

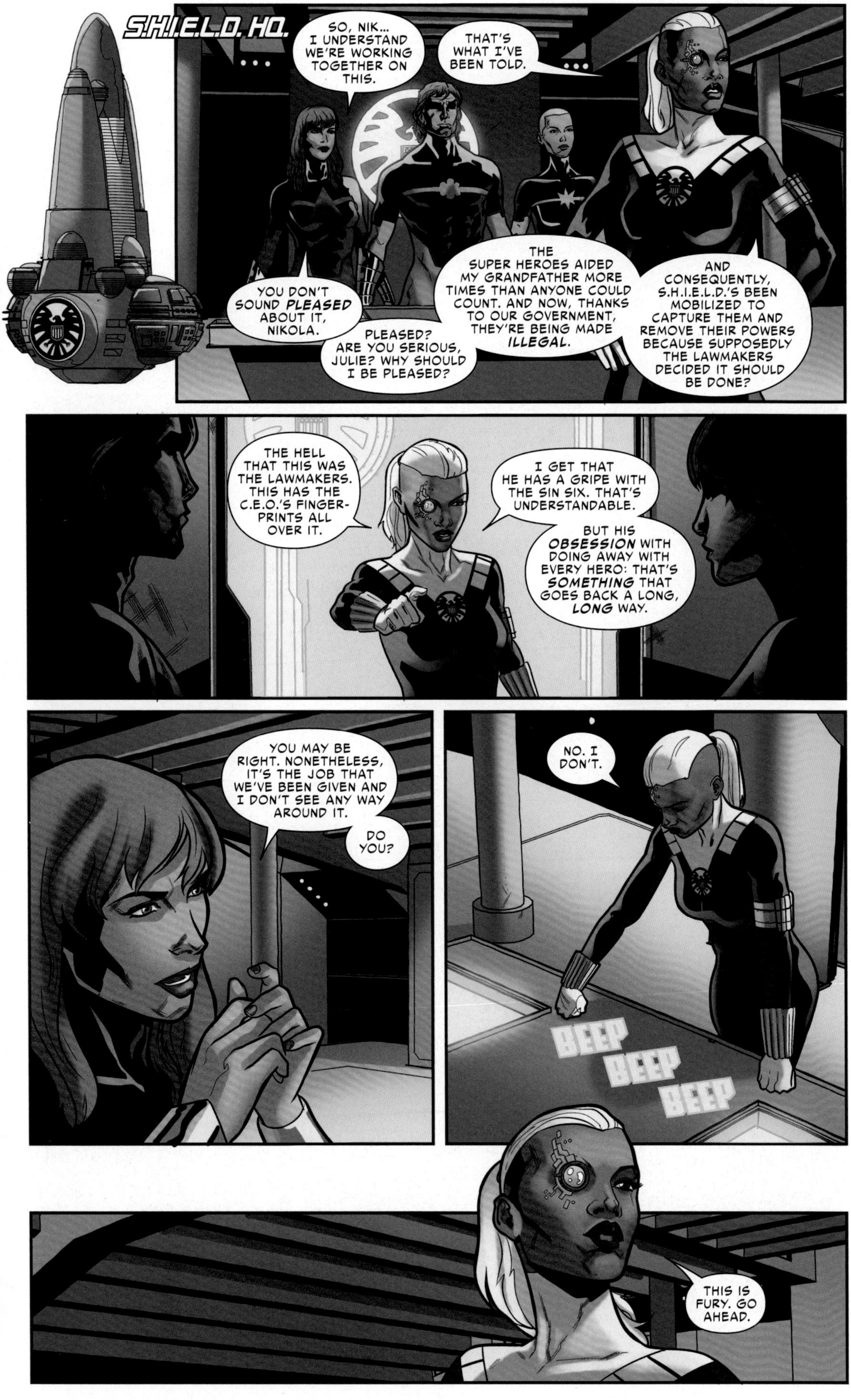
S.H.I.E.L.D. HQ.
SO, NIK... I UNDERSTAND WE'RE WORKING TOGETHER ON THIS.
THAT'S WHAT I'VE BEEN TOLD.
YOU DON'T SOUND PLEASED ABOUT IT, NIKOLA.
PLEASED? ARE YOU SERIOUS, JULIE? WHY SHOULD I BE PLEASED?
THE SUPER HEROES AIDED MY GRANDFATHER MORE TIMES THAN ANYONE COULD COUNT. AND NOW, THANKS TO OUR GOVERNMENT, THEY'RE BEING MADE ILLEGAL.
AND CONSEQUENTLY, S.H.I.E.L.D.'S BEEN MOBILIZED TO CAPTURE THEM AND REMOVE THEIR POWERS BECAUSE SUPPOSEDLY THE LAWMAKERS DECIDED IT SHOULD BE DONE?
THE HELL THAT THIS WAS THE LAWMAKERS. THIS HAS THE C.E.O.'S FINGER-PRINTS ALL OVER IT.
I GET THAT HE HAS A GRIPE WITH THE SIN SIX. THAT'S UNDERSTANDABLE.
BUT HIS OBSESSION WITH DOING AWAY WITH EVERY HERO: THAT'S SOMETHING THAT GOES BACK A LONG, LONG WAY.
YOU MAY BE RIGHT. NONETHELESS, IT'S THE JOB THAT WE'VE BEEN GIVEN AND I DON'T SEE ANY WAY AROUND IT.
DO YOU?
NO. I DON'T.
BEEP
BEEP
BEEP
THIS IS FURY. GO AHEAD.

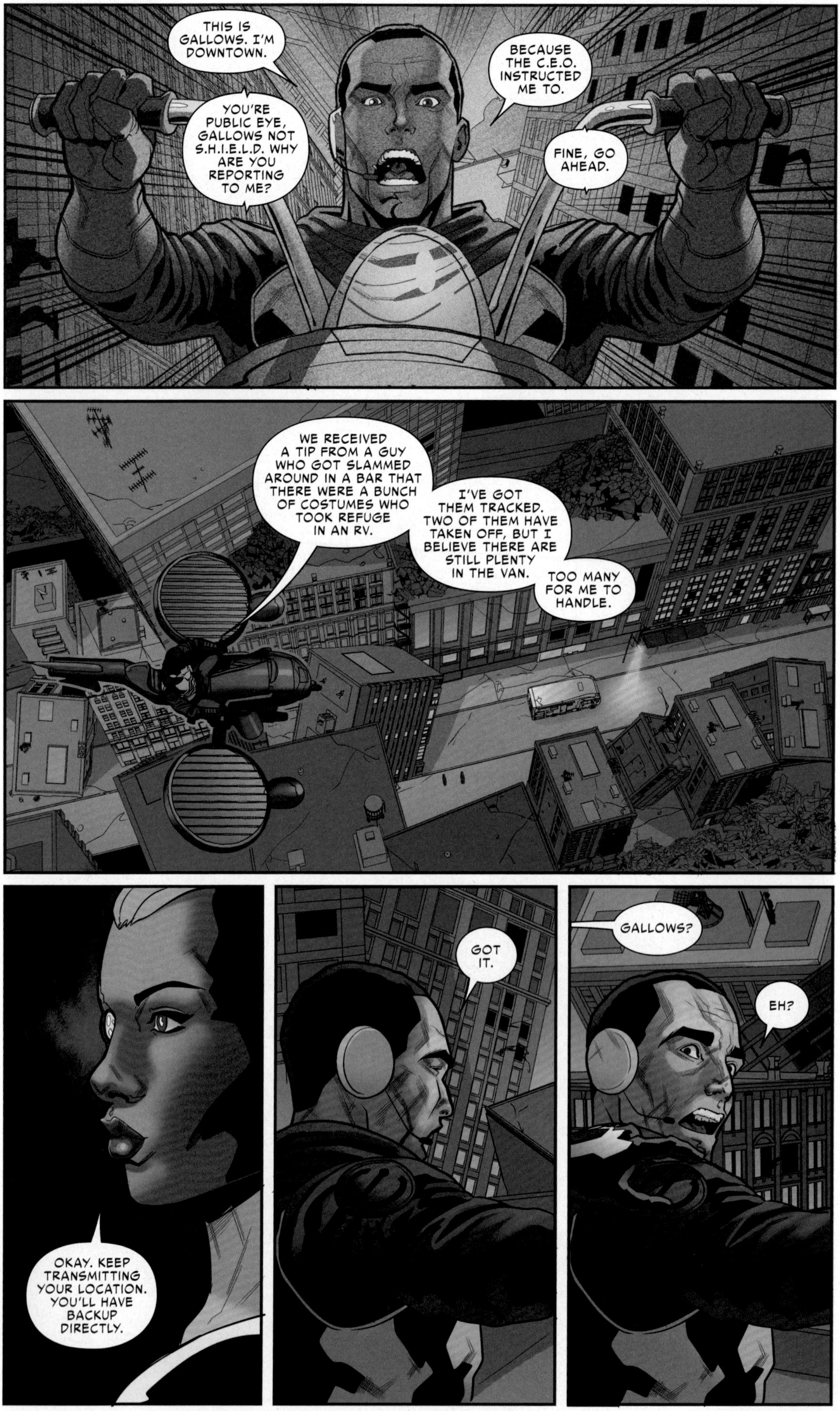
THIS IS GALLOWS. I'M DOWNTOWN.
YOU'RE PUBLIC EYE, GALLOWS NOT S.H.I.E.L.D. WHY ARE YOU REPORTING TO ME?
BECAUSE THE C.E.O. INSTRUCTED ME TO.
FINE, GO AHEAD.
WE RECEIVED A TIP FROM A GUY WHO GOT SLAMMED AROUND IN A BAR THAT THERE WERE A BUNCH OF COSTUMES WHO TOOK REFUGE IN AN RV.
I'VE GOT THEM TRACKED. TWO OF THEM HAVE TAKEN OFF, BUT I BELIEVE THERE ARE STILL PLENTY IN THE VAN.
TOO MANY FOR ME TO HANDLE.
OKAY. KEEP TRANSMITTING YOUR LOCATION. YOU'LL HAVE BACKUP DIRECTLY.
GOT IT.
GALLOWS?
EH?

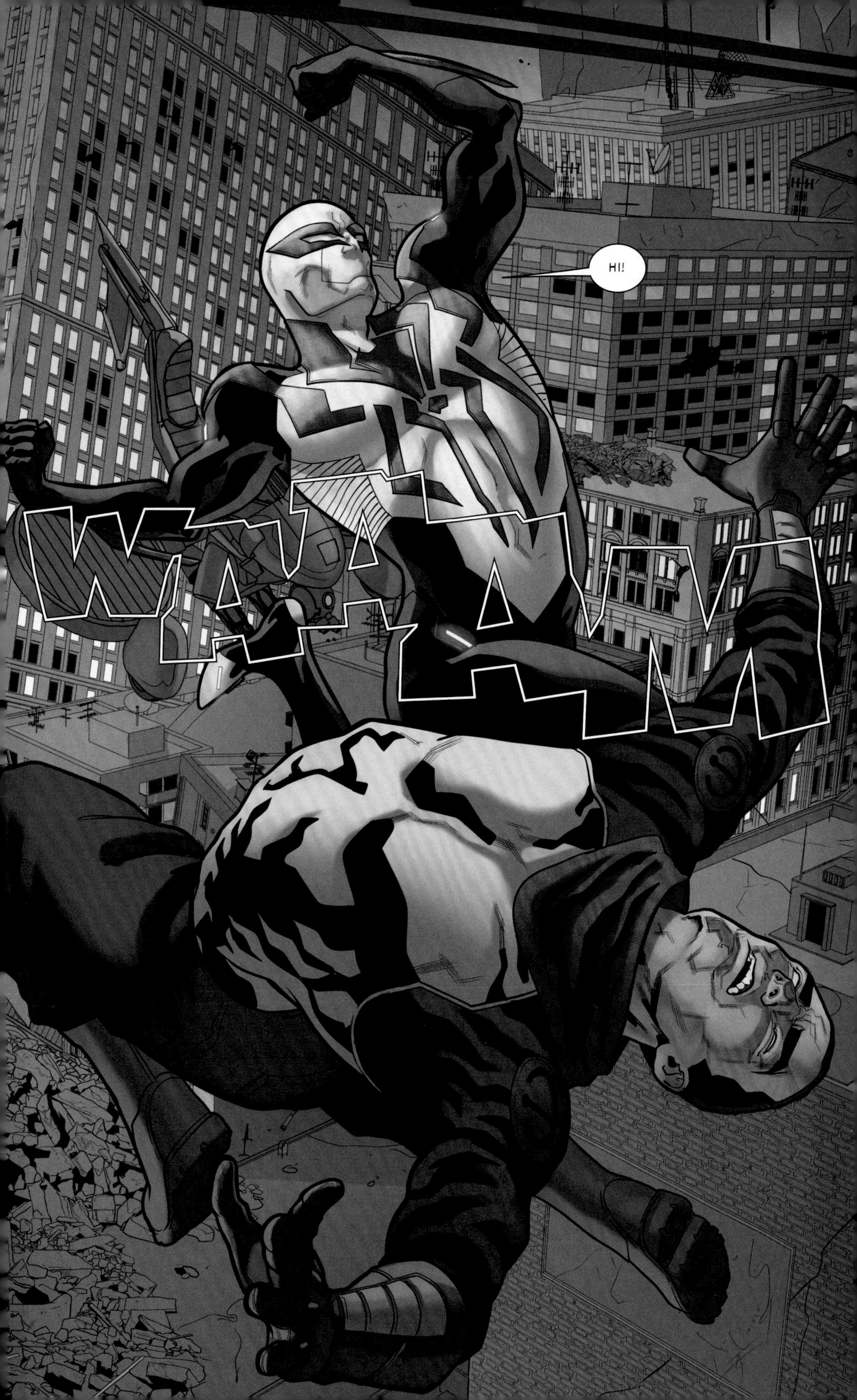
HI!
WHAM

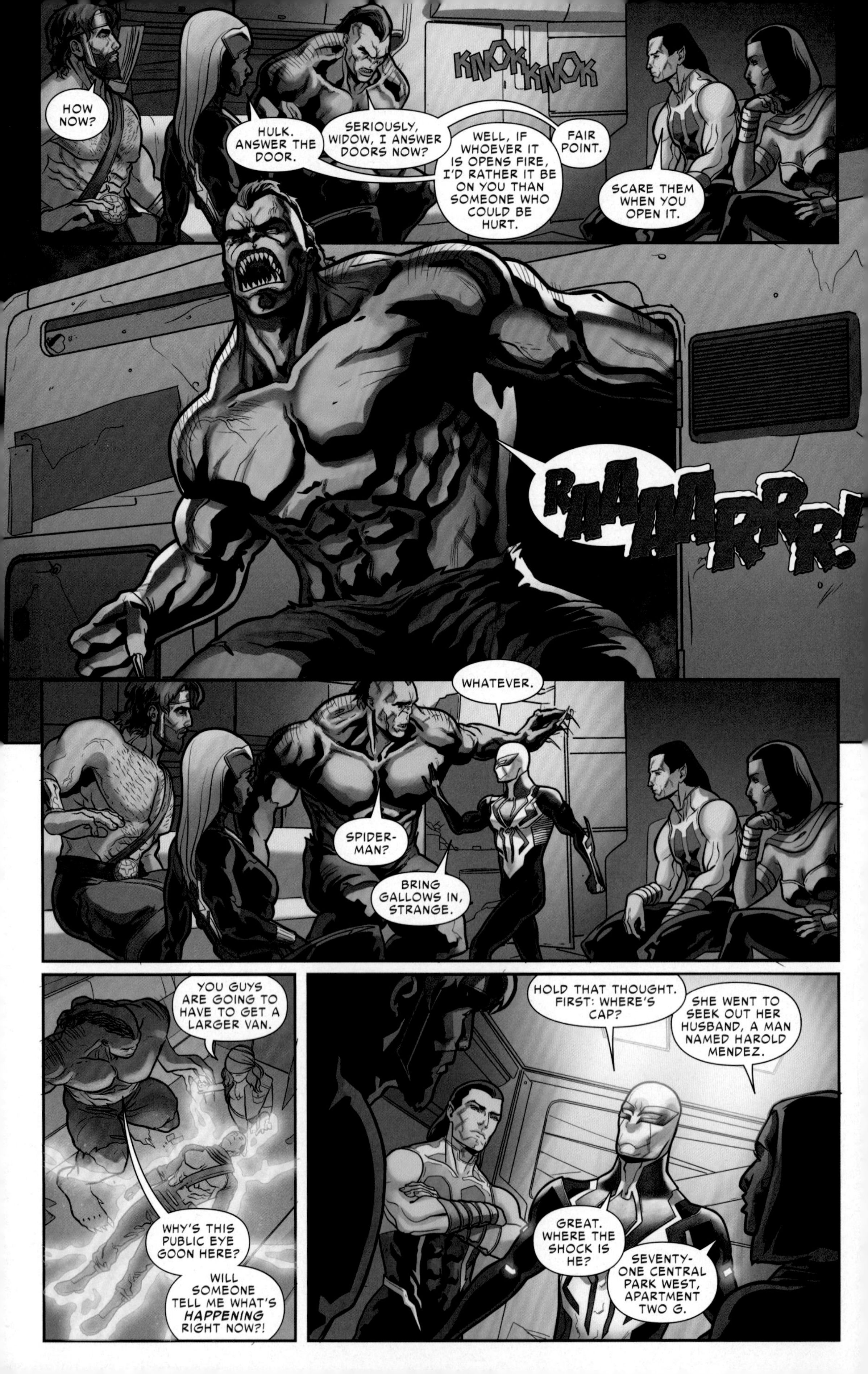
KNOKKNOK
HOW NOW?
HULK. ANSWER THE DOOR.
SERIOUSLY, WIDOW, I ANSWER DOORS NOW?
WELL, IF WHOEVER IT IS OPENS FIRE, I'D RATHER IT BE ON YOU THAN SOMEONE WHO COULD BE HURT.
FAIR POINT.
SCARE THEM WHEN YOU OPEN IT.
RAAARRRR!
WHATEVER.
SPIDER-MAN?
BRING GALLOWS IN, STRANGE.
YOU GUYS ARE GOING TO HAVE TO GET A LARGER VAN.
WHY'S THIS PUBLIC EYE GOON HERE?
WILL SOMEONE TELL ME WHAT'S *HAPPENING* RIGHT NOW?!
HOLD THAT THOUGHT. FIRST: WHERE'S CAP?
SHE WENT TO SEEK OUT HER HUSBAND, A MAN NAMED HAROLD MENDEZ.
GREAT. WHERE THE SHOCK IS HE?
SEVENTY-ONE CENTRAL PARK WEST, APARTMENT TWO G.

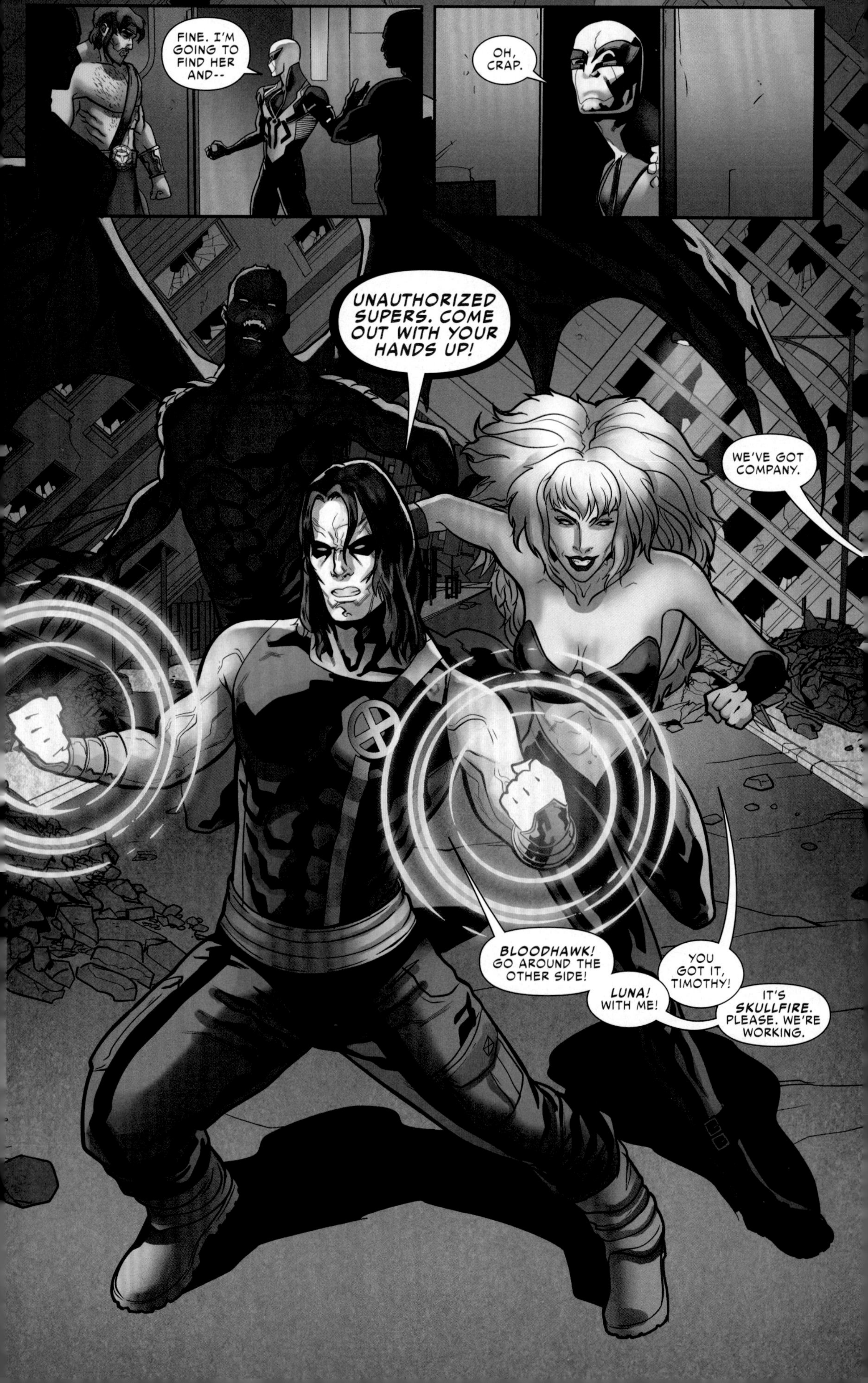
FINE. I'M GOING TO FIND HER AND--
OH, CRAP.
UNAUTHORIZED SUPERS. COME OUT WITH YOUR HANDS UP!
WE'VE GOT COMPANY.
BLOODHAWK! GO AROUND THE OTHER SIDE!
LUNA! WITH ME!
YOU GOT IT, TIMOTHY!
IT'S SKULLFIRE. PLEASE. WE'RE WORKING.

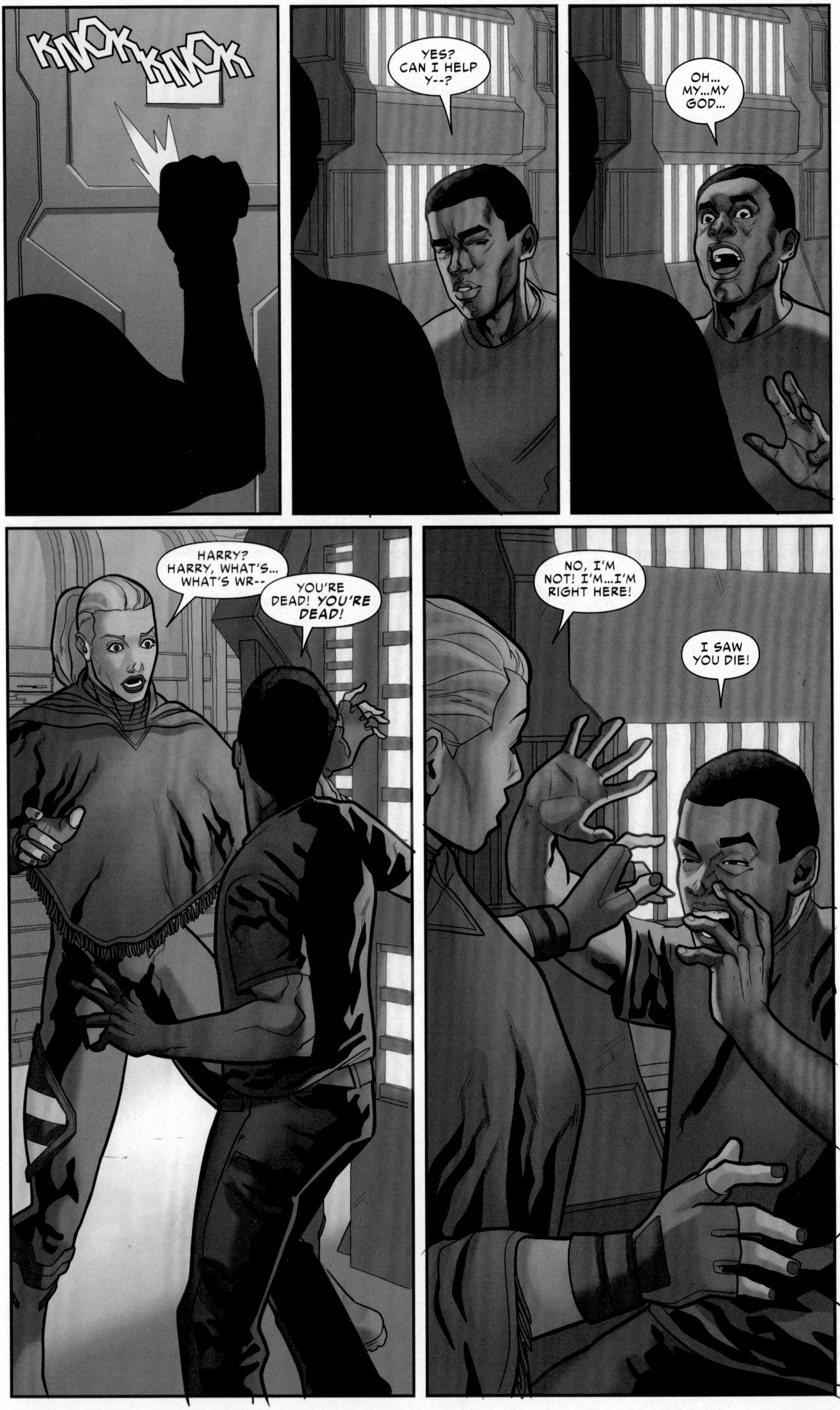
KNOK KNOK
YES? CAN I HELP Y--?
OH... MY...MY GOD...
HARRY? HARRY, WHAT'S... WHAT'S WR--
YOU'RE DEAD! *YOU'RE DEAD!*
NO, I'M NOT! I'M...I'M RIGHT HERE!
I SAW YOU DIE!

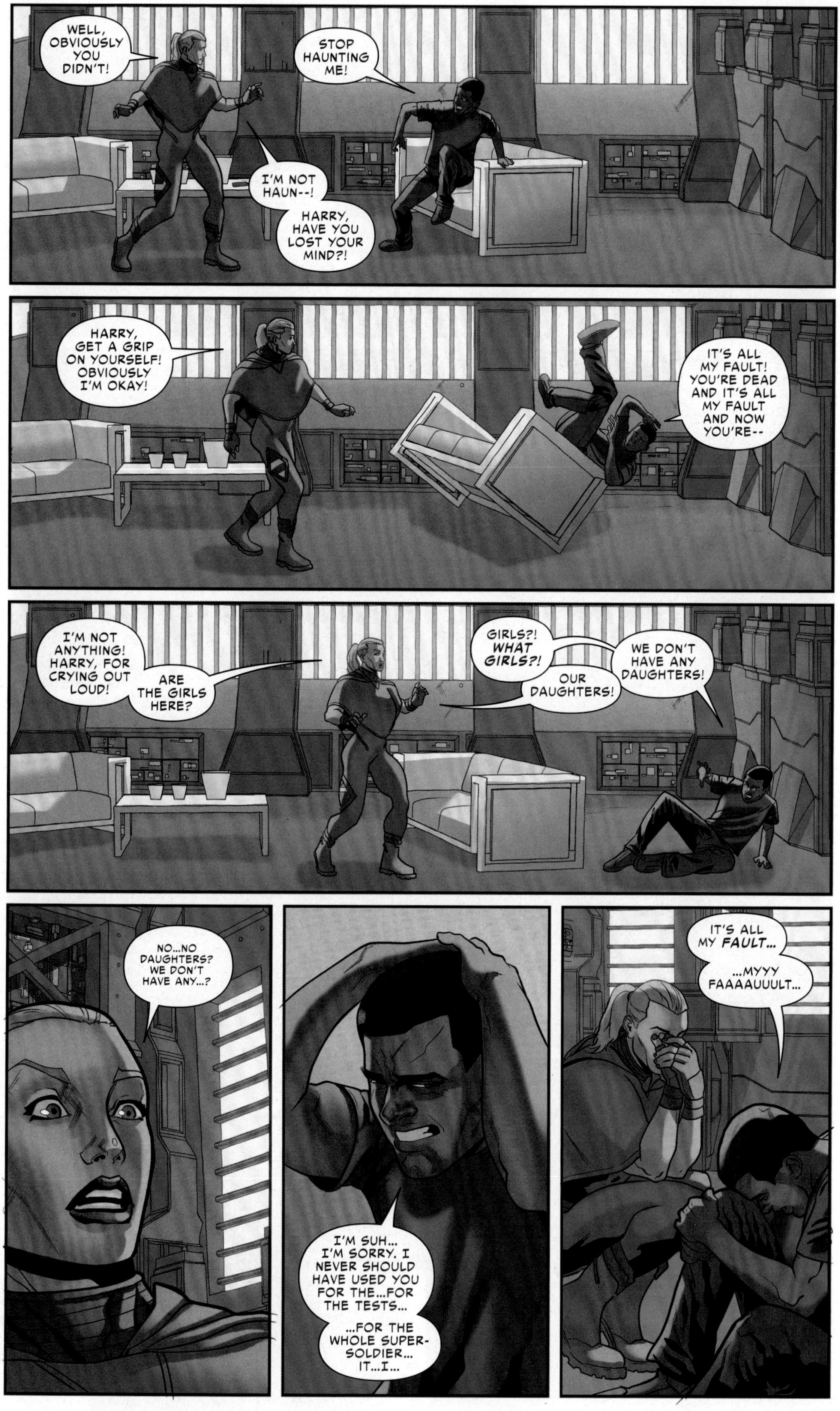
WELL, OBVIOUSLY YOU DIDN'T!
STOP HAUNTING ME!
I'M NOT HAUN--!
HARRY, HAVE YOU LOST YOUR MIND?!
HARRY, GET A GRIP ON YOURSELF! OBVIOUSLY I'M OKAY!
IT'S ALL MY FAULT! YOU'RE DEAD AND IT'S ALL MY FAULT AND NOW YOU'RE--
I'M NOT ANYTHING! HARRY, FOR CRYING OUT LOUD!
ARE THE GIRLS HERE?
GIRLS?! WHAT GIRLS?!
OUR DAUGHTERS!
WE DON'T HAVE ANY DAUGHTERS!
NO...NO DAUGHTERS? WE DON'T HAVE ANY...?
I'M SUH... I'M SORRY. I NEVER SHOULD HAVE USED YOU FOR THE...FOR THE TESTS...
...FOR THE WHOLE SUPER-SOLDIER... IT...I...
IT'S ALL MY FAULT...
...MYYY FAAAAUUULT...

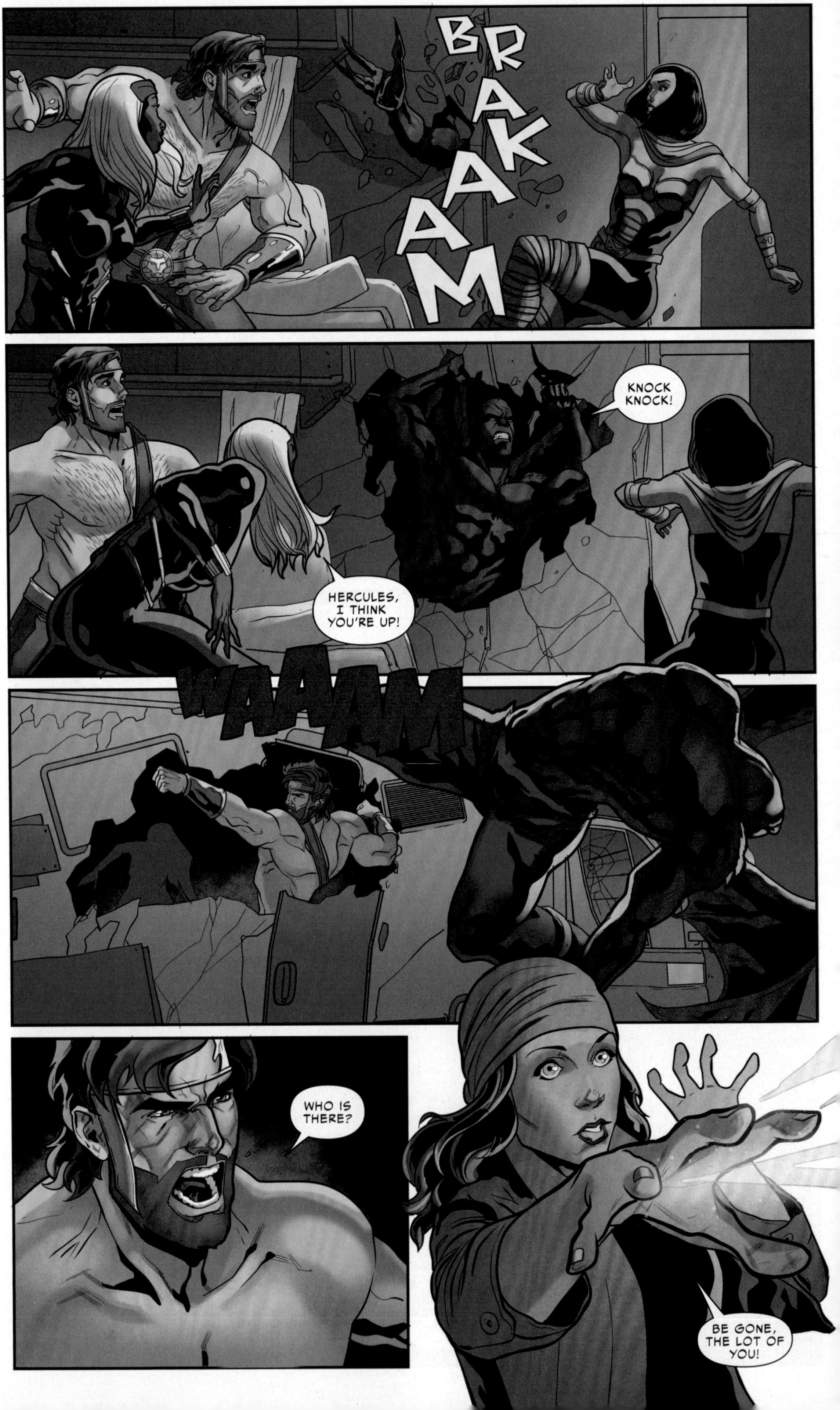
BRAKAAM
KNOCK KNOCK!
HERCULES, I THINK YOU'RE UP!
WAAAM
WHO IS THERE?
BE GONE, THE LOT OF YOU!

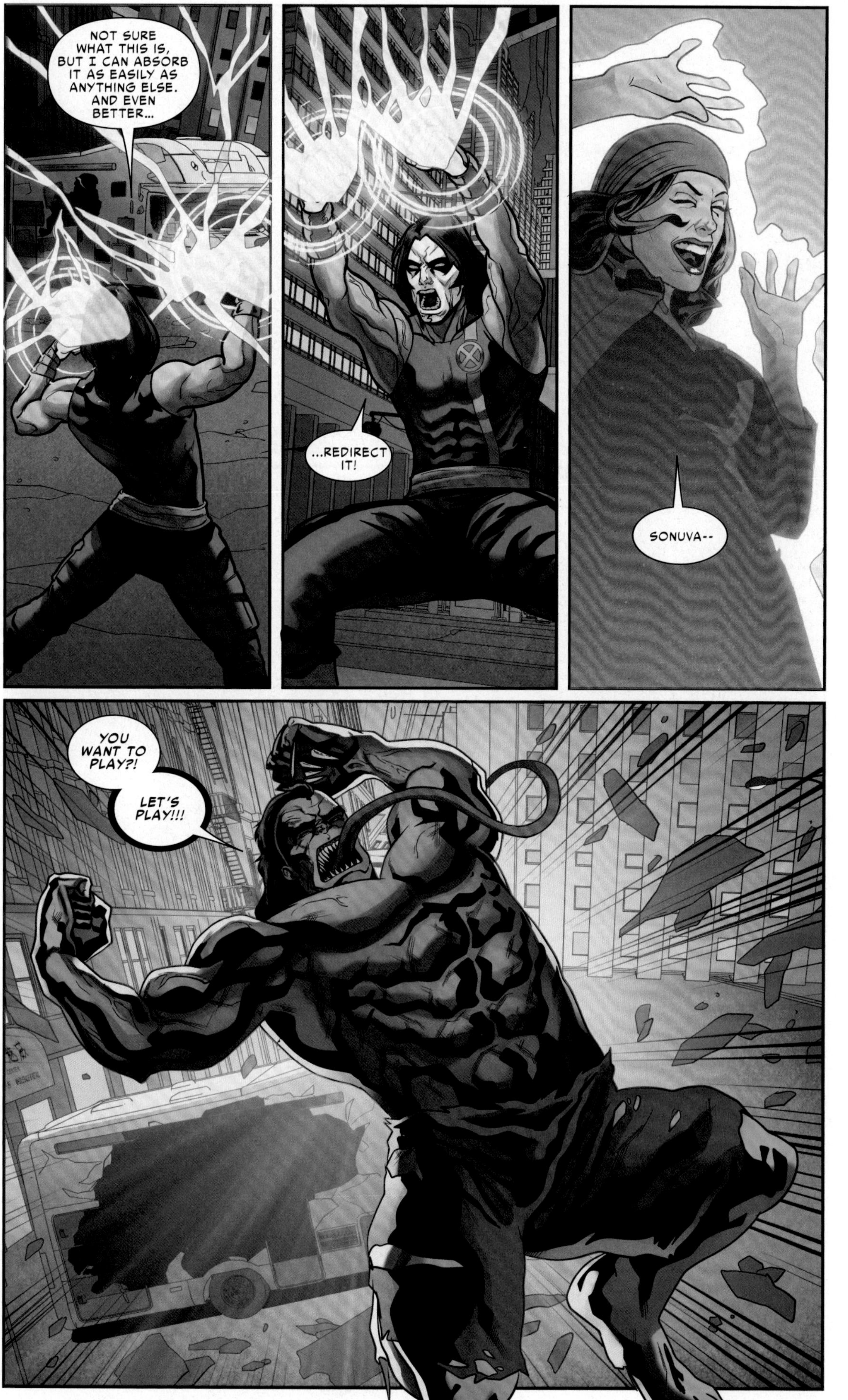
NOT SURE WHAT THIS IS, BUT I CAN ABSORB IT AS EASILY AS ANYTHING ELSE. AND EVEN BETTER...
...REDIRECT IT!
SONUVA--
YOU WANT TO PLAY?!
LET'S PLAY!!!

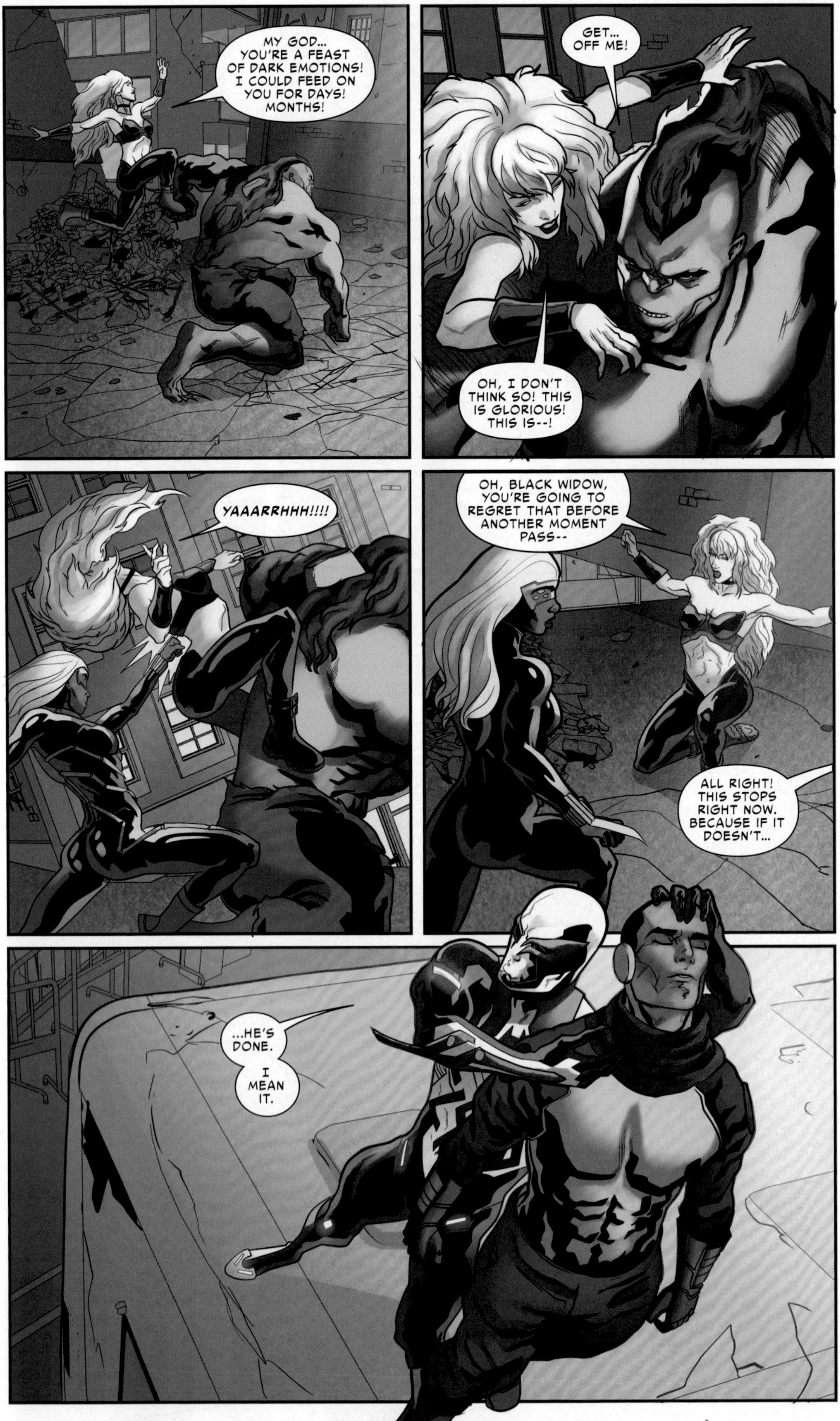
MY GOD... YOU'RE A FEAST OF DARK EMOTIONS! I COULD FEED ON YOU FOR DAYS! MONTHS!
GET... OFF ME!
OH, I DON'T THINK SO! THIS IS GLORIOUS! THIS IS--!
YAAARRHHH!!!!
OH, BLACK WIDOW, YOU'RE GOING TO REGRET THAT BEFORE ANOTHER MOMENT PASS--
ALL RIGHT! THIS STOPS RIGHT NOW. BECAUSE IF IT DOESN'T...
...HE'S DONE.
I MEAN IT.

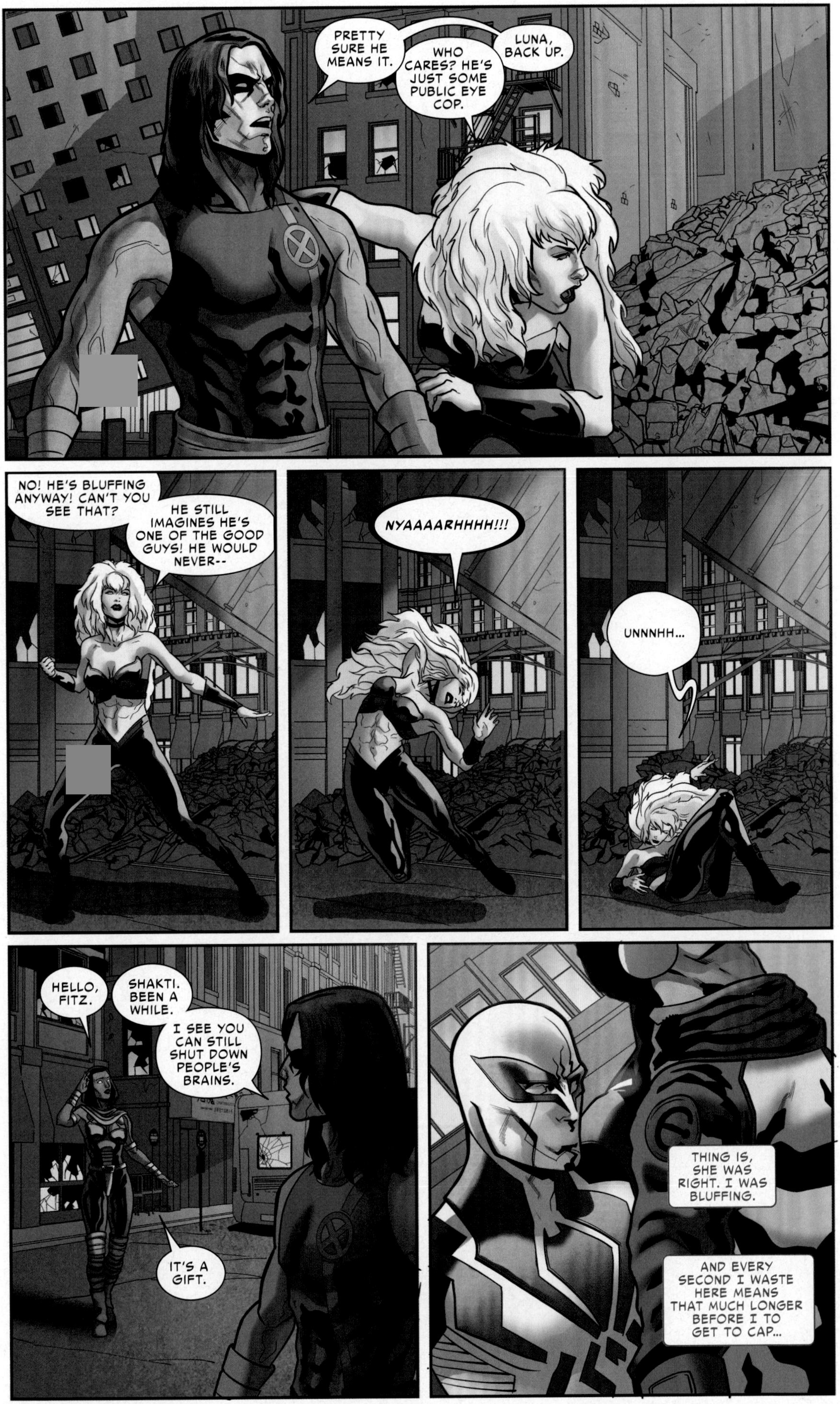
PRETTY SURE HE MEANS IT.
LUNA, BACK UP.
WHO CARES? HE'S JUST SOME PUBLIC EYE COP.
NO! HE'S BLUFFING ANYWAY! CAN'T YOU SEE THAT?
HE STILL IMAGINES HE'S ONE OF THE GOOD GUYS! HE WOULD NEVER--
NYAAAARHHHH!!!
UNNNHH...
HELLO, FITZ.
SHAKTI. BEEN A WHILE.
I SEE YOU CAN STILL SHUT DOWN PEOPLE'S BRAINS.
IT'S A GIFT.
THING IS, SHE WAS RIGHT. I WAS BLUFFING.
AND EVERY SECOND I WASTE HERE MEANS THAT MUCH LONGER BEFORE I TO GET TO CAP...

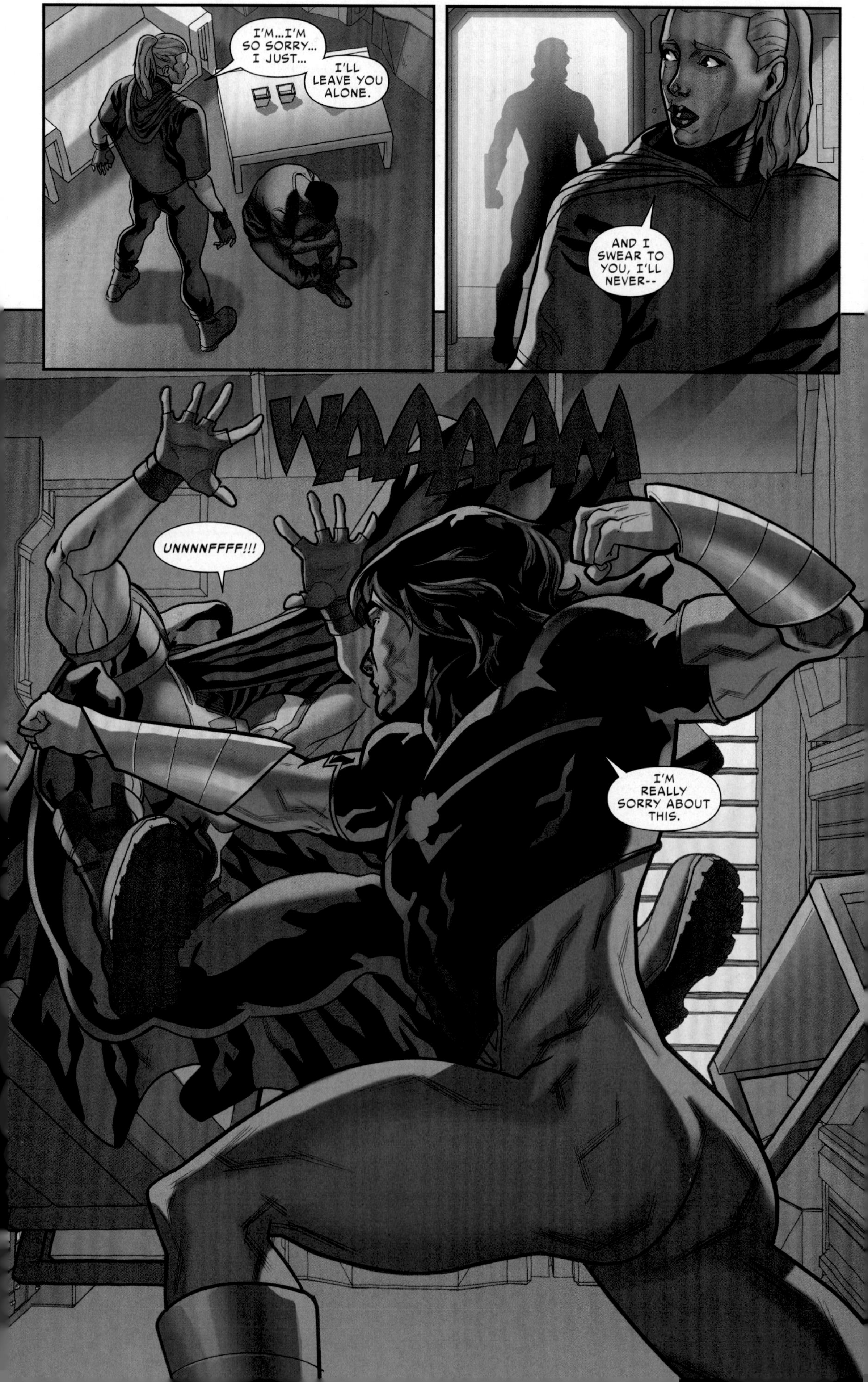
I'M...I'M SO SORRY... I JUST...
I'LL LEAVE YOU ALONE.
AND I SWEAR TO YOU, I'LL NEVER--
WAAAAM
UNNNNFFFF!!!
I'M REALLY SORRY ABOUT THIS.

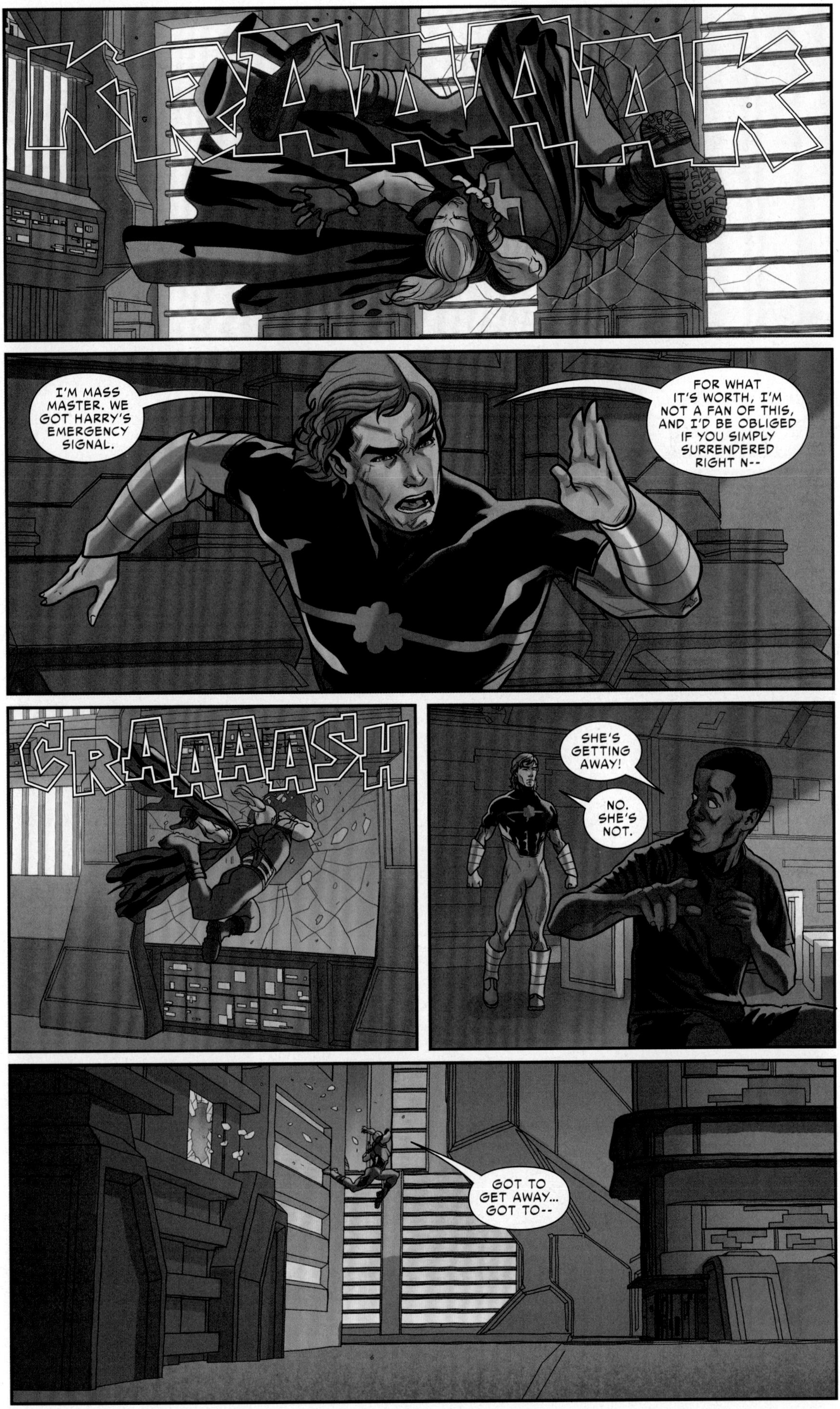
KRAAAAAK
I'M MASS MASTER. WE GOT HARRY'S EMERGENCY SIGNAL.
FOR WHAT IT'S WORTH, I'M NOT A FAN OF THIS, AND I'D BE OBLIGED IF YOU SIMPLY SURRENDERED RIGHT N--
CRAAAASH
SHE'S GETTING AWAY!
NO. SHE'S NOT.
GOT TO GET AWAY... GOT TO--

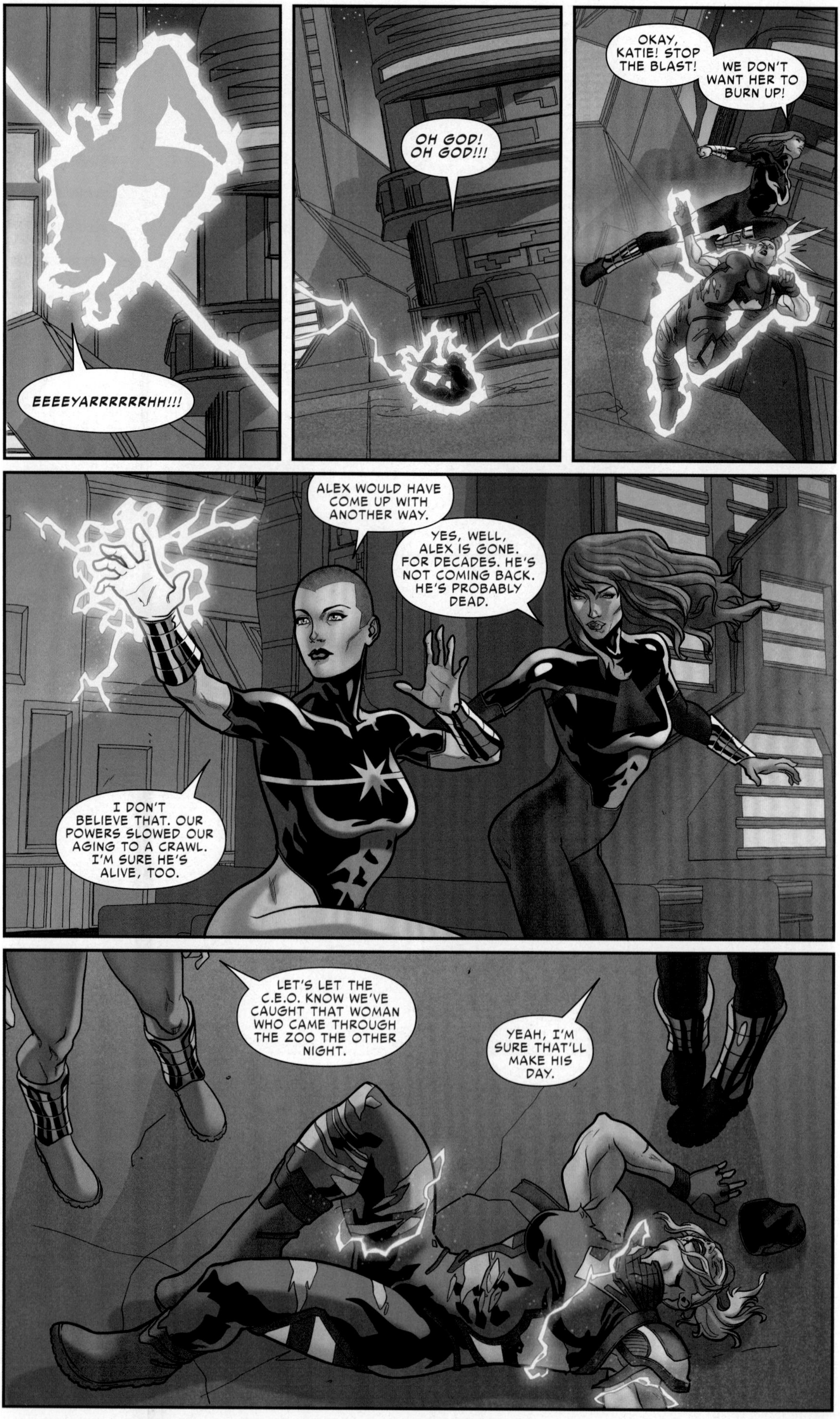
EEEEYARRRRRRHH!!!
OH GOD! OH GOD!!!
OKAY, KATIE! STOP THE BLAST!
WE DON'T WANT HER TO BURN UP!
ALEX WOULD HAVE COME UP WITH ANOTHER WAY.
YES, WELL, ALEX IS GONE. FOR DECADES. HE'S NOT COMING BACK. HE'S PROBABLY DEAD.
I DON'T BELIEVE THAT. OUR POWERS SLOWED OUR AGING TO A CRAWL. I'M SURE HE'S ALIVE, TOO.
LET'S LET THE C.E.O. KNOW WE'VE CAUGHT THAT WOMAN WHO CAME THROUGH THE ZOO THE OTHER NIGHT.
YEAH, I'M SURE THAT'LL MAKE HIS DAY.

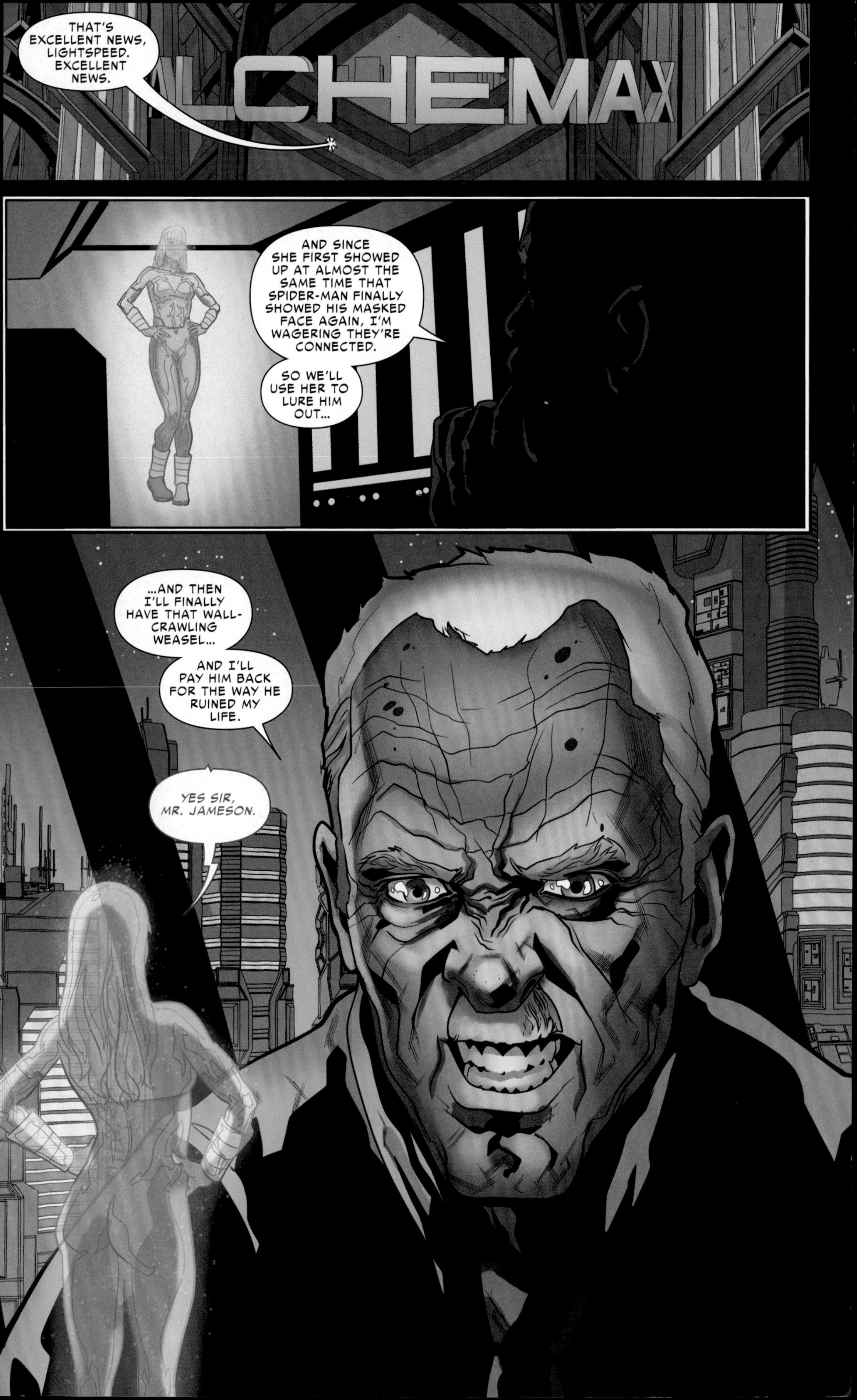
ALCHEMAX
THAT'S EXCELLENT NEWS, LIGHTSPEED. EXCELLENT NEWS.
AND SINCE SHE FIRST SHOWED UP AT ALMOST THE SAME TIME THAT SPIDER-MAN FINALLY SHOWED HIS MASKED FACE AGAIN, I'M WAGERING THEY'RE CONNECTED.
SO WE'LL USE HER TO LURE HIM OUT...
...AND THEN I'LL FINALLY HAVE THAT WALL-CRAWLING WEASEL...
AND I'LL PAY HIM BACK FOR THE WAY HE RUINED MY LIFE.
YES SIR, MR. JAMESON.

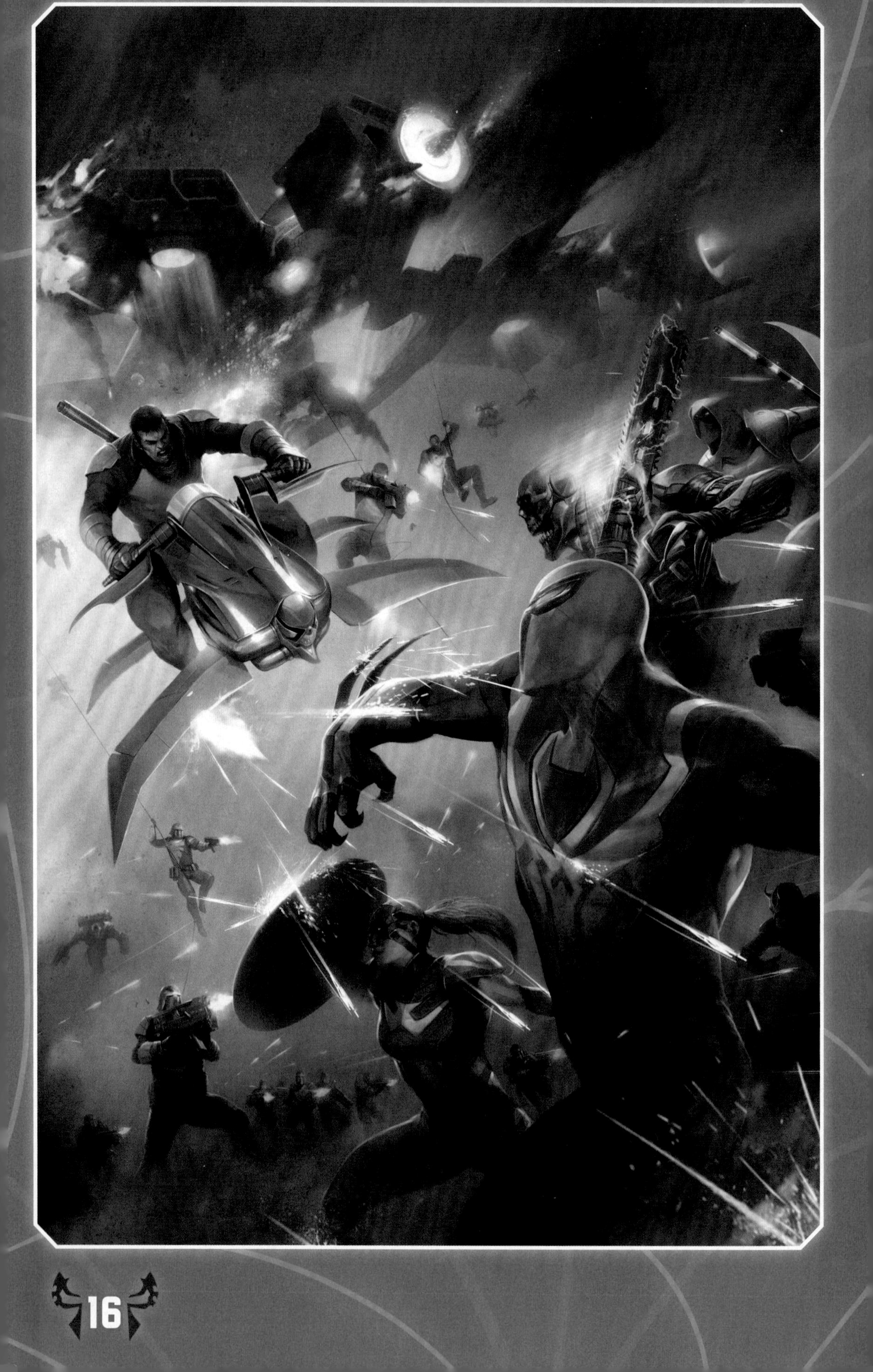

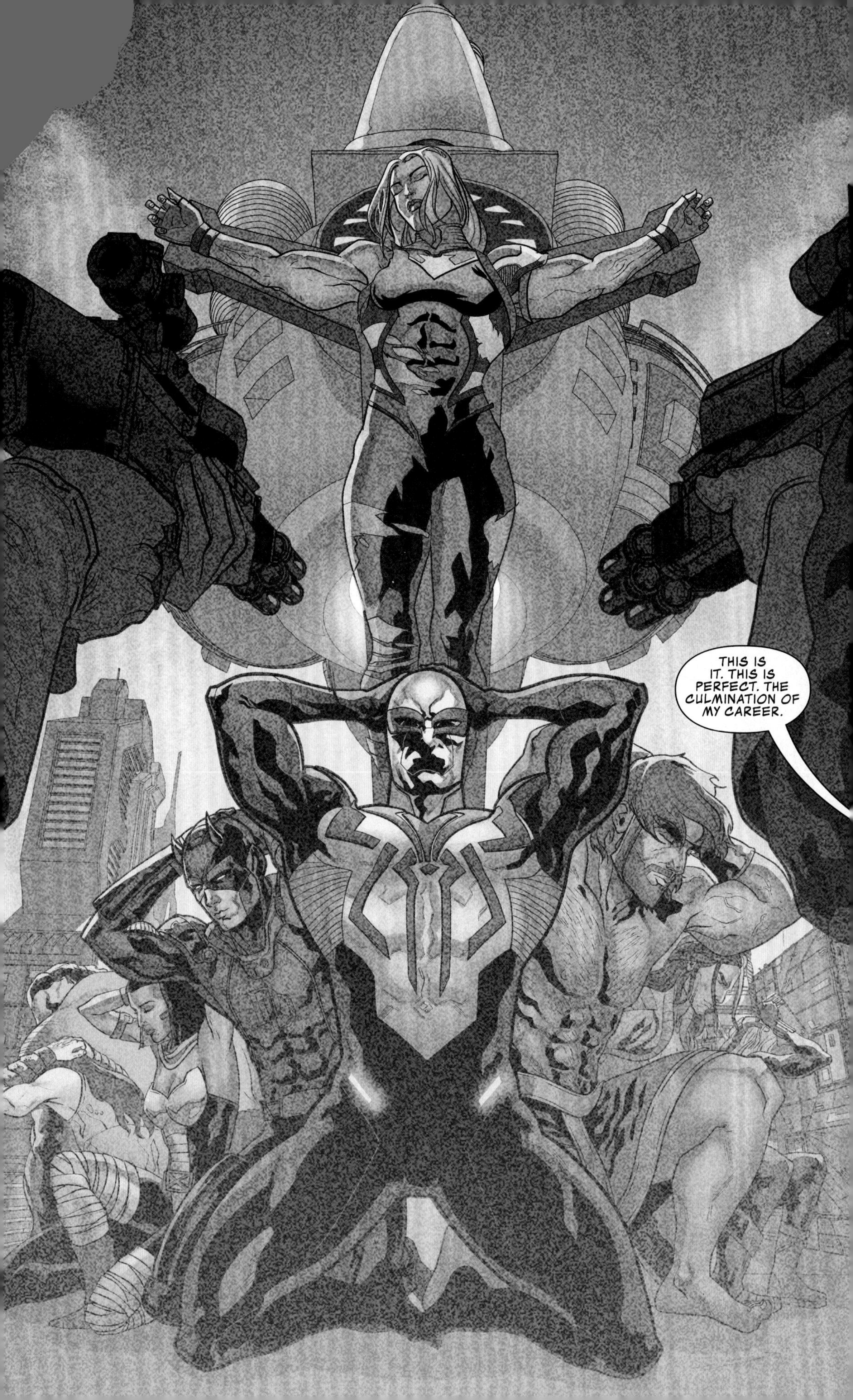
THIS IS IT. THIS IS PERFECT. THE CULMINATION OF MY CAREER.

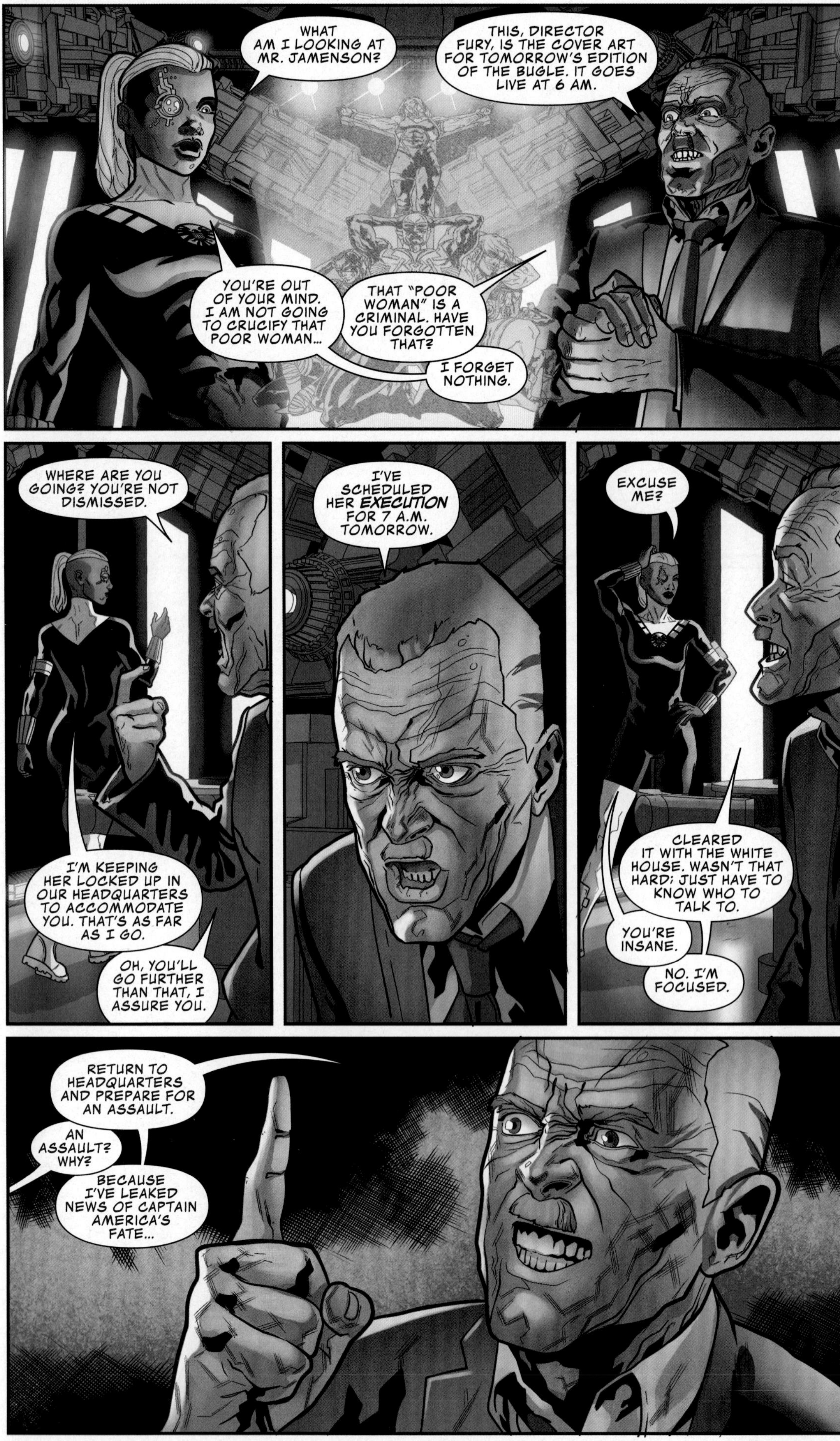
WHAT AM I LOOKING AT MR. JAMENSON?
THIS, DIRECTOR FURY, IS THE COVER ART FOR TOMORROW'S EDITION OF THE BUGLE. IT GOES LIVE AT 6 AM.
YOU'RE OUT OF YOUR MIND. I AM NOT GOING TO CRUCIFY THAT POOR WOMAN...
THAT "POOR WOMAN" IS A CRIMINAL. HAVE YOU FORGOTTEN THAT?
I FORGET NOTHING.
WHERE ARE YOU GOING? YOU'RE NOT DISMISSED.
I'M KEEPING HER LOCKED UP IN OUR HEADQUARTERS TO ACCOMMODATE YOU. THAT'S AS FAR AS I GO.
OH, YOU'LL GO FURTHER THAN THAT, I ASSURE YOU.
I'VE SCHEDULED HER EXECUTION FOR 7 A.M. TOMORROW.
EXCUSE ME?
CLEARED IT WITH THE WHITE HOUSE. WASN'T THAT HARD; JUST HAVE TO KNOW WHO TO TALK TO.
YOU'RE INSANE.
NO. I'M FOCUSED.
RETURN TO HEADQUARTERS AND PREPARE FOR AN ASSAULT.
AN ASSAULT? WHY?
BECAUSE I'VE LEAKED NEWS OF CAPTAIN AMERICA'S FATE...

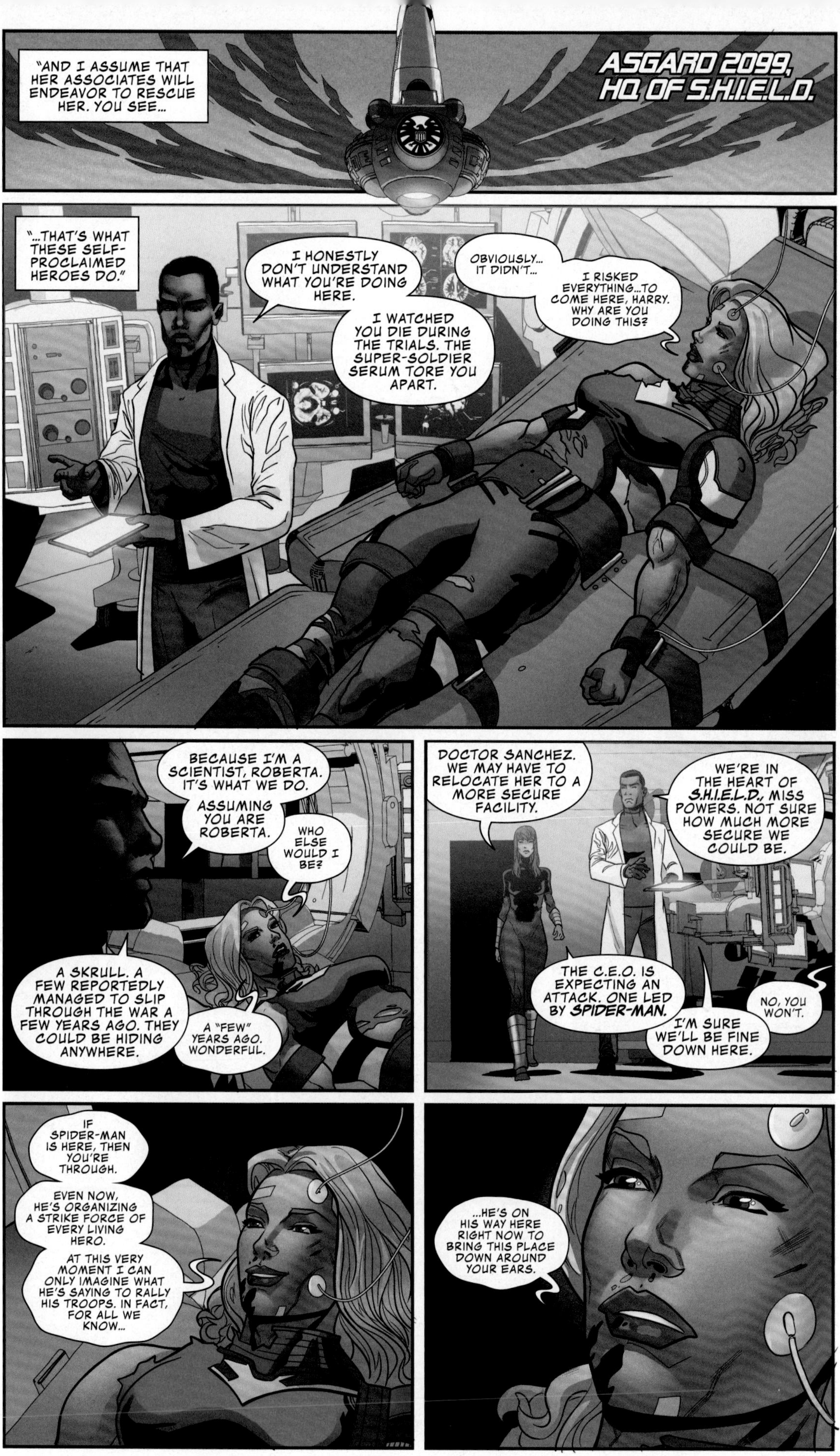
"AND I ASSUME THAT HER ASSOCIATES WILL ENDEAVOR TO RESCUE HER. YOU SEE...
ASGARD 2099, HQ OF S.H.I.E.L.D.
"...THAT'S WHAT THESE SELF-PROCLAIMED HEROES DO."
I HONESTLY DON'T UNDERSTAND WHAT YOU'RE DOING HERE.
I WATCHED YOU DIE DURING THE TRIALS. THE SUPER-SOLDIER SERUM TORE YOU APART.
OBVIOUSLY... IT DIDN'T...
I RISKED EVERYTHING...TO COME HERE, HARRY. WHY ARE YOU DOING THIS?
BECAUSE I'M A SCIENTIST, ROBERTA. IT'S WHAT WE DO.
ASSUMING YOU ARE ROBERTA.
WHO ELSE WOULD I BE?
A SKRULL. A FEW REPORTEDLY MANAGED TO SLIP THROUGH THE WAR A FEW YEARS AGO. THEY COULD BE HIDING ANYWHERE.
A "FEW" YEARS AGO. WONDERFUL.
DOCTOR SANCHEZ. WE MAY HAVE TO RELOCATE HER TO A MORE SECURE FACILITY.
WE'RE IN THE HEART OF S.H.I.E.L.D., MISS POWERS. NOT SURE HOW MUCH MORE SECURE WE COULD BE.
THE C.E.O. IS EXPECTING AN ATTACK. ONE LED BY SPIDER-MAN.
I'M SURE WE'LL BE FINE DOWN HERE.
NO, YOU WON'T.
IF SPIDER-MAN IS HERE, THEN YOU'RE THROUGH.
EVEN NOW, HE'S ORGANIZING A STRIKE FORCE OF EVERY LIVING HERO.
AT THIS VERY MOMENT I CAN ONLY IMAGINE WHAT HE'S SAYING TO RALLY HIS TROOPS. IN FACT, FOR ALL WE KNOW...
...HE'S ON HIS WAY HERE RIGHT NOW TO BRING THIS PLACE DOWN AROUND YOUR EARS.

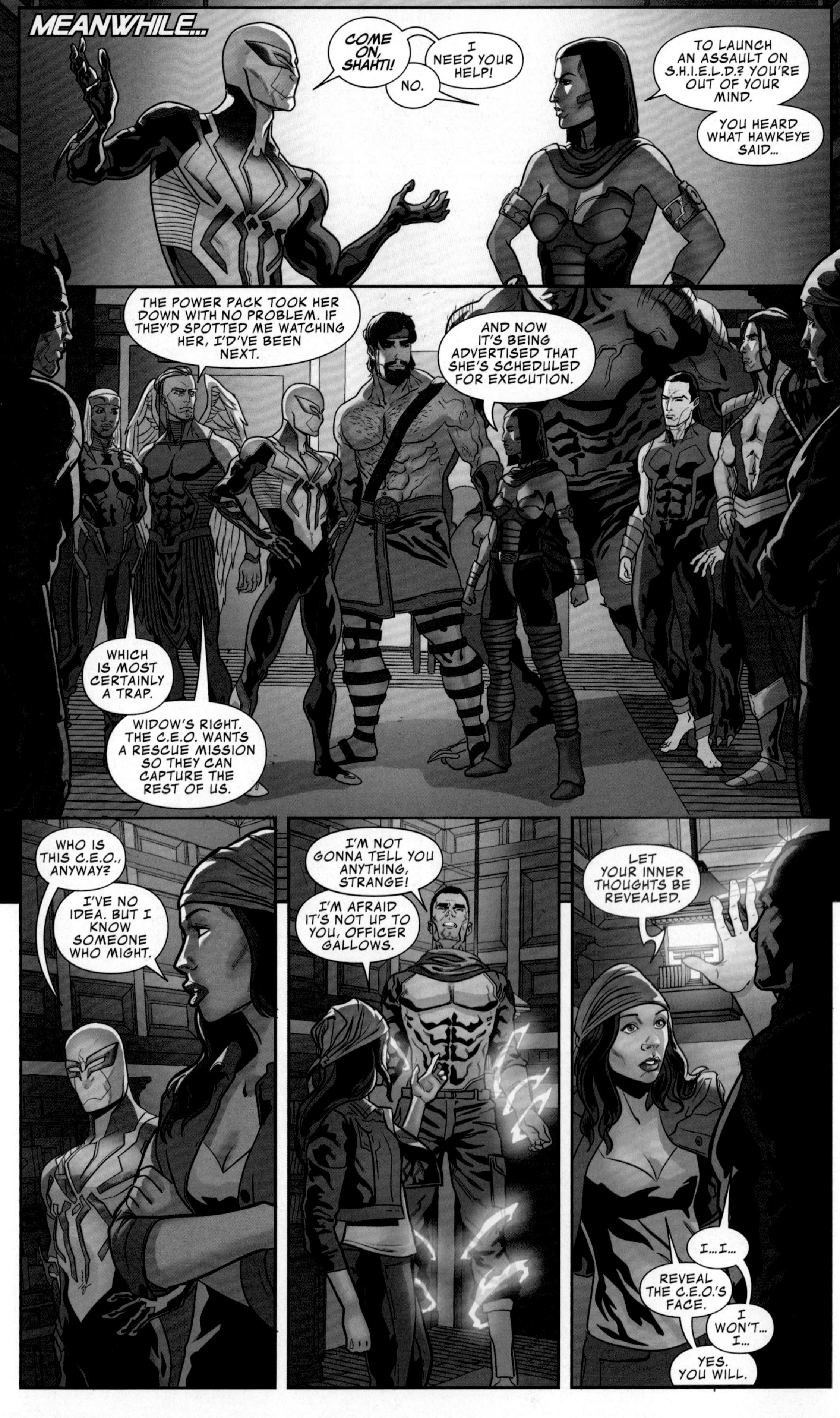
MEANWHILE...
COME ON, SHAKTI!
NO.
I NEED YOUR HELP!
TO LAUNCH AN ASSAULT ON S.H.I.E.L.D.? YOU'RE OUT OF YOUR MIND.
YOU HEARD WHAT HAWKEYE SAID...
THE POWER PACK TOOK HER DOWN WITH NO PROBLEM. IF THEY'D SPOTTED ME WATCHING HER, I'D'VE BEEN NEXT.
AND NOW IT'S BEING ADVERTISED THAT SHE'S SCHEDULED FOR EXECUTION.
WHICH IS MOST CERTAINLY A TRAP.
WIDOW'S RIGHT. THE C.E.O. WANTS A RESCUE MISSION SO THEY CAN CAPTURE THE REST OF US.
WHO IS THIS C.E.O., ANYWAY?
I'VE NO IDEA. BUT I KNOW SOMEONE WHO MIGHT.
I'M NOT GONNA TELL YOU ANYTHING, STRANGE!
I'M AFRAID IT'S NOT UP TO YOU, OFFICER GALLOWS.
LET YOUR INNER THOUGHTS BE REVEALED.
I... I...
REVEAL THE C.E.O.'S FACE.
I WON'T... I...
YES. YOU WILL.

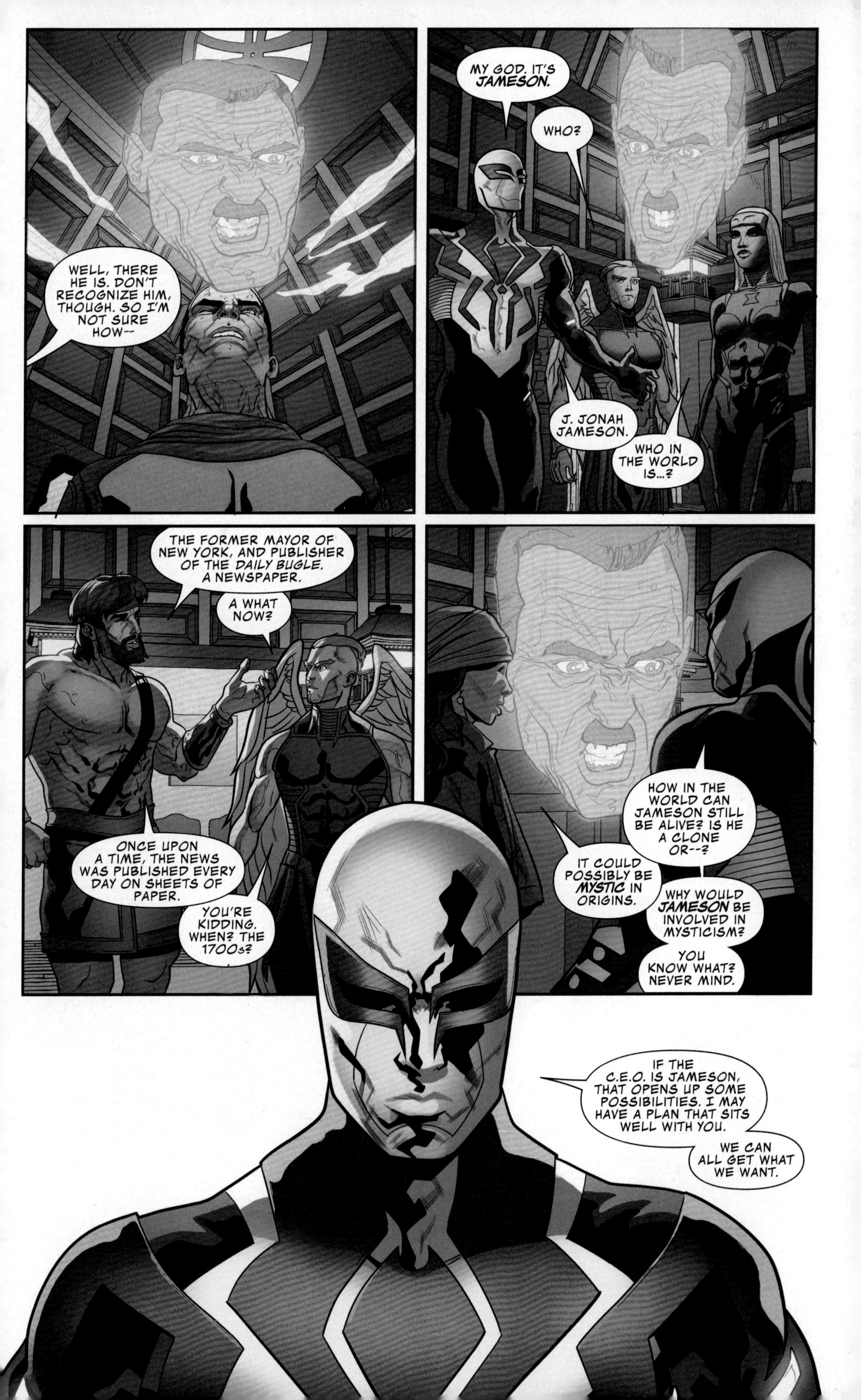
WELL, THERE HE IS. DON'T RECOGNIZE HIM, THOUGH. SO I'M NOT SURE HOW--
MY GOD. IT'S *JAMESON.*
WHO?
J. JONAH JAMESON.
WHO IN THE WORLD IS...?
THE FORMER MAYOR OF NEW YORK, AND PUBLISHER OF THE *DAILY BUGLE.* A NEWSPAPER.
A WHAT NOW?
ONCE UPON A TIME, THE NEWS WAS PUBLISHED EVERY DAY ON SHEETS OF PAPER.
YOU'RE KIDDING. WHEN? THE 1700s?
HOW IN THE WORLD CAN JAMESON STILL BE ALIVE? IS HE A CLONE OR--?
IT COULD POSSIBLY BE *MYSTIC* IN ORIGINS.
WHY WOULD *JAMESON* BE INVOLVED IN MYSTICISM?
YOU KNOW WHAT? NEVER MIND.
IF THE C.E.O. IS JAMESON, THAT OPENS UP SOME POSSIBILITIES. I MAY HAVE A PLAN THAT SITS WELL WITH YOU.
WE CAN ALL GET WHAT WE WANT.

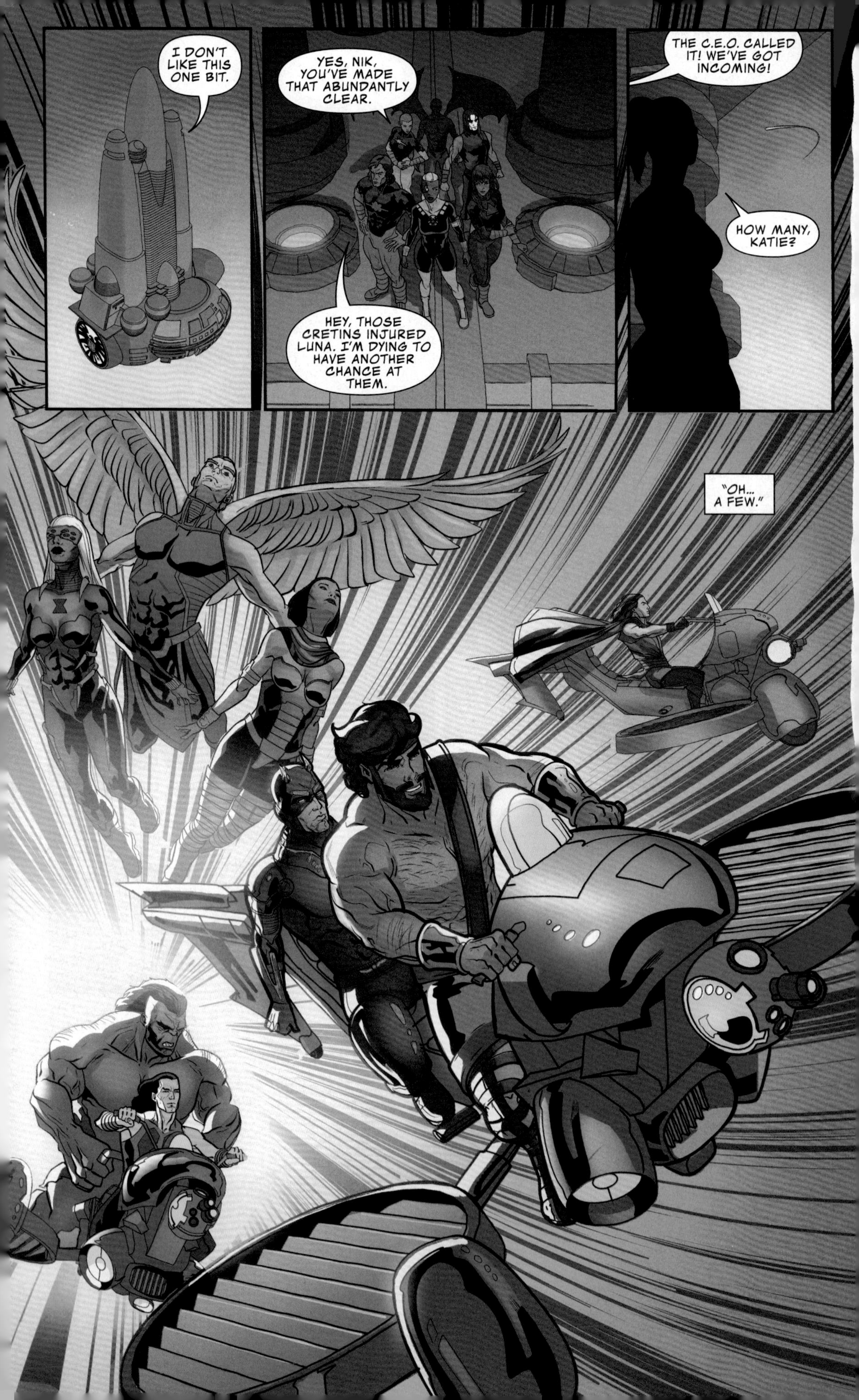
I DON'T LIKE THIS ONE BIT.
YES, NIK, YOU'VE MADE THAT ABUNDANTLY CLEAR.
HEY, THOSE CRETINS INJURED LUNA. I'M DYING TO HAVE ANOTHER CHANCE AT THEM.
THE C.E.O. CALLED IT! WE'VE GOT INCOMING!
HOW MANY, KATIE?
"OH... A FEW."

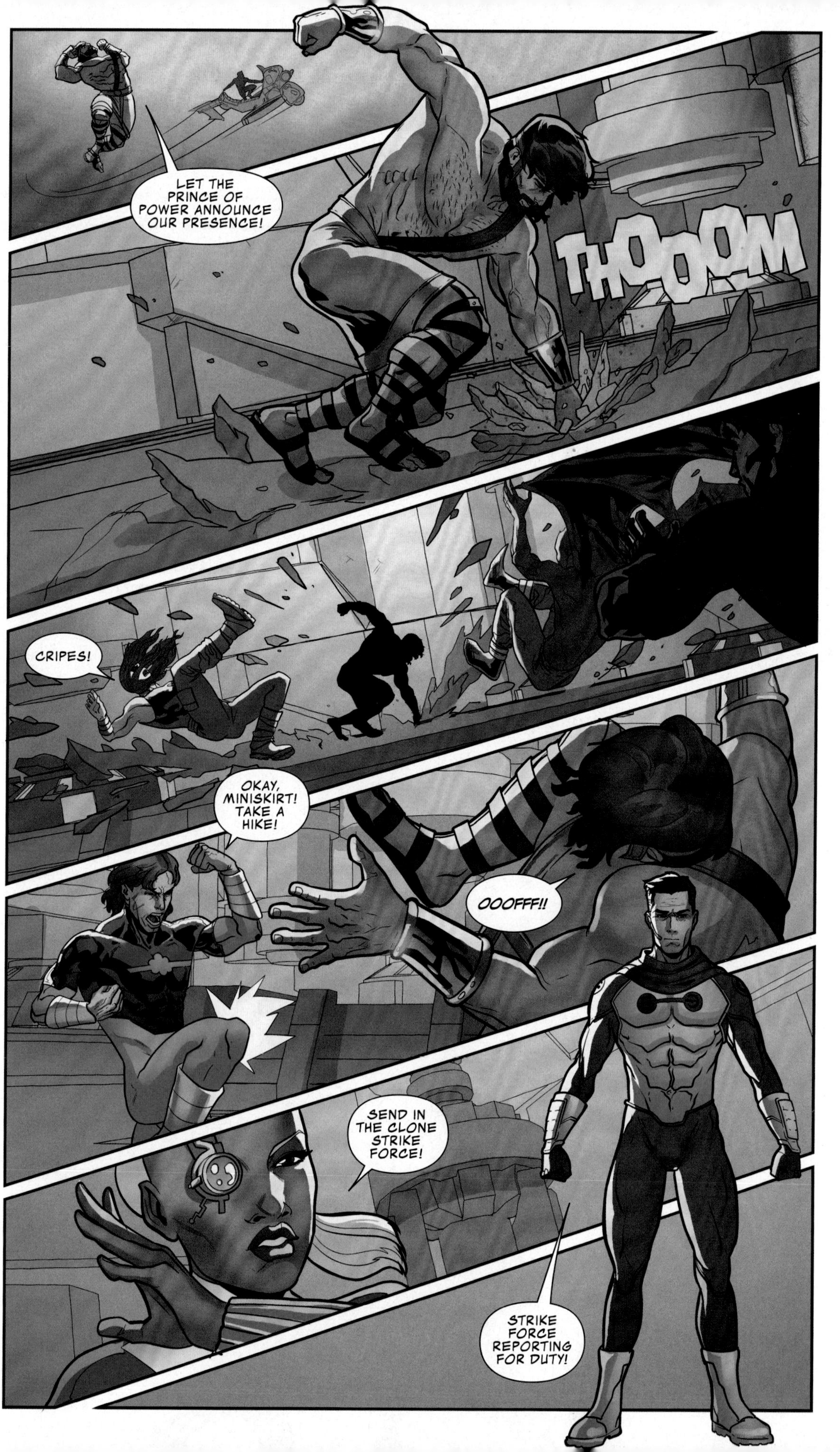
LET THE PRINCE OF POWER ANNOUNCE OUR PRESENCE!
THOOOM
CRIPES!
OKAY, MINISKIRT! TAKE A HIKE!
OOOFFF!!
SEND IN THE CLONE STRIKE FORCE!
STRIKE FORCE REPORTING FOR DUTY!

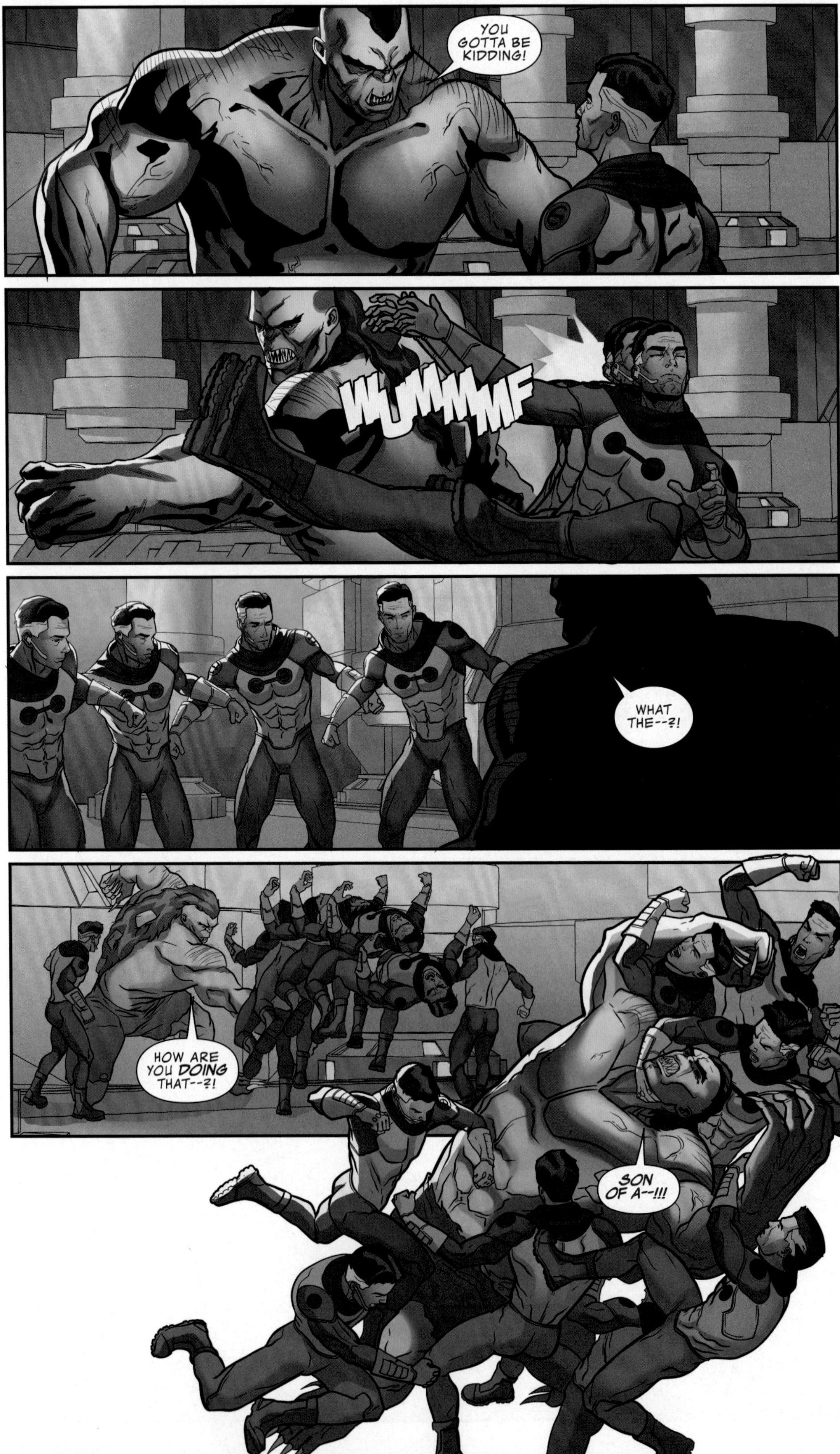
YOU GOTTA BE KIDDING!
WUMMMF
WHAT THE--?!
HOW ARE YOU DOING THAT--?!
SON OF A--!!!

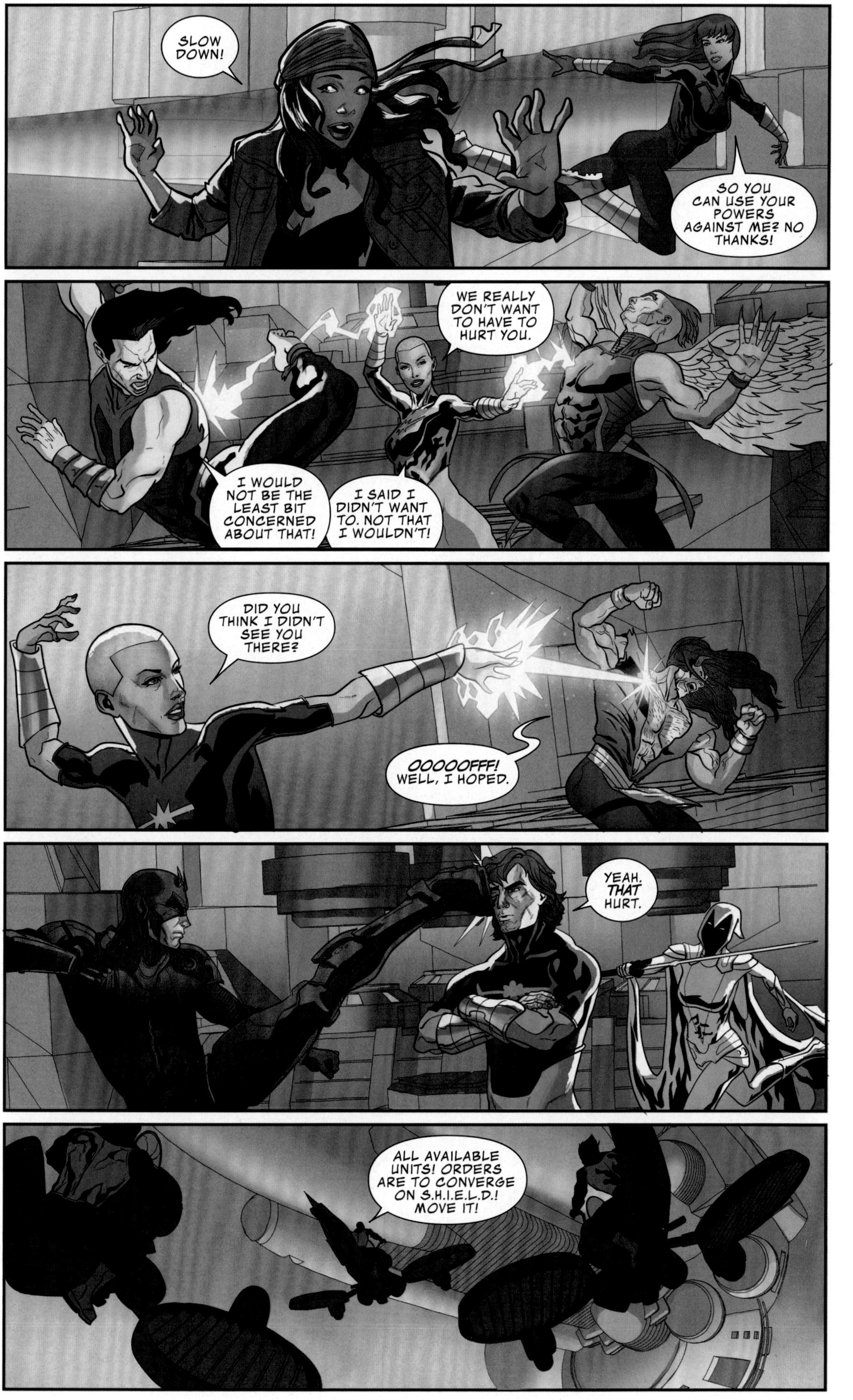
SLOW DOWN!
SO YOU CAN USE YOUR POWERS AGAINST ME? NO THANKS!
WE REALLY DON'T WANT TO HAVE TO HURT YOU.
I WOULD NOT BE THE LEAST BIT CONCERNED ABOUT THAT!
I SAID I DIDN'T WANT TO. NOT THAT I WOULDN'T!
DID YOU THINK I DIDN'T SEE YOU THERE?
OOOOOFFF! WELL, I HOPED.
YEAH. *THAT* HURT.
ALL AVAILABLE UNITS! ORDERS ARE TO CONVERGE ON S.H.I.E.L.D.! MOVE IT!

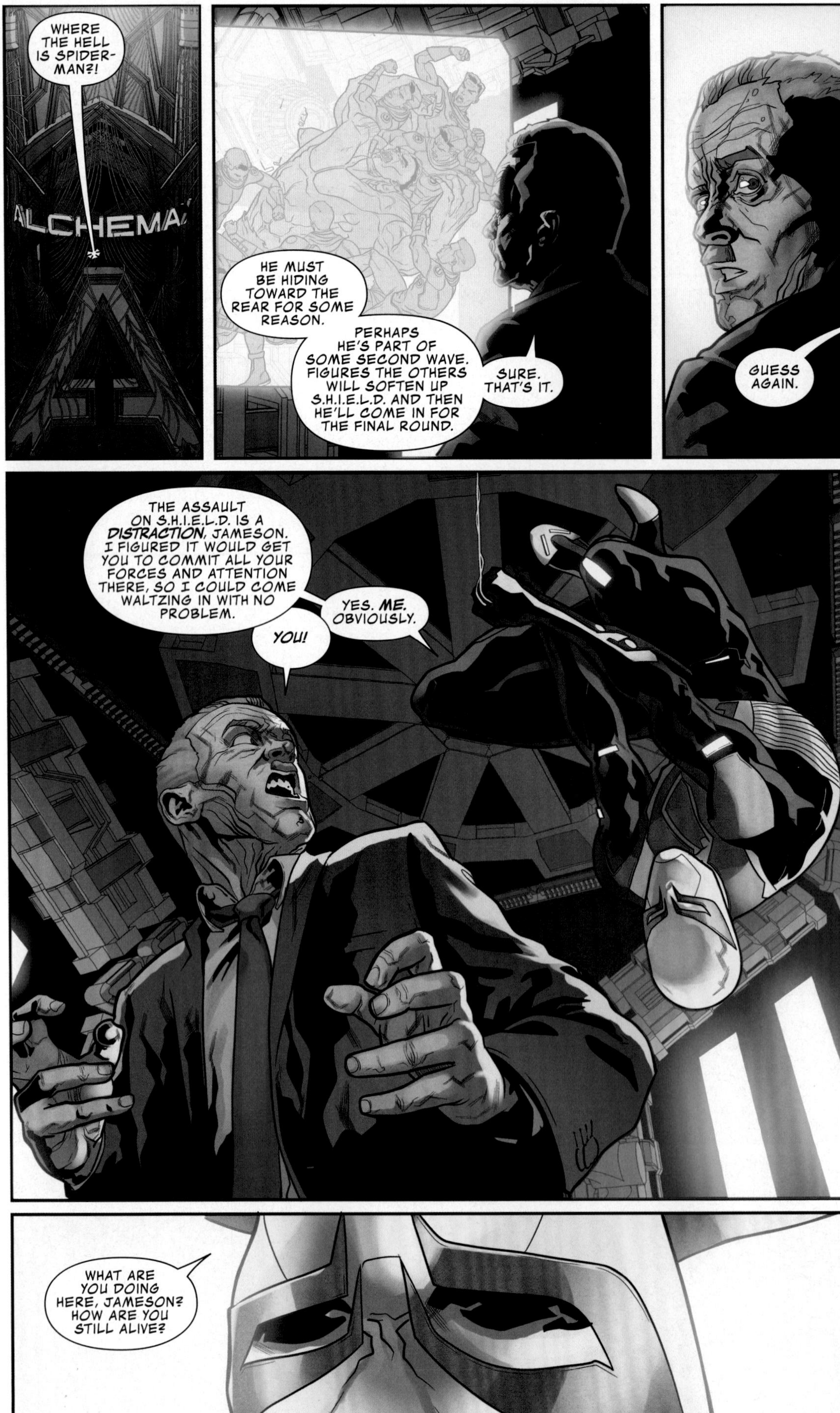
WHERE THE HELL IS SPIDER-MAN?!
ALCHEMAX
HE MUST BE HIDING TOWARD THE REAR FOR SOME REASON.
PERHAPS HE'S PART OF SOME SECOND WAVE. FIGURES THE OTHERS WILL SOFTEN UP S.H.I.E.L.D. AND THEN HE'LL COME IN FOR THE FINAL ROUND.
SURE. THAT'S IT.
GUESS AGAIN.
YOU!
YES. **ME.** OBVIOUSLY.
THE ASSAULT ON S.H.I.E.L.D. IS A ***DISTRACTION***, JAMESON. I FIGURED IT WOULD GET YOU TO COMMIT ALL YOUR FORCES AND ATTENTION THERE, SO I COULD COME WALTZING IN WITH NO PROBLEM.
WHAT ARE YOU DOING HERE, JAMESON? HOW ARE YOU STILL ALIVE?

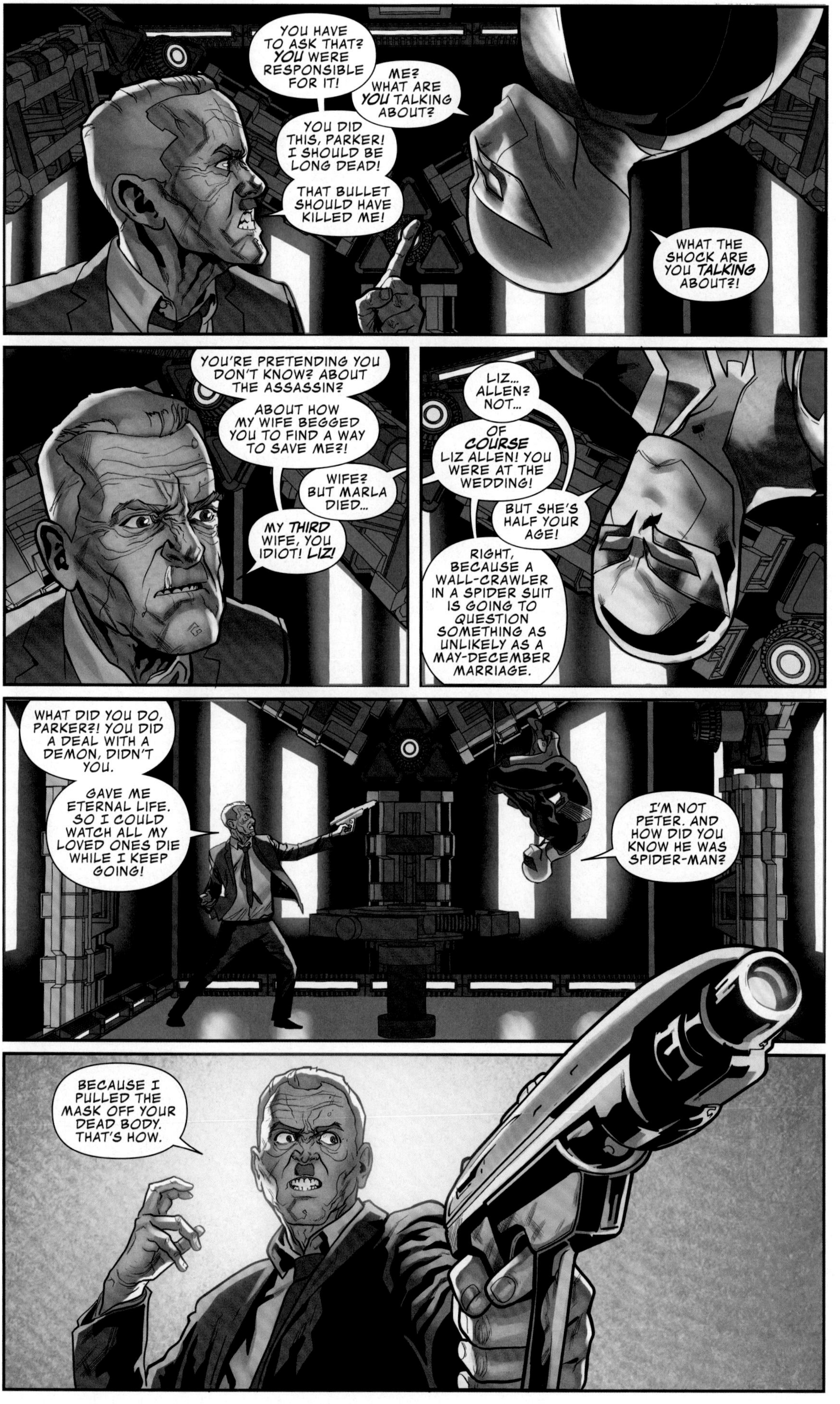

YOU HAVE TO ASK THAT? YOU WERE RESPONSIBLE FOR IT!
ME? WHAT ARE YOU TALKING ABOUT?
YOU DID THIS, PARKER! I SHOULD BE LONG DEAD!
THAT BULLET SHOULD HAVE KILLED ME!
WHAT THE SHOCK ARE YOU TALKING ABOUT?!
YOU'RE PRETENDING YOU DON'T KNOW? ABOUT THE ASSASSIN?
ABOUT HOW MY WIFE BEGGED YOU TO FIND A WAY TO SAVE ME?!
WIFE? BUT MARLA DIED...
MY THIRD WIFE, YOU IDIOT! LIZ!
LIZ... ALLEN? NOT...
OF COURSE LIZ ALLEN! YOU WERE AT THE WEDDING!
BUT SHE'S HALF YOUR AGE!
RIGHT, BECAUSE A WALL-CRAWLER IN A SPIDER SUIT IS GOING TO QUESTION SOMETHING AS UNLIKELY AS A MAY-DECEMBER MARRIAGE.
WHAT DID YOU DO, PARKER?! YOU DID A DEAL WITH A DEMON, DIDN'T YOU.
GAVE ME ETERNAL LIFE. SO I COULD WATCH ALL MY LOVED ONES DIE WHILE I KEEP GOING!
I'M NOT PETER. AND HOW DID YOU KNOW HE WAS SPIDER-MAN?
BECAUSE I PULLED THE MASK OFF YOUR DEAD BODY. THAT'S HOW.

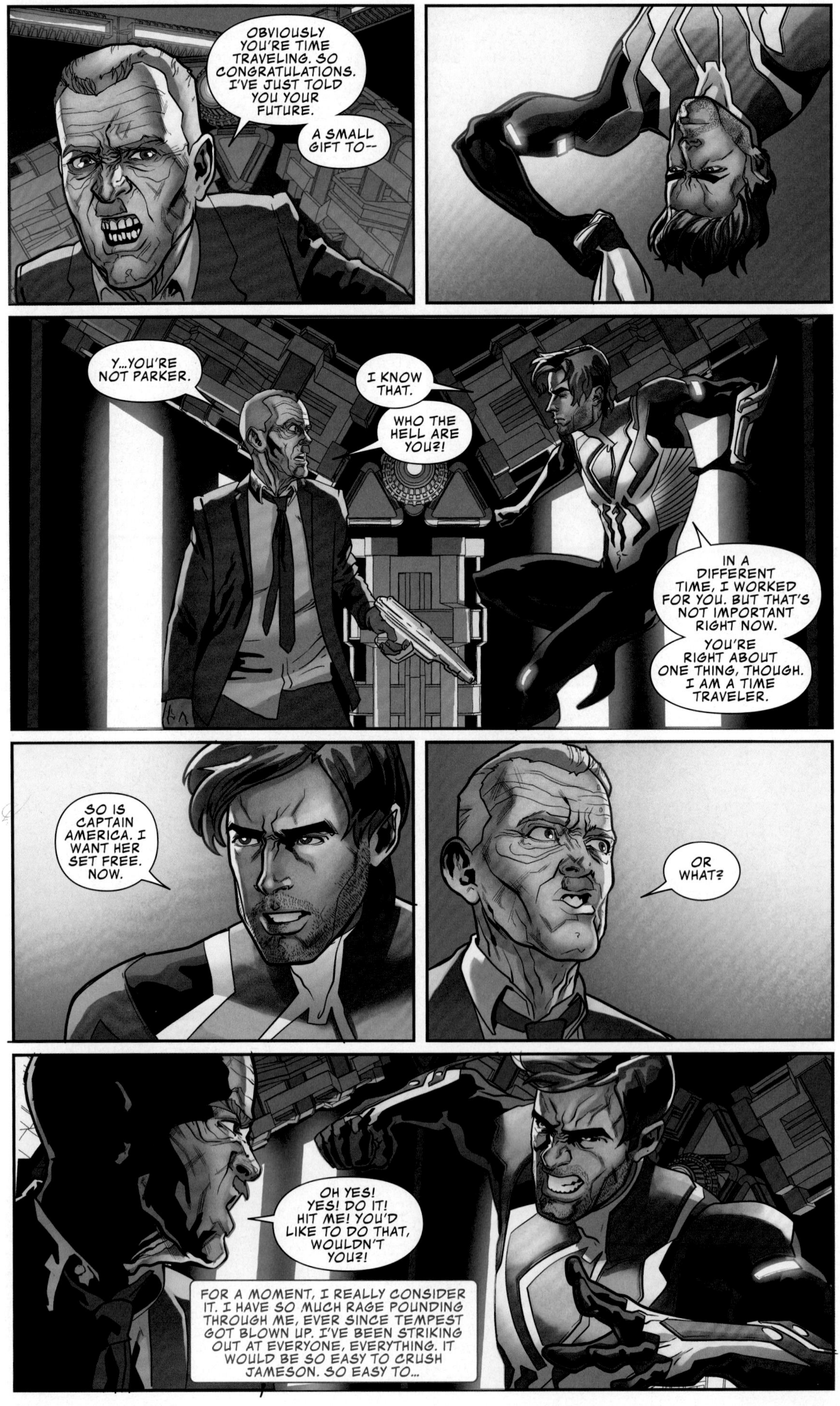
OBVIOUSLY YOU'RE TIME TRAVELING. SO CONGRATULATIONS. I'VE JUST TOLD YOU YOUR FUTURE.
A SMALL GIFT TO--
Y...YOU'RE NOT PARKER.
I KNOW THAT.
WHO THE HELL ARE YOU?!
IN A DIFFERENT TIME, I WORKED FOR YOU. BUT THAT'S NOT IMPORTANT RIGHT NOW.
YOU'RE RIGHT ABOUT ONE THING, THOUGH. I AM A TIME TRAVELER.
SO IS CAPTAIN AMERICA. I WANT HER SET FREE. NOW.
OR WHAT?
OH YES! YES! DO IT! HIT ME! YOU'D LIKE TO DO THAT, WOULDN'T YOU?!
FOR A MOMENT, I REALLY CONSIDER IT. I HAVE SO MUCH RAGE POUNDING THROUGH ME, EVER SINCE TEMPEST GOT BLOWN UP. I'VE BEEN STRIKING OUT AT EVERYONE, EVERYTHING. IT WOULD BE SO EASY TO CRUSH JAMESON. SO EASY TO...

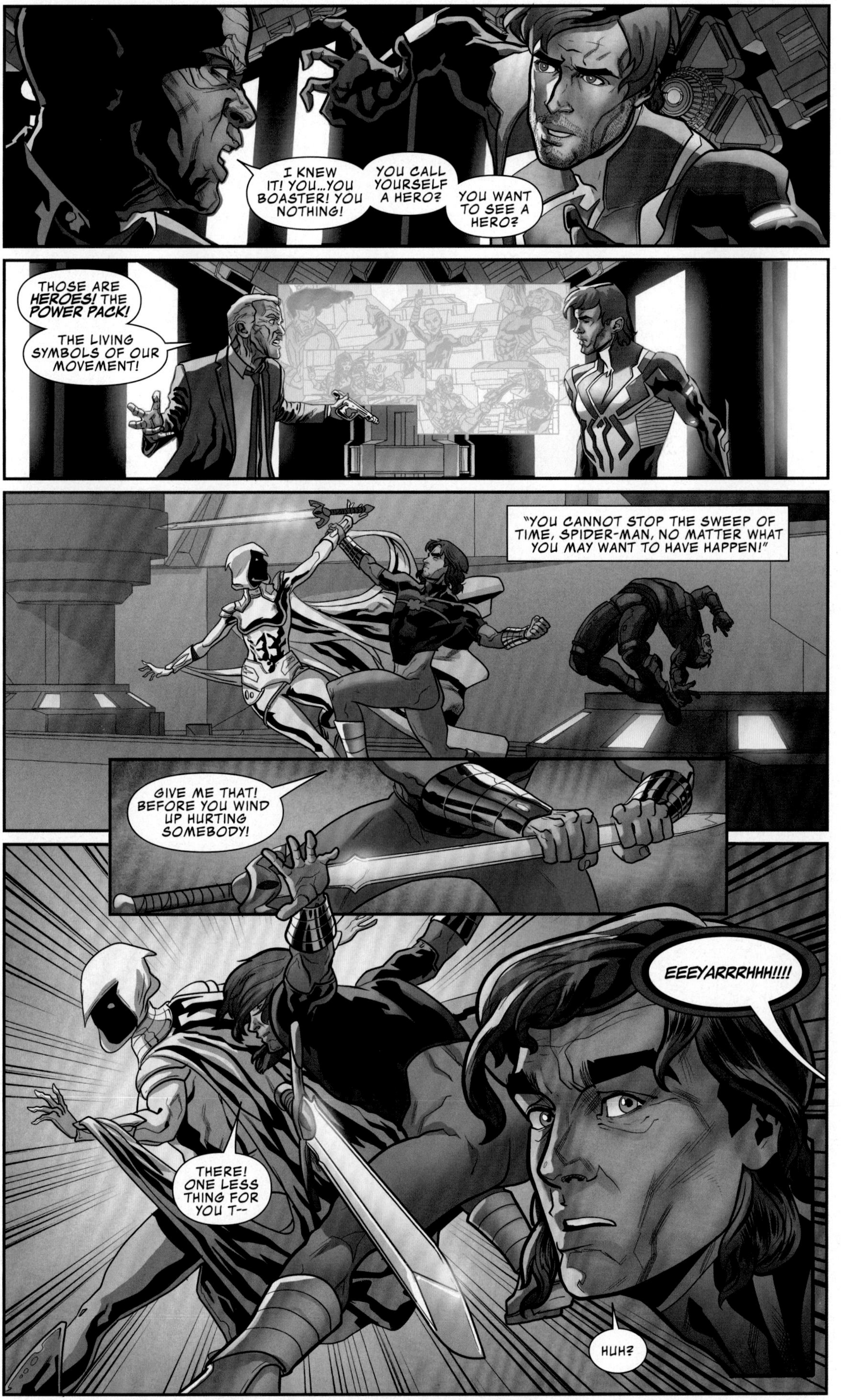
I KNEW IT! YOU...YOU BOASTER! YOU NOTHING!
YOU CALL YOURSELF A HERO?
YOU WANT TO SEE A HERO?
THOSE ARE HEROES! THE POWER PACK!
THE LIVING SYMBOLS OF OUR MOVEMENT!
"YOU CANNOT STOP THE SWEEP OF TIME, SPIDER-MAN, NO MATTER WHAT YOU MAY WANT TO HAVE HAPPEN!"
GIVE ME THAT! BEFORE YOU WIND UP HURTING SOMEBODY!
EEEYARRRHHH!!!!
THERE! ONE LESS THING FOR YOU T--
HUH?

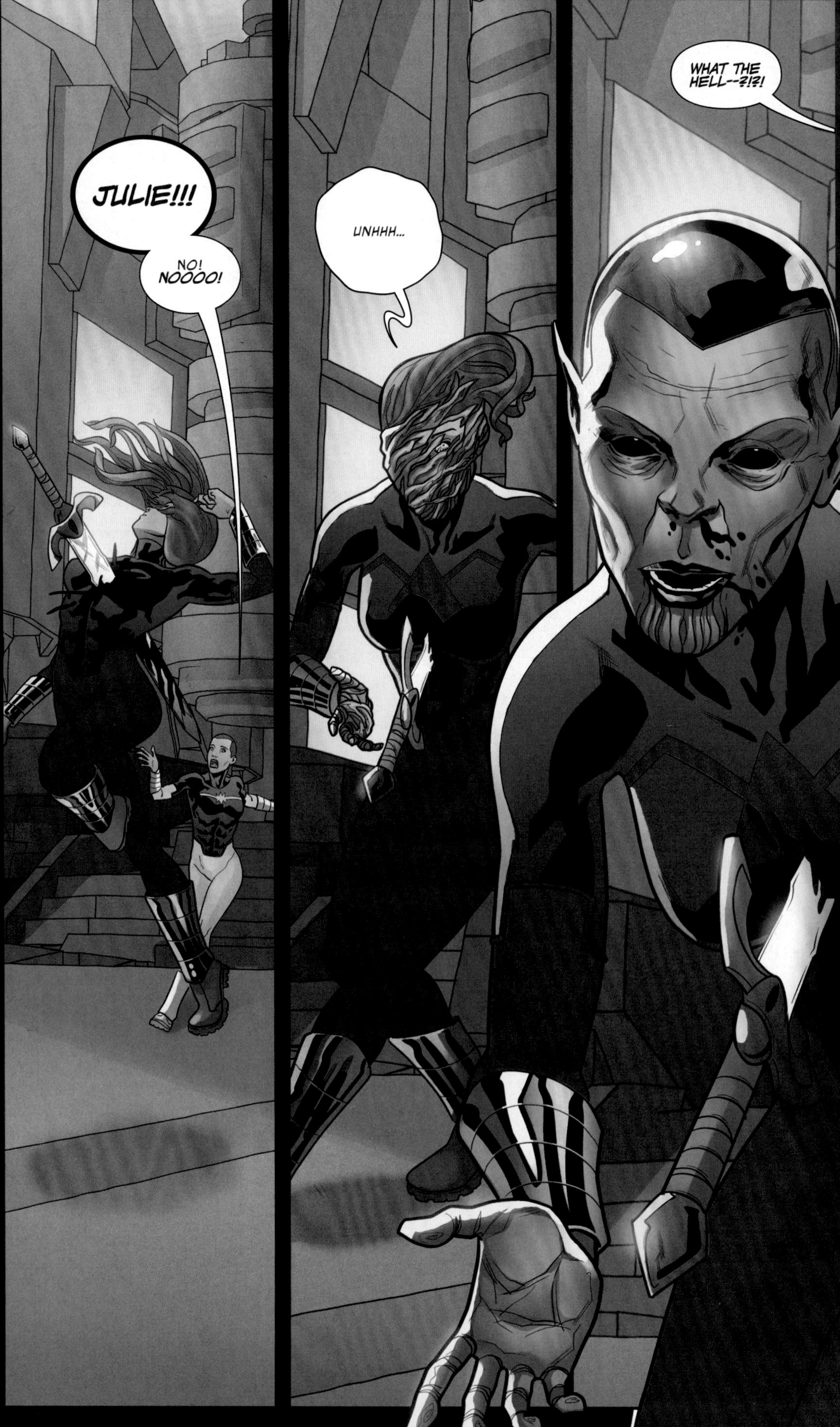
JULIE!!!
NO! NOOOO!
UNHHH...
WHAT THE HELL--?!?!

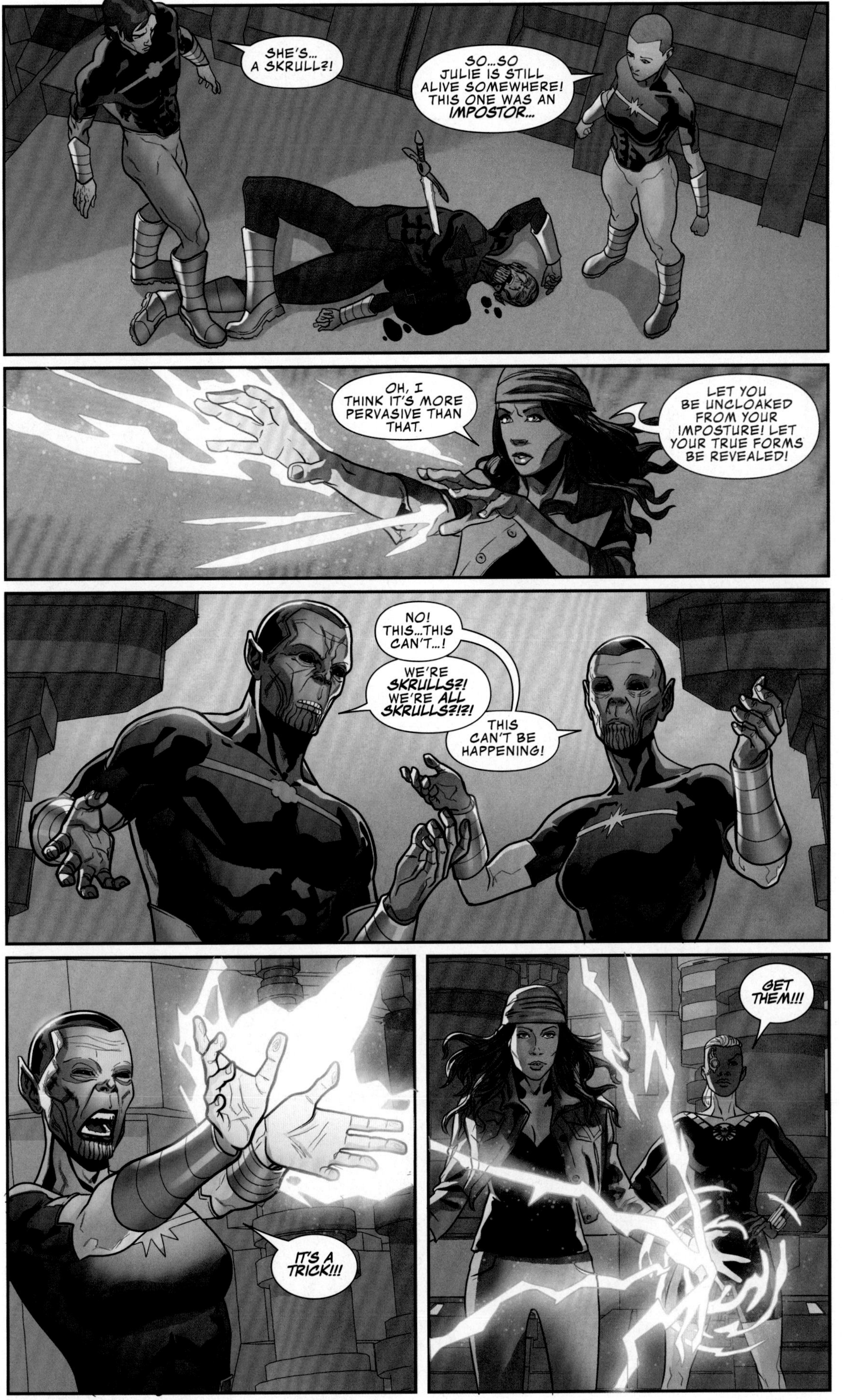
SHE'S... A SKRULL?!
SO...SO JULIE IS STILL ALIVE SOMEWHERE! THIS ONE WAS AN IMPOSTOR...
OH, I THINK IT'S MORE PERVASIVE THAN THAT.
LET YOU BE UNCLOAKED FROM YOUR IMPOSTURE! LET YOUR TRUE FORMS BE REVEALED!
NO! THIS...THIS CAN'T...!
WE'RE SKRULLS?! WE'RE ALL SKRULLS?!?!
THIS CAN'T BE HAPPENING!
IT'S A TRICK!!!
GET THEM!!!

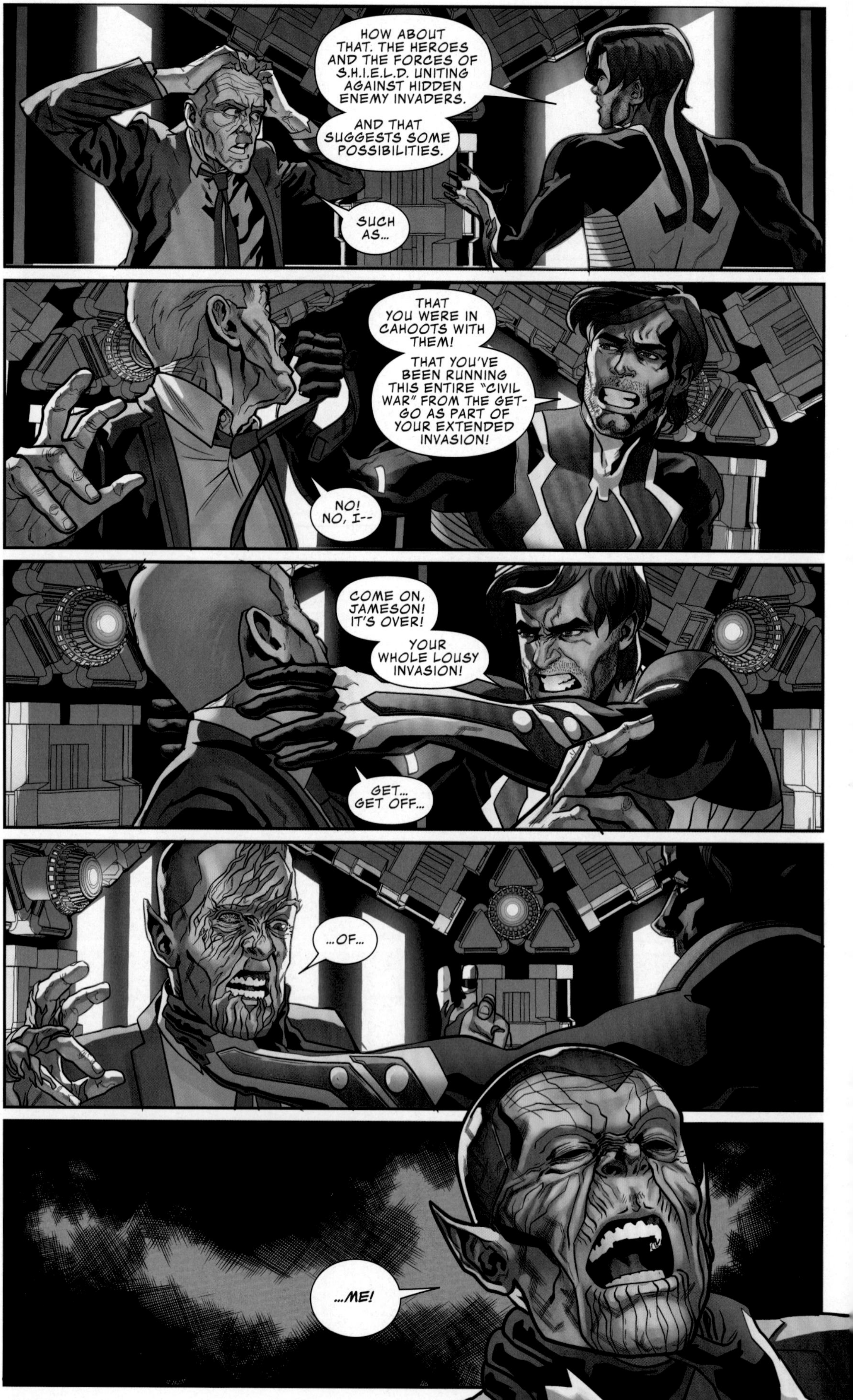
HOW ABOUT THAT. THE HEROES AND THE FORCES OF S.H.I.E.L.D. UNITING AGAINST HIDDEN ENEMY INVADERS.
AND THAT SUGGESTS SOME POSSIBILITIES.
SUCH AS...
THAT YOU WERE IN CAHOOTS WITH THEM!
THAT YOU'VE BEEN RUNNING THIS ENTIRE "CIVIL WAR" FROM THE GET-GO AS PART OF YOUR EXTENDED INVASION!
NO! NO, I--
COME ON, JAMESON! IT'S OVER!
YOUR WHOLE LOUSY INVASION!
GET... GET OFF...
...OF...
...ME!

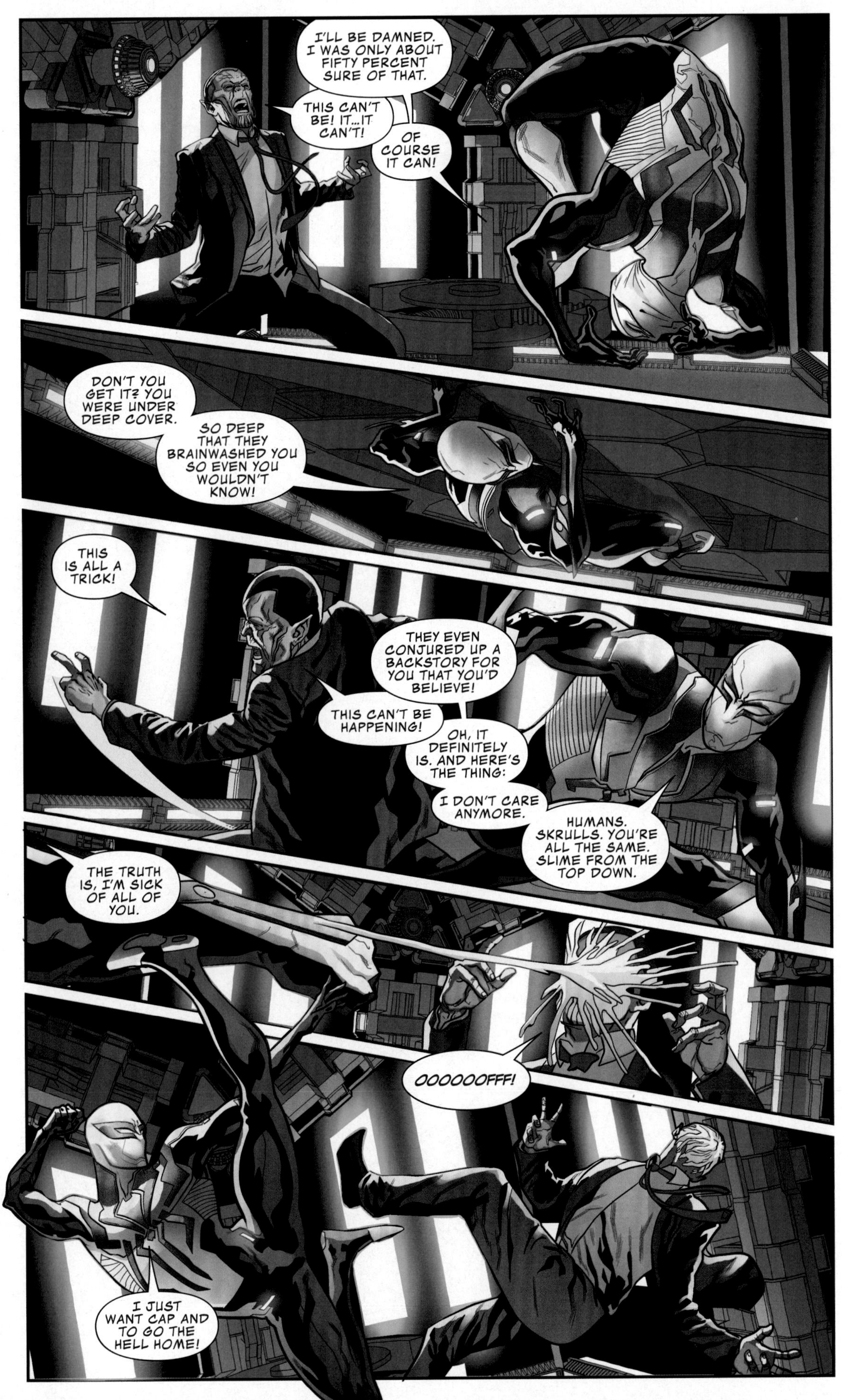
I'LL BE DAMNED. I WAS ONLY ABOUT FIFTY PERCENT SURE OF THAT.
THIS CAN'T BE! IT...IT CAN'T!
OF COURSE IT CAN!
DON'T YOU GET IT? YOU WERE UNDER DEEP COVER.
SO DEEP THAT THEY BRAINWASHED YOU SO EVEN YOU WOULDN'T KNOW!
THIS IS ALL A TRICK!
THEY EVEN CONJURED UP A BACKSTORY FOR YOU THAT YOU'D BELIEVE!
THIS CAN'T BE HAPPENING!
OH, IT DEFINITELY IS. AND HERE'S THE THING:
I DON'T CARE ANYMORE.
HUMANS. SKRULLS. YOU'RE ALL THE SAME. SLIME FROM THE TOP DOWN.
THE TRUTH IS, I'M SICK OF ALL OF YOU.
OOOOOOFFF!
I JUST WANT CAP AND TO GO THE HELL HOME!

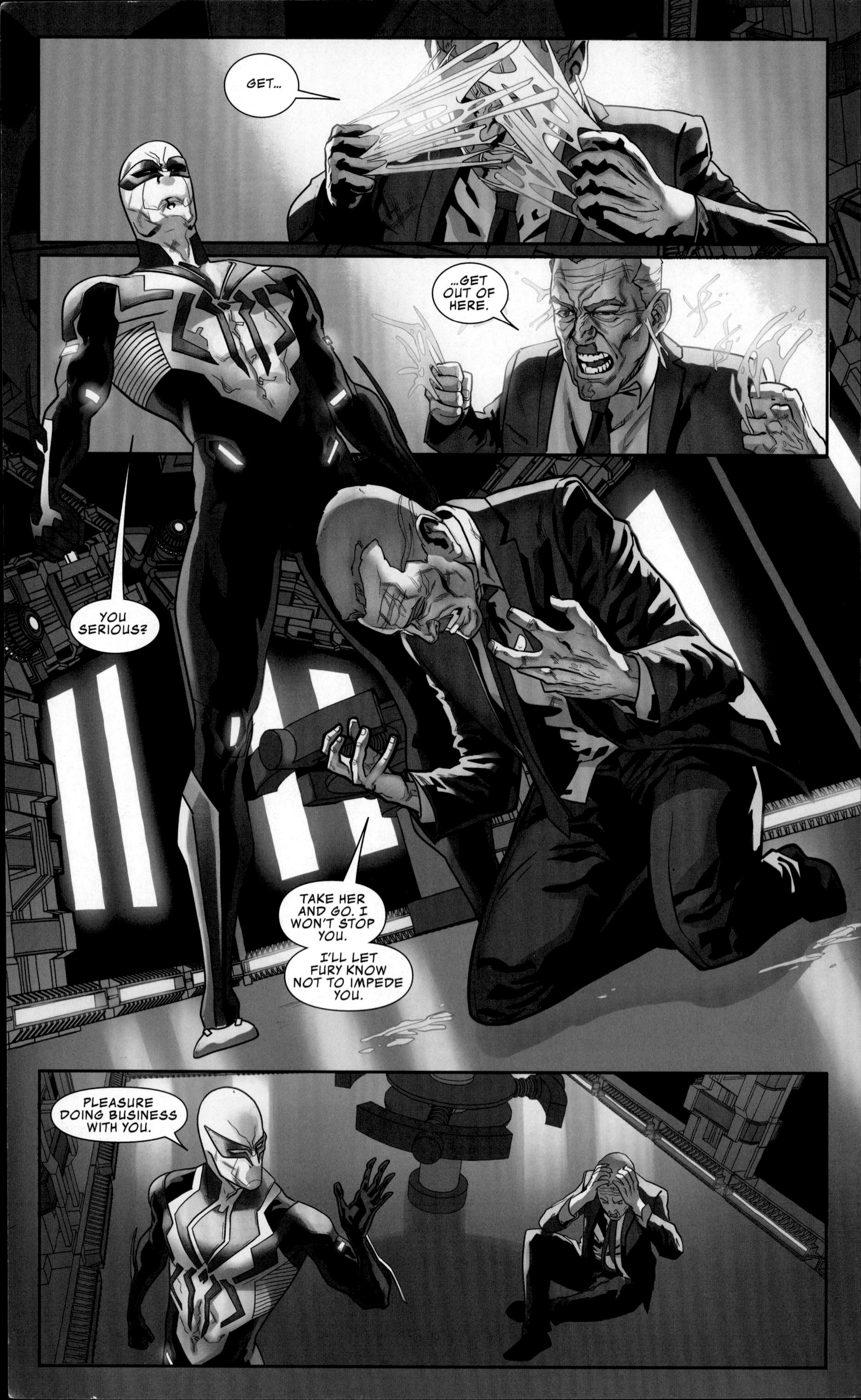
GET...
...GET OUT OF HERE.
YOU SERIOUS?
TAKE HER AND GO. I WON'T STOP YOU.
I'LL LET FURY KNOW NOT TO IMPEDE YOU.
PLEASURE DOING BUSINESS WITH YOU.

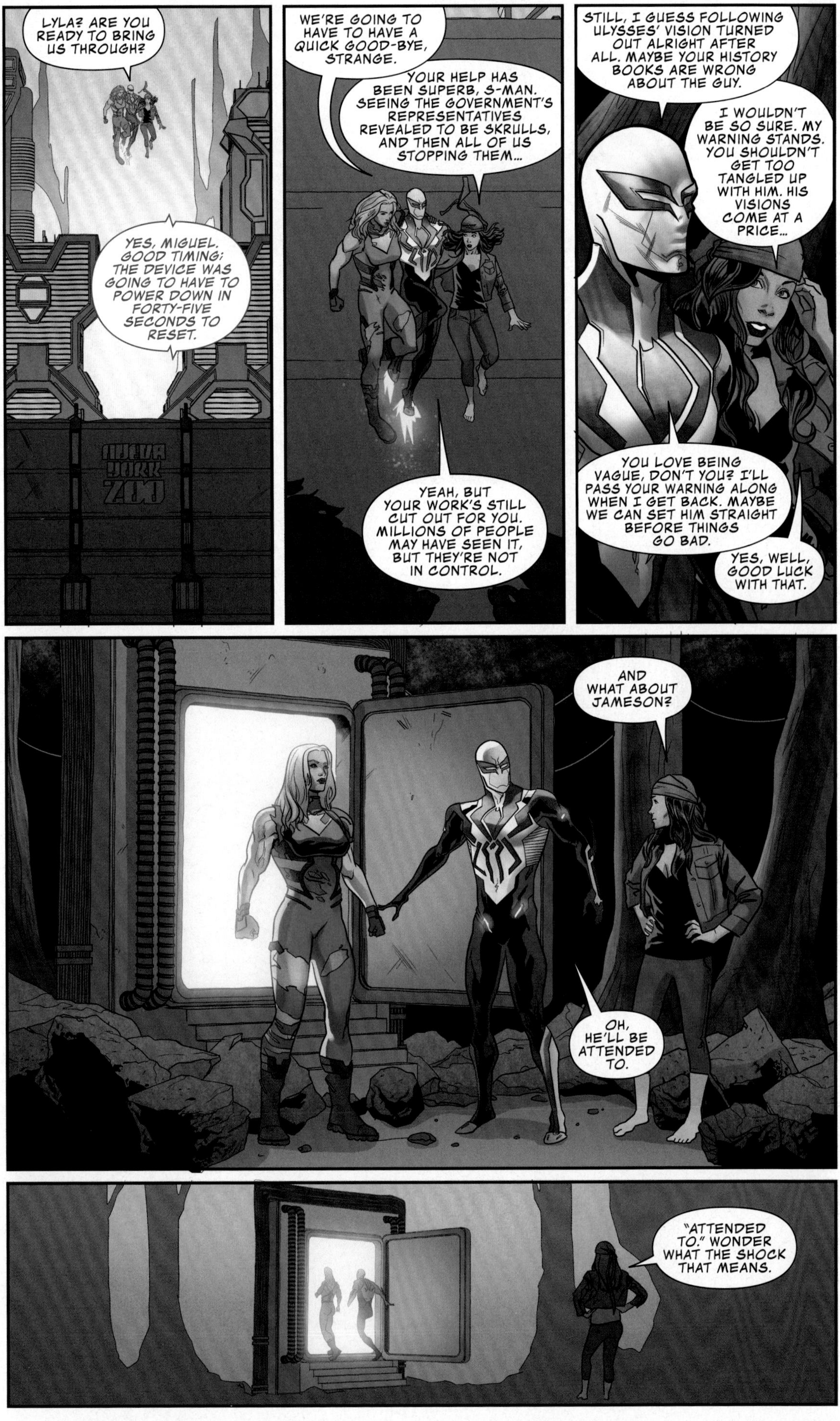
LYLA? ARE YOU READY TO BRING US THROUGH?
YES, MIGUEL. GOOD TIMING; THE DEVICE WAS GOING TO HAVE TO POWER DOWN IN FORTY-FIVE SECONDS TO RESET.
WE'RE GOING TO HAVE TO HAVE A QUICK GOOD-BYE, STRANGE.
YOUR HELP HAS BEEN SUPERB, S-MAN. SEEING THE GOVERNMENT'S REPRESENTATIVES REVEALED TO BE SKRULLS, AND THEN ALL OF US STOPPING THEM...
YEAH, BUT YOUR WORK'S STILL CUT OUT FOR YOU. MILLIONS OF PEOPLE MAY HAVE SEEN IT, BUT THEY'RE NOT IN CONTROL.
STILL, I GUESS FOLLOWING ULYSSES' VISION TURNED OUT ALRIGHT AFTER ALL. MAYBE YOUR HISTORY BOOKS ARE WRONG ABOUT THE GUY.
I WOULDN'T BE SO SURE. MY WARNING STANDS. YOU SHOULDN'T GET TOO TANGLED UP WITH HIM. HIS VISIONS COME AT A PRICE...
YOU LOVE BEING VAGUE, DON'T YOU? I'LL PASS YOUR WARNING ALONG WHEN I GET BACK. MAYBE WE CAN SET HIM STRAIGHT BEFORE THINGS GO BAD.
YES, WELL, GOOD LUCK WITH THAT.
AND WHAT ABOUT JAMESON?
OH, HE'LL BE ATTENDED TO.
"ATTENDED TO." WONDER WHAT THE SHOCK THAT MEANS.

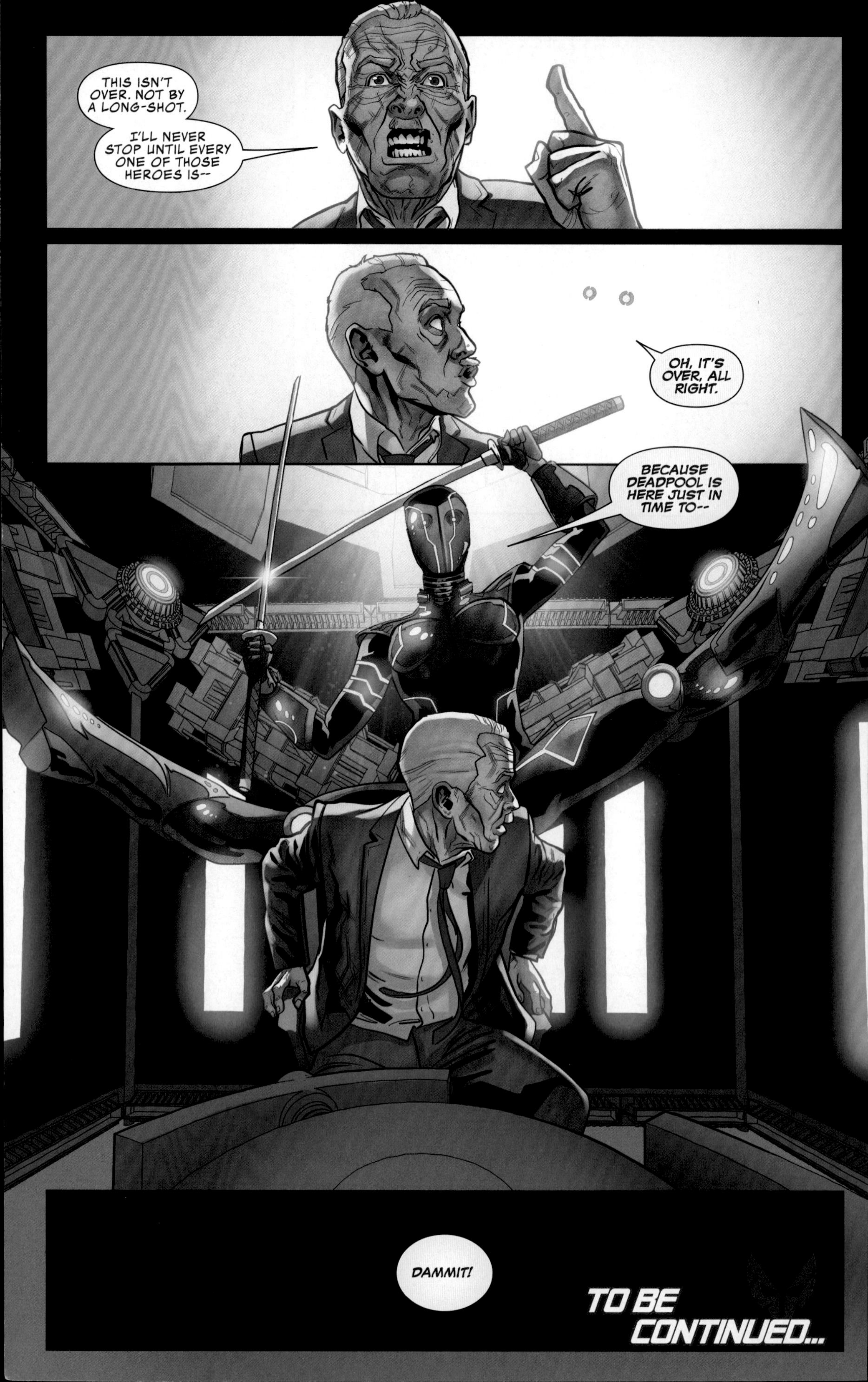

THIS ISN'T OVER. NOT BY A LONG-SHOT.
I'LL NEVER STOP UNTIL EVERY ONE OF THOSE HEROES IS--
OH, IT'S OVER, ALL RIGHT.
BECAUSE DEADPOOL IS HERE JUST IN TIME TO--
DAMMIT!
TO BE CONTINUED...

#11 cover sketches by FRANCESCO MATTINA

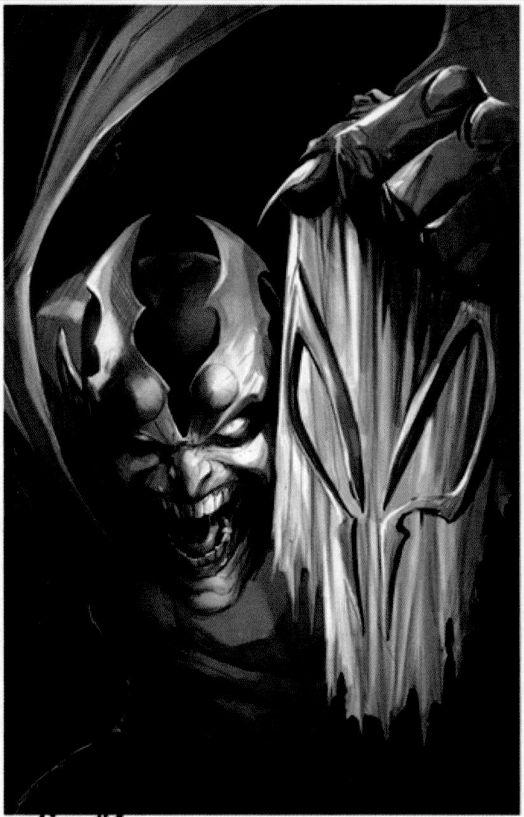

option#1

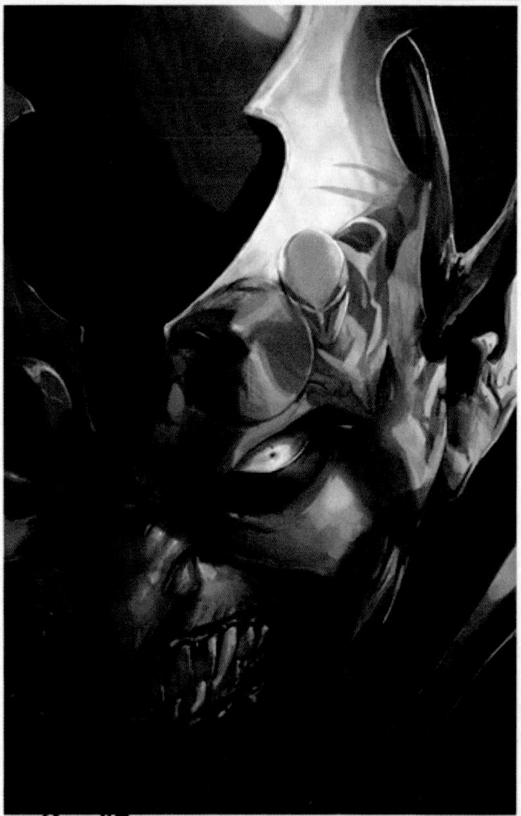

option#2

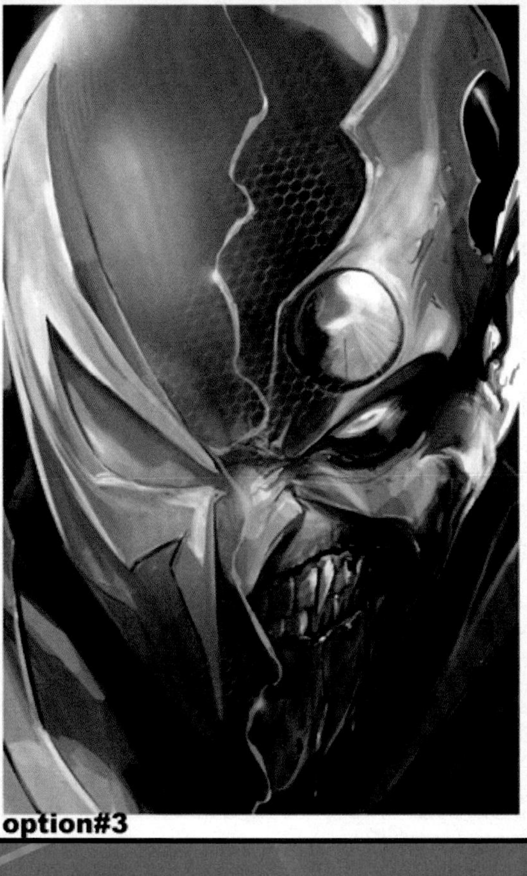

option#3

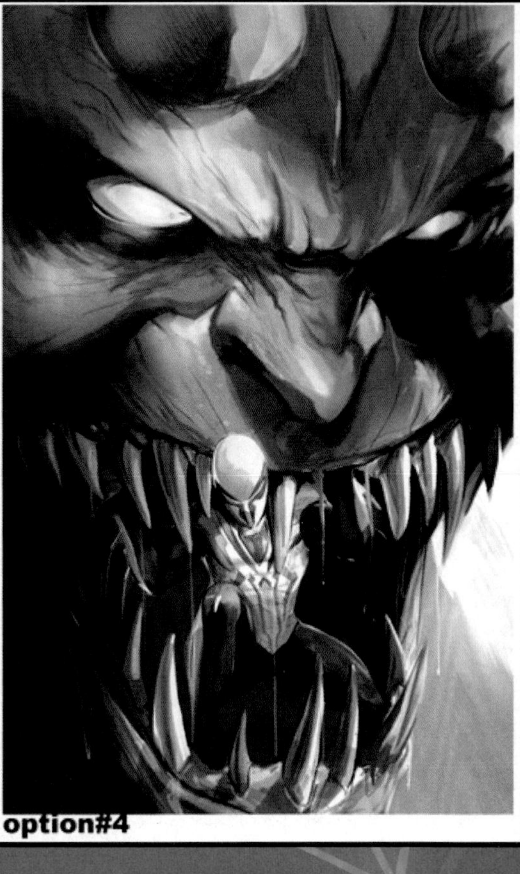

option#4

#12 cover sketches by FRANCESCO MATTINA

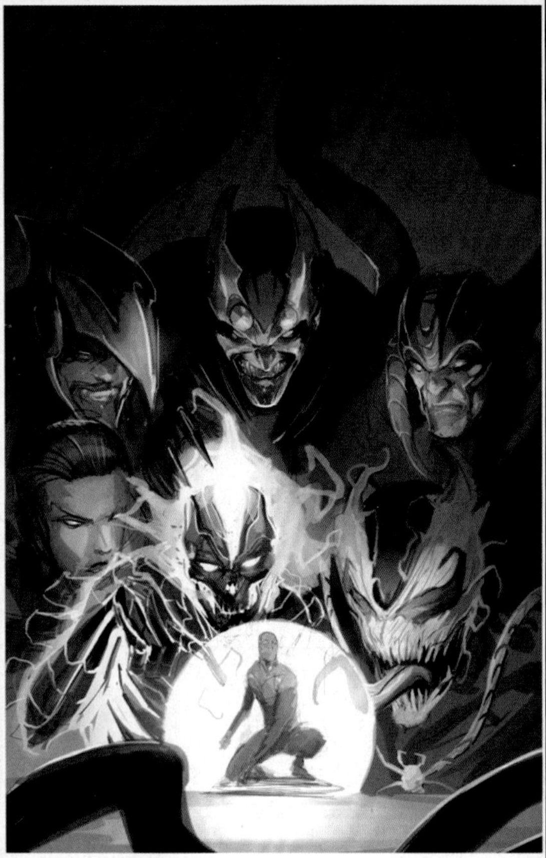

option#2

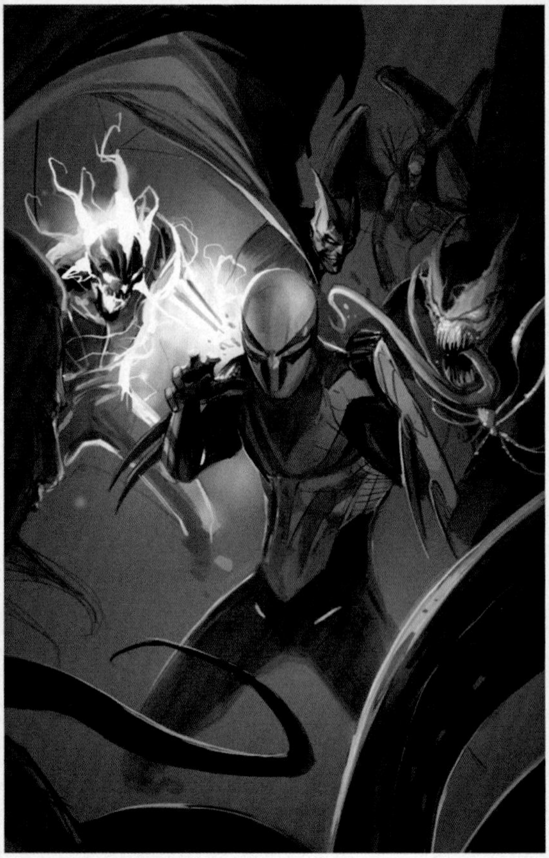

option#3

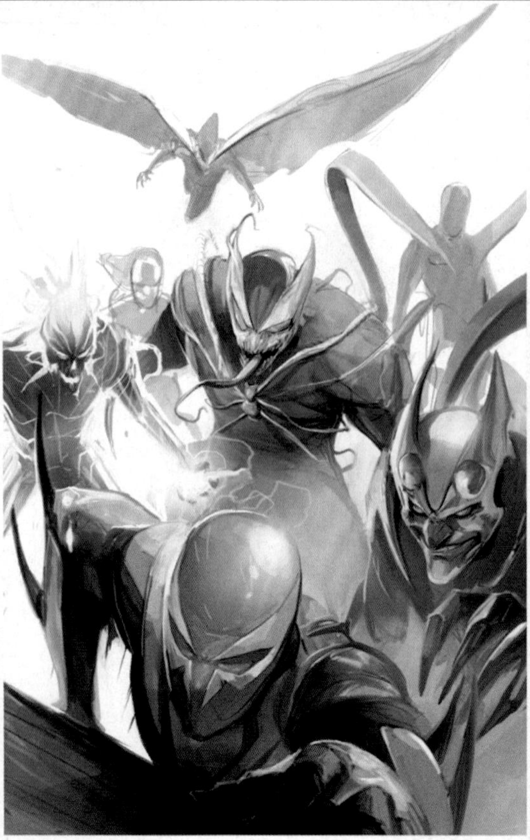

option#4

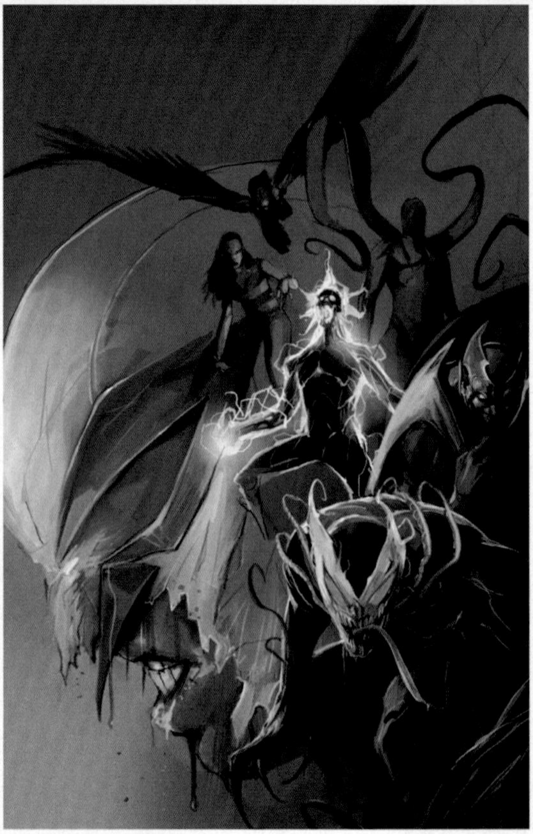

option#5

#14 cover sketches by FRANCESCO MATTINA

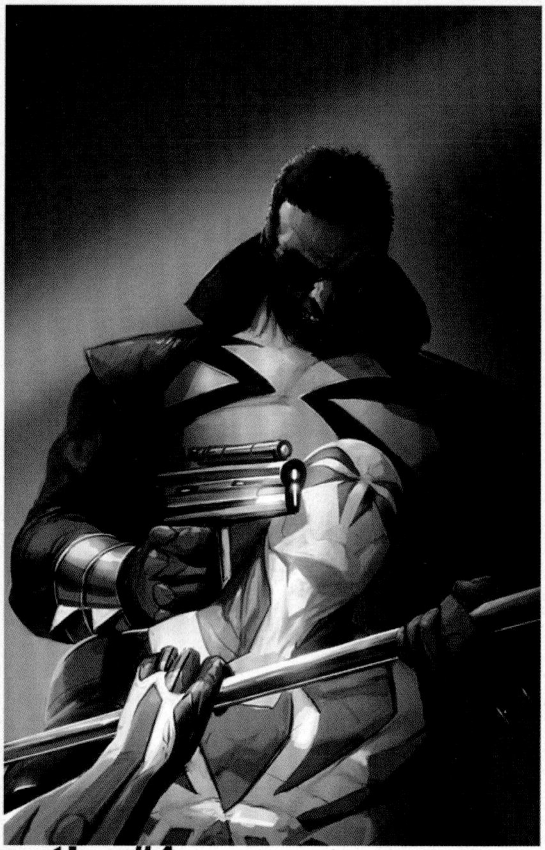

option#1

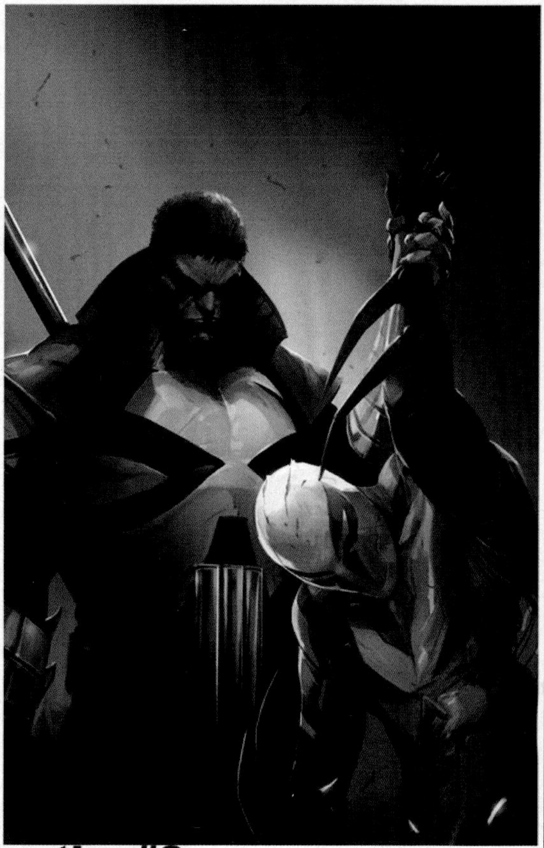

option#2

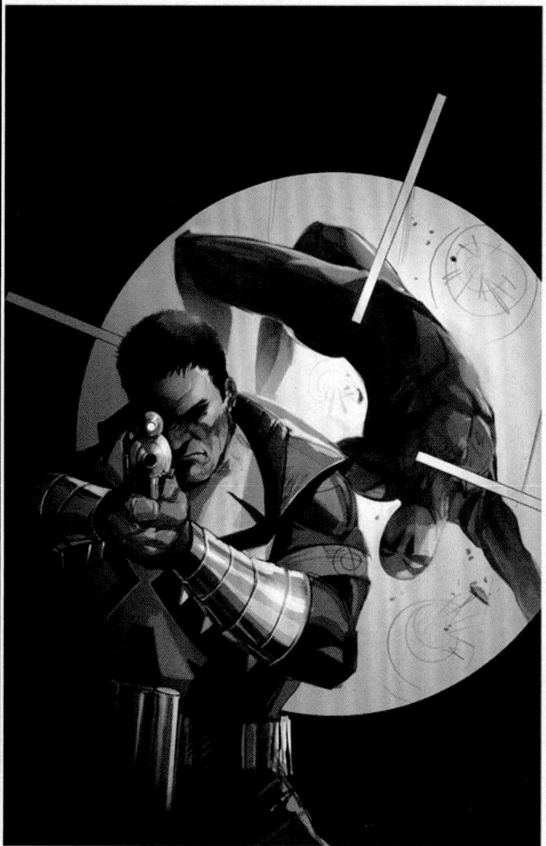

option#3

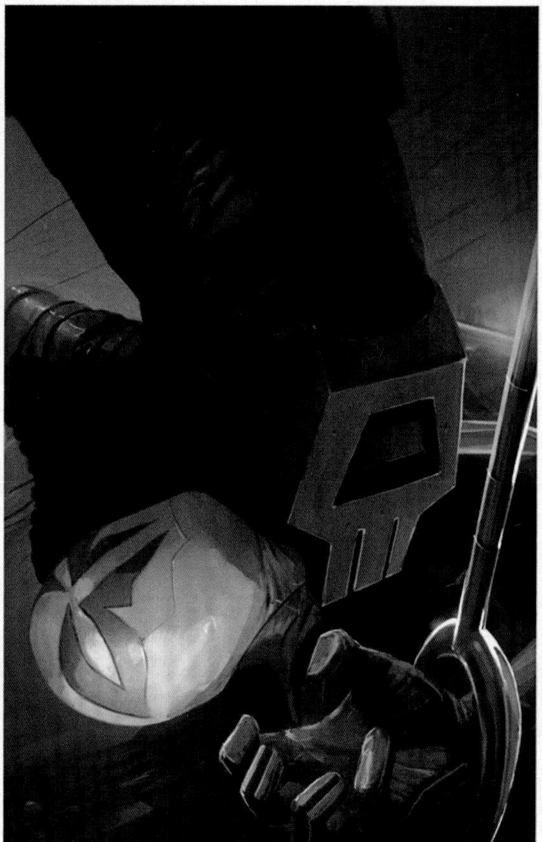

option#4

character sketches by WILL SLINEY

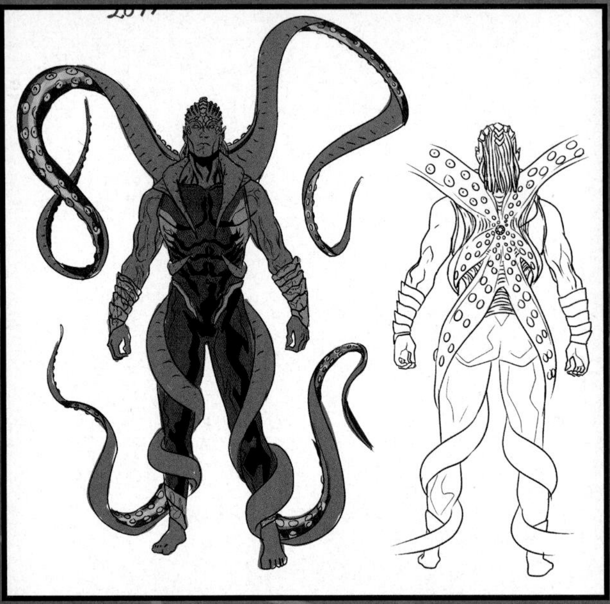

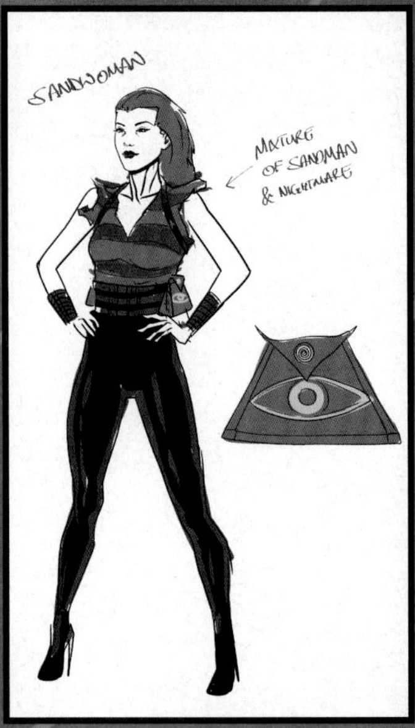
SANDWOMAN
MIXTURE OF SANDMAN & NIGHTMARE

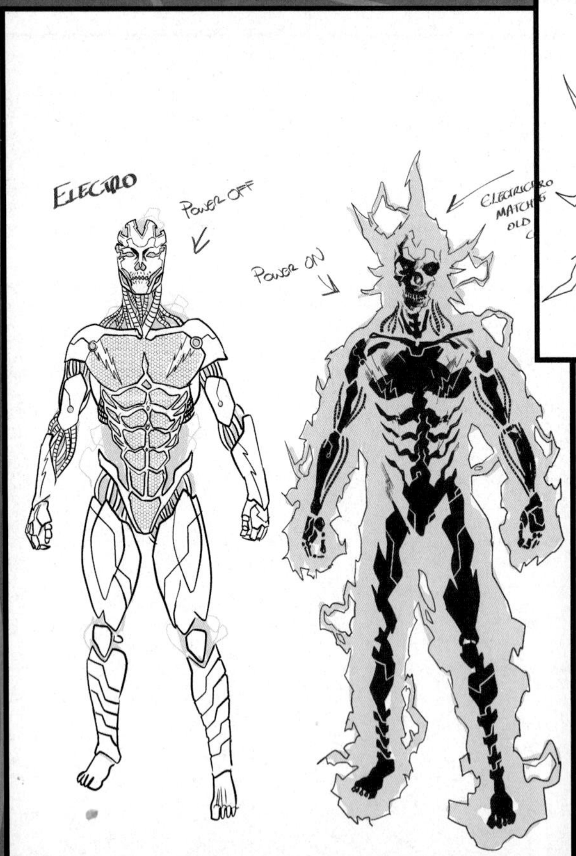
ELECTRO
POWER OFF
POWER ON

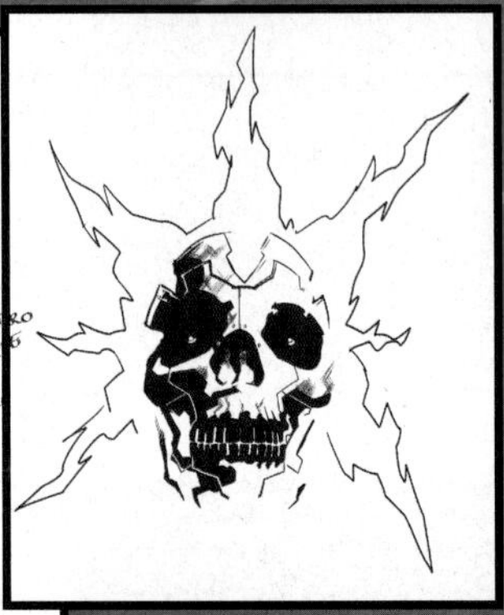

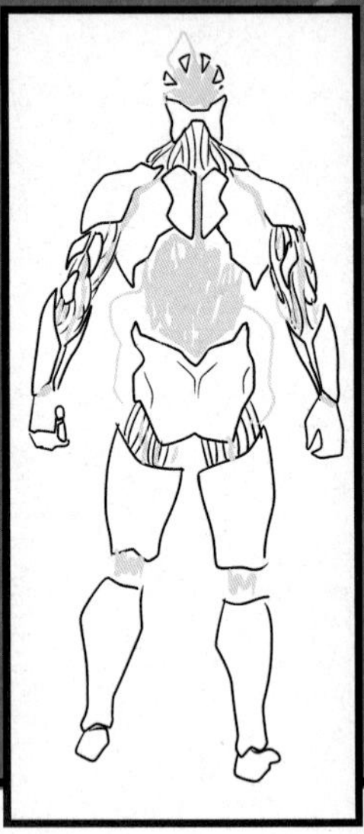

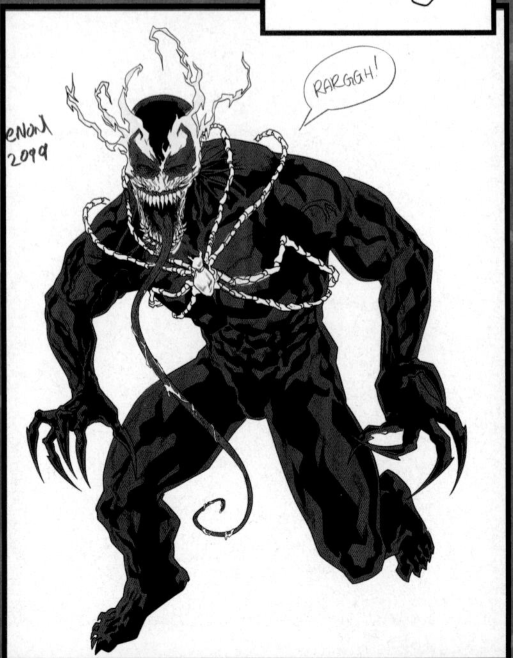
RARGGGH!

#11, pages 1-3 script
by PETER DAVID and
pages 2-3 inks
by WILL SLINEY

Page 1

Panel 1.1: Completely black.

Balloon 1: * Unnhhhh *

Goblin 2: Wakey wakey.

Panel 1.2: Same POV as a blurred face is looking at us.

Goblin 3: Eggs and bakey.

Panel 1.3: And the image clears up: It's the Goblin 2099.

Goblin 4: Actually, I can't tell if your eyes are open because, y'know: mask.

Panel 1.4: Reverse angle to reveal Spidey startling awake.

Spidey 5: Holy--!!

Spidey 6: Goblin!

Panel 1.5: The Goblin smiles dementedly.

Goblin 7: Holy Goblin. I like that, for reasons you can't even begin to imagine.

Goblin 8: Have you met my associates?

Goblin9: Some of them, I'm sure.

Goblin 10: We call ourselves...

Pages 2 to 3

DOUBLE PAGED SPLASH: We are in the main chamber of the Sinister Six. Remember the senate chamber from "Star Wars: Phantom Menace"? Like that, except not remotely so massive. But sizeable. Spidey is bound hand and foot to a large X, held there through oversized cuffs. The Six are scattered around the room and the balloons should go above them as introductions: [Colorist note: Sandwoman should have pale skin and green hair. Although we're not making a point of it at this juncture, she is Nightmare's daughter.]

Goblin 1: The Sinister Six.

Goblin 2: You know Venom, of course. And he purports to know you, although he refuses to divulge your identity. We've left your mask on out of deference to him.

Goblin 3: And Doctor Octopus, you've also met. A former Atlantean scientist; quite the genius in xenobiology.

Goblin 4: Then there's the Vulture. Always an independent operator before joining up with our little band.

Goblin 5: Then there's Electro. As you can see, he's not quite human. An android, actually. Previously a simple worker until a generator accident triggered his self-awareness and also gave him impressive electrical powers.

Goblin 6: And that fellow there is the Sandwoman. She seems harmless enough, I know...but I would not suggest you allow her to sprinkle her sand on you. It will end quite badly.

Goblin 7: So...that's everyone. And believe me, we all know you. Very well.

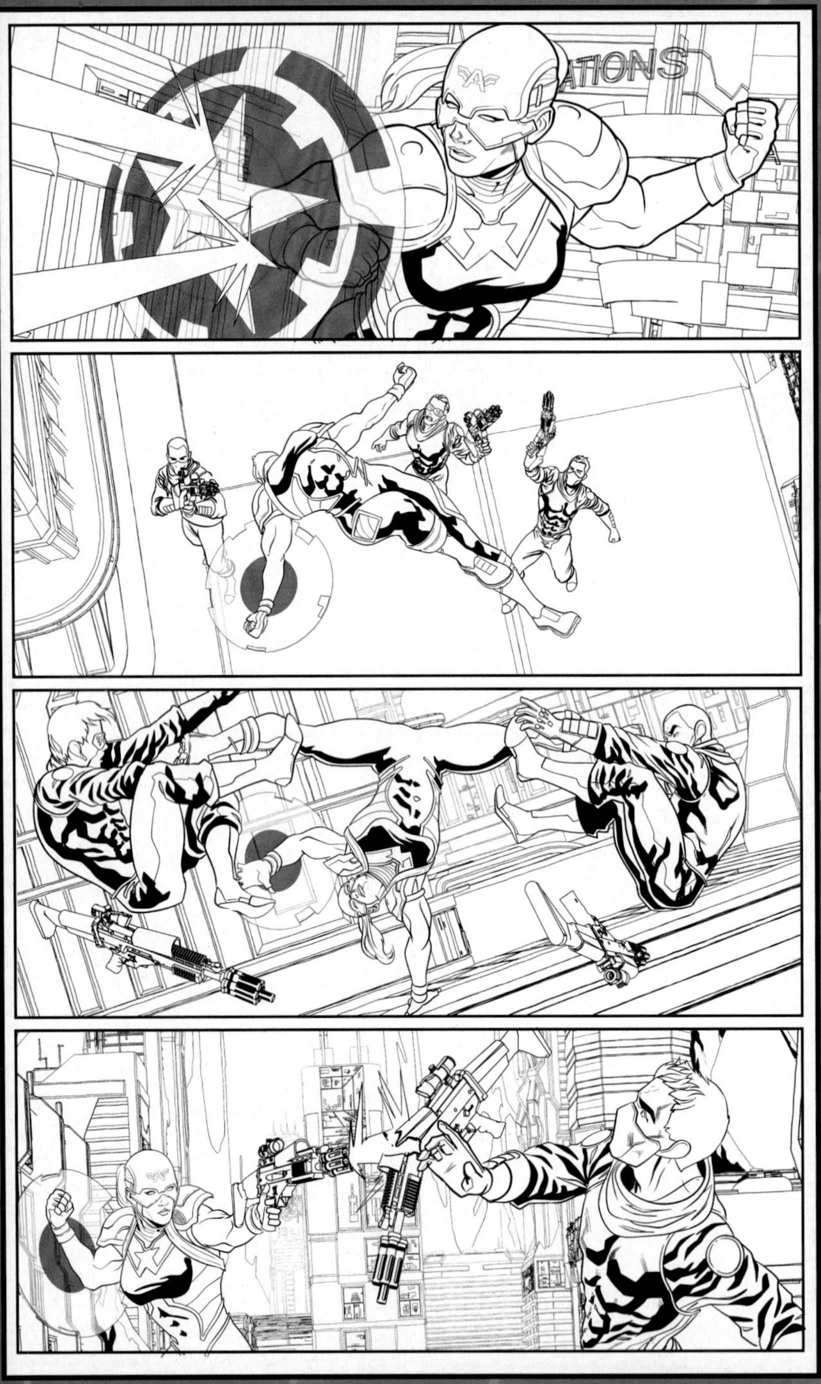
ATIONS

#13, page 9 script by **PETER DAVID** and inks by **WILL SLINEY**

Page 9

Panel A: The holographic shield snaps into place, deflecting blasts from their rifles.

Cap 1: So we're going to do this, huh.

Panel B: She somersaults over their heads.

Cop 2: What in the--?!

Panel C: She pivots in midair, slamming her feet into two of them, taking them out.

Sfx: THUUD THWAAAK

Panel D: She picks up a fallen blaster.

Cap 3: This didn't have to be this way.

Panel E: And she shoots, blasting the third guy's gun out of his hands.

Sfx: ZAAAAK

Cop 4: Arrhhh!!!

Cap 5: I'm sorry about that. But you really shouldn't have attacked me.

Cap 6: Now if you'll excuse me, I'll be on my—